THE SOVIET UNION AND THE THIRD WORLD

Also by E. J. Feuchtwanger

DISRAELI, DEMOCRACY AND THE TORY PARTY
PRUSSIA: MYTH AND REALITY
GLADSTONE
UPHEAVAL AND CONTINUITY: A CENTURY OF
  GERMAN HISTORY (*editor*)
SOVIET MILITARY POWER AND PERFORMANCE
  (*editor with John Erickson*)

THE SOVIET UNION AND THE THIRD WORLD

Edited by
E. J. Feuchtwanger and Peter Nailor

St. Martin's Press   New York

ISBN 0–312–74909–0

Library of Congress Cataloging in Publication Data

Main entry under title:

The Soviet Union and the Third World.

Includes index.
1. Soviet Union—Foreign relations—1975– —
Addresses, essays, lectures. I. Feuchtwanger,
E. J. II. Nailor, Peter.
DK274.S651963 1981   327.47   81–2552
ISBN 0–312–74909–0   AACR2

Contents

Notes on the Contributors

Jonathan Alford is Deputy Director of the International Institute for Strategic Studies.

Christopher Clapham is Senior Lecturer in the Department of Politics at the University of Lancaster.

Karen Dawisha is Lecturer in the Department of Politics at the University of Southampton.

E. J. Feuchtwanger is Reader in History at the University of Southampton.

Michael Leifer is Reader in the Department of International Relations at the London School of Economics.

James Mayall is Senior Lecturer in the Department of International Relations at the London School of Economics.

Peter Nailor is Professor of History at the Royal Naval College, Greenwich.

Otto Pick is Professor of International Relations at the University of Surrey.

Brian Pockney is Director of Russian Studies in the Department of Linguistic and International Studies at the University of Surrey.

Peter Wiles is Professor of Russian Social and Economic Studies at the London School of Economics. **Yukimasa Chudo, Barry Lynch, Alan Smith** and **Nicos Zafiris** have been associated with him in a major research investigation into Soviet and Communist Third World commercial and trading policies.

Malcolm Yapp is Senior Lecturer in the Department of History of the Near and Middle East at the School of Oriental and African Studies, University of London.

Editors' Preface

The choice of topics in this book has been governed by the aim of shedding light on an important area of Soviet policy rather than by the desire to cover comprehensively the relationships of all Third World countries, if such could be precisely defined, with the Soviet Union. Thus, besides military and strategic considerations, Soviet trade with the Third World figures prominently. In addition to a general chapter on Soviet trade with the Third World, there is a separate chapter by Professor Wiles and his team of researchers dealing with the question how far Third World countries which can be broadly defined as Marxist–Leninist are being pulled into the Soviet orbit by their commercial ties with the Eastern bloc. It is such economic dependence which may well be the most enduring basis for Soviet influence in the Third World. Political and military ties can be, as the case of Egypt strikingly illustrates, short-lived.

In the second part of the book a number of case studies drawn from various Third World regions highlight the course of Soviet policy in the recent past. Some deal with countries contiguous to the Soviet Union where there is often a long history of Russian influence and aspirations; in other regions, such as Africa, it is the recent acquisition of a global capability that has given the Soviet Union the option of projecting influence.

The editors hope that the book makes a general contribution towards illustrating the aims and intentions of Soviet foreign policy.

Part I General Aspects

1 Introduction: Political and Ideological Aspects

Otto Pick

The new Soviet Constitution approved in 1977 is very precise about the goals of Soviet foreign policy. In Article 28 it states clearly and without reservation: 'The foreign policy of the USSR is aimed at ensuring international conditions favourable for building Communism in the USSR, safeguarding the State interests of the Soviet Union, consolidating the position of world socialism, supporting the struggle of people for national liberation and social progress, preventing wars of aggression, achieving complete and universal disarmament, and consistently implementing the principle of peaceful co-existence of States with different social systems.'

This represents a rather unusual example of drafting constitutions, for most written constitutions do not instruct the Government on the precise nature of its foreign policy goals. The so-called Brezhnev Constitution does this and the order in which these goals are stated is not without significance. The Russians say what they mean: to ensure conditions favourable for building Communism in the USSR and to safeguard the interests of the Soviet Union by consolidating the position of world socialism is right at the top of their list of priorities. From the Soviet point of view, these are obviously reasonable and legitimate goals to pursue; the only surprise is that some commentators in the West refuse to believe that the Russians mean what they say.

The old theories of the balance of power have been discredited in the eyes of numerous academic practitioners of international relations but they persist in the practices and perceptions of the politicians who, perhaps unfortunately, bear the responsibility for mismanaging the international system. Official Soviet theory, however, prefers to speak of the correlation of forces, and semantically this is perhaps a more subtle definition than the 'balance of power'. It expresses more clearly the comprehensive characteristics of the basic concept which is supposed to determine foreign policy. Anything that happens any-where in the world affects the correlation in some way, and everything is systematically connected with everything else. The determinist philosophy, developed by Marx and Engels from Hegelian roots and refined by Lenin with specific reference to international relations, which forms the ideological framework of reference within which situations are judged and decisions taken, proclaims that, because of the inherent defects of the capitalist and 'imperialist' systems, the correlation of forces must inexorably develop in favour of the 'socialist' world, whatever that may mean nowadays.

There are those who argue that ideology is dead, and that Moscow is merely interested in maintaining and advancing the national interest of the Russian state. However, the elegance of the theory of correlation of forces is such that it has provided a conceptually flexible tool enabling its practitioners to define, pursue and rationalise their policies simultaneously at the complementary levels of ideology and power politics. In some ways, it has confused both them and their preferred opponents, as, in the final analysis, it does not differentiate between these two levels. There is both logic and purpose in this overlap between ideology and practical politics, but the logic is frequently misunderstood by Western commentators.

Managing the correlation of forces puts a premium on seizing every possible opportunity to adjust the system – opportunism is built into the concept. At times the pursuit of apparently opportunistic goals, which appear to conflict with fundamental ideological principles, serves to confuse the issue for all concerned. Mistakes are made and sometimes cannot be retrieved, perceptions are distorted by the con-straints of narrowly defined ideological premises, but given time the basic thrust of foreign policy can usually be restored without much difficulty.

Soviet policy in Africa and Asia has followed this pattern with a predictable degree of consistency. In many ways, it provides an almost tailor-made opportunity to advance the Soviet national interest with-out compromising the requirements of revolutionary theory. At the 1920 Conference of the Comintern – in the early days of relative ideological innocence – Lenin spoke eloquently about the connection between the revolutionary struggle of the working class and the situ-ation of oppressed colonial peoples. To him, the national liberation of the colonial peoples was a two-stage process – the first stage of rapprochement involves the victims of colonialism in the beginnings of their national liberation struggle against their oppressors who are, by definition, capitalist imperialists. In doing so, they move towards a common approach to the struggle against colonialism, and this tendency is reinforced as the conflict develops. Furthermore, their fight begins to converge with the efforts of the proletariat in industrialised societies which has either already won through to the socialist revolution (within the Marxist definition of socialism) or is about to do so. A community of interests is developed between the national liberation struggle and the socialist revolution. At this stage of the struggle, the theory accepts that in the absence of an industrial working class, the fight must be led by the 'national bourgeoisie' (nationalist, but not socialist) and that concessions to the prejudices and vested interests of this social group may have to be made. In due course, in consequence of economic and social changes, a working class leadership will emerge.

The second stage is reached after the battle for national liberation has been won, when the recently liberated colonial peoples move on to socialising their societies and ultimately achieve the blissful state of complete merger with the world socialist camp.

Soviet commentators use the example of the USSR itself to illustrate the validity of Lenin's thesis – the success of the 1917 revolution in European Russia, the Ukraine and Byelorussia assisted the colonial peoples of Central Asia and the Caucausus to complete their struggle for national liberation, enabling them to merge in the socialist society of the USSR as a whole. According to this ideological model, the Soviet Union is therefore the obvious ally upon whom the new states of the Third World have to rely. Decolonisation leading to political independence is not the end of the struggle, for capitalism has merely changed the scale and methods it uses to exploit the Third World. Soviet commentators today naturally stress the nature of the West's involvement in Africa and Asia, arguing that colonialism has been replaced by neo-colonialism, that the capitalist imperialists have merely changed the scale and methods of plunder and that only socialism offers any hope for the developing nations of the Third World. In a statement to the 25th Congress of the Soviet Communist Party in 1976, Brezhnev himself described the national liberation struggle as part of the international class struggle of the oppressed against their oppressors. He went on: 'Our Party, the Communist Party of the Soviet Union, supports peoples fighting for their freedom. In doing so, the Soviet Union does not look for advantages, does not hunt for concessions, does not seek political domination and does not covet military bases.'

The pragmatic and often opportunistic nature of Soviet action in the Third World has provided superficial support to the view that Soviet foreign policy underwent a fundamental change in 1956 when Khrushchev allegedly decided to dispense with ideology. The new pragmatism is frequently contrasted to the alleged dogmatism of the Stalinist period, but this is a crude oversimplification prompted by an understandable desire to rationalise international relations in terms familiar to Western diplomats. Lenin's and Stalin's record is no less pragmatic than Khrushchev's or Brezhnev's. In its earliest days, the Soviet State was quite ready to provide practical support to non-proletarian nationalists like Amanullah in Afghanistan, Kemal Ataturk in Turkey or Chiang Kai-shek in China, while the Comintern was encouraged to throw itself into paroxysms of revolutionary fervour. Even if the Soviet leaders were consciously determined to practice pragmatism to the exclusion of all other considerations, they still could not escape from the limitations imposed by their ideological training and background. It provides a prism, which affects and often distorts their perception of the world at large; they have no other mental discipline of thinking about political questions than the one in which they have been trained. This is the only political language they know and it therefore exerts considerable direct and indirect influence upon the formation of their policies and the making of their decisions. Although their view of the world may be a travesty of the true state of affairs, they have at least a schematic and coherent picture which must be a comfort to them.

Yet there are times when this theoretical framework cannot meet the exigencies of the real world. The Sino-Soviet split and the rise of revolutionary Islam create obvious difficulties today. Which brand of socialism – the Chinese or the Russian – is to benefit from the continuous transformation of the correlation of forces? It can be argued that Soviet policy in Africa has a twofold aim: to contain the spread of Chinese influence while trying to reduce the positions of the West. The Chinese possess several advantages, particularly in Africa – they are an Asian people who have themselves been the victims of imperialism. The behaviour of the Chinese working in Africa contrasts favourably with the boorish antics of some Russian experts and, despite its relative poverty, the Chinese government has been prepared to grant credits on more generous terms than the Russians. On the other hand, Chinese policy in Indochina has caused some concern in South-East Asia, and the situation in Cambodia has revealed both the USSR and the Chinese People's Republic as powers engaged in a traditional 'imperialist' contest for spheres of influence. Further afield, the Chinese cannot match the global power of the Soviet Union; and Moscow's growing confidence in its military capabilities, reflected in more adventurous policies, must worry Peking as much as Washington.

The renaissance of militant Islam poses a problem of a different order. It meets many of the criteria laid down for national liberation movements, but it is socially regressive and rejects Marxism as an essentially Western doctrine. A statement, attributed to Khomeini in 1942 and emblazoned on the banners draped around the occupied American Embassy in Teheran in November 1979 by Iranian students, makes the position quite clear; 'The U.S. is worse than Britain, Britain is worse than the U.S., the U.S.S.R. is worse than both. Each is filthier than the other.'

It seems, at the time of writing, rather unlikely that the Moslem populations of Soviet Central Asia will be attracted by the Ayatollah's Revolution, but Soviet attempts to establish a 'socialist' government in Afghanistan have come up against tribal opposition articulated in extreme Islamic terms which must remind the Russians of the misfortunes suffered by the British at the hands of similar opponents throughout the nineteenth century.

The Soviet Union, however, has an enviable record of extricating itself from difficult colonial situations. Its policy of simultaneously backing both the Somalis and the Ethiopians in the Horn of Africa almost defeated its own purpose, but at the last minute, thanks to its tremendous military reinforcement capability, the USSR was able to retrieve the situation and to give its backing to the Ethiopian *regime*, which had by then clearly emerged as the more promising 'revolutionary' prospect. The impressive naval and air transport capabilities, which the USSR has developed in recent years, have provided the foundations for interventionist policies in Africa. The decision to encourage the despatch of a Cuban expeditionary force to assist national liberation movements and 'progressive' *regimes* in Africa illustrate the extent to which opportunism can be reconciled with ideological premises. The Cubans are obviously more acceptable in Africa than the Russians would be. Castro's involvement with the global 'class war' has now been used to transform the orientation of the so-called uncommitted nations and the socialist world's support for the national liberation struggle has been projected as a permanent factor in contemporary international relations.

Even though ideological considerations are of considerable significance in the formulation and rationalisation of Soviet goals in Africa and Asia, it would be a fallacy to interpret Soviet policies in terms of a conspiracy theory. The attraction of the ideological analysis of national liberation movements rests primarily on the ease with which opportunities can be seized and used. Most of the opportunities available to the Soviet Union in the Third World have been created by the West – by Western policy failures, by the historical record of the former colonial powers and the resultant guilt complexes and by the pressure of public opinion in pluralist societies. The USSR suffers from none of these inhibitions.

Historically, the Soviet interest in Africa is relatively recent. Asia and the Middle East were in the fore-front of Tsarist Russia's political ambitions throughout the nineteenth century. The push toward the Dardanelles alternated with expansion in Central Asia – in the direction of the Indian sub-continent – and the building of the Trans-Siberian Railway manifested Russia's belief in their Asian destiny. Lenin was obsessed with revolution in Asia; for him the road to London and Paris went through Delhi and Peking. Yet he foresaw the difficulties and what he wrote in 1920 might have been inspired by the Ayatollah Khomeini: 'Our policies towards West European countries must be very cautious, but out policy in the East must be even more cautious and patient, for here we are dealing with countries that are much more backward, are under the oppressive influence of religion, of religious fanaticism . . . are imbued with distrust of the Russian people.' On the other hand, Africa was a relatively closed book. The first Institute for the Study of African Affairs was founded in Moscow in 1959. In Stalin's day, Soviet African studies were dominated by old-fashioned anthropologists with political pretensions, of whom Academician Potekhin was the most prominent one. This, of course, has changed, and today, the Soviet leaders are able to draw upon reasonable professional resources in their assessment of African developments.

The Middle East represents a completely different dimension; it is much more obviously relevant to the global policies of the Soviet government. Partly, Soviet interest in the area is an inheritance from the Tsars, and the Soviet Union has succeeded where Imperial Russia failed. It has become a Mediterranean power, partly by judicious exploitation of the Arab–Israeli conflict and partly as a result of the Soviet naval build-up in the area. The break with Egypt has reduced the Soviet Union's potential for action, and represents one of the few opportunities for diplomatic initiative offered by Soviet errors of judgment which the United States has been able to seize in recent years. Soviet interest in the Middle East, and incidentally in the Horn of Africa, goes beyond support for national liberation movements. It is, of course, closely linked to the global energy crisis, from which the USSR cannot isolate itself. Although still a net exporter of energy and the world's largest oil producer, the USSR faces its own energy crisis in the 1980s and easy access to Middle Eastern oil may then acquire a new significance. (*Pravda*, on 12 November 1979, urged energy consumers to exercise 'strict economy' and pointed out that 'the energy needs of our national economy have been growing'.) Soviet consumption is going up all the time; some of the oilfields now in use are nearing exhaustion and the opening up of new sources in Siberia and the Barents Sea bristles with technological difficulties.

In discussing Soviet policies in the Third World, the long-standing attempt to present the Soviet experience as a valid and indeed unique model of economic and social development is of some relevance. The Soviet argument is a simple one – the USSR raised itself from being the world's biggest underdeveloped country in 1917 to its present status by transforming its social and economic base, and developing countries today could do the same by following the Soviet example, especially as they now have the benefit of support and economic aid from the powerful 'socialist camp'. The details of Soviet economic policies are discussed elsewhere in this volume, but it does seem that the help which the USSR is prepared to give to Afro-Asian countries consists largely of arms supplies. The Soviet supply of military hardware to less developed countries represents about double the amount of funds expended on economic development as such.

The other aspect of the economic model offered by the Soviet Union appeals to many Third World intellectuals – the claim that the progress towards socialism is founded upon a truly scientific analysis of social and economic development. Marxist dialectic presents this process as inevitable, because of the allegedly perfect nature of the analysis on which it is based. Of course, this purely dogmatic approach minimises the problems posed by tribalism and the types of leadership which have emerged in black Africa and in some Asian and Middle Eastern states. In many of these countries, the governing *elites* consist of army officers, who are prepared to use the apparatus of the Leninist state, but are not especially in sympathy with the Marxist reasoning from which it is allegedly derived. In many African countries, 'socialist' rhetoric is used to provide a respectable facade for personal or tribal dictatorships of the crudest kind. It is an acceptable facade, for it is untainted by colonial associations, even though it is of Western origin.

In fact, a revolutionary situation in strictly Marxist terms exists only in the Republic of South Africa, where there is a large black industrial working class in a society dominated by white capital. Elsewhere in black Africa, the Leninist concept of the national liberation struggle provides the only theoretical guideline for Soviet policy.

Strategic advantage obviously leads the list of Soviet priorities. This is of necessity a very vague definition of political and military objectives, which inevitably relates closely to the national interest of the USSR, regardless of ideological concerns. In Asia, the advantage currently being sought is the exclusion, or at least the diminution, of Chinese influence. Soviet policies in Indochina, for example, demonstrate this trend very clearly. In Africa it has been maintained that Soviet control over the Horn would enable the Soviet Navy to threaten the maritime lines of communication on which the West depends for its supplies of oil from the Middle East. It can, of course, be argued that any determined effort by the Soviet Navy to translate this threat into action would represent a major *casus belli* and that this alone would deter the USSR from running risks of such magnitude. On the other hand, the very existence of such a threat might deter the West from opposing Soviet policies. Obviously, the Soviet Union is interested in reducing the freedom of action which its preferred opponents might be able to exercise, and the spread of the Soviet presence in the Third World is therefore significant insofar as it serves to squeeze out Western or Chinese influence.

On the ideological front, Lenin's belief that the loss of colonial empires would inevitably lead to the collapse of the 'capitalist' system has been disproved by the course of events. Marxists, of course, argue that nothing has really changed, that colonialism has just given way to neo-colonialism, but this argument is really too simplistic. To some it appeared that Lenin would be proved right after all by the energy crisis, but in effect the OPEC cartel has emerged as a new imperialist force, exacting tribute not only from the 'capitalist' world, but also from the Fourth World – the oil-deficient countries of what used to be called the Third World.

There is, of course, a simple explanation for Soviet policies in the Third World which is not much affected by ideological considerations. The USSR is a world power, and as such it sees itself pursuing a global range of interests. To concede an absence of direct Soviet interests in any part of the world would be an admission of diminished status. As a world superpower, the USSR is convinced that it must have policies for all contingencies in all parts of the world and its ideology maintains that it must obtain advantages wherever and whenever it can. Opportunities presented by Western mistakes and failures must be seized – it would be ideologically and practically inadmissible to ignore them. Of course, errors are committed and miscalculations occur in the pursuit of these self-fulfilling goals, but that, too, is part of the games which great powers play. Beneath the elaborate superstructure of ideological motivation and great power interests, Soviet policy in the Third World may, after all, be just an exercise in role-playing.

2 The New Military Instruments

Jonathan Alford

THE OLD AND THE NEW

In many respects the Soviet Union is not using 'new' military instruments in the Third World at all; she is actually using very old military instruments indeed, instruments which do not seem to differ in any substantive way from those that have been used by imperial powers, since the days of the Roman Empire, to extend influence and protect distant interests. All imperial powers have sought to make use of others bound to them by self-interest or by threat of retribution to fight their wars for them. And many powers have, over the centuries, hired mercenaries or subvented other countries to provide soldiers to fight in their service.

This is not intended as a historical study, but the parallels seem exact enough to allow one to cast doubt as to the 'newness' of what the Soviet Union appears to be doing in the Third World. It may be new for Russia, a country which has always had an abundance of manpower and not much interest in non-contiguous areas, but it is not a new way for the world.

However, what is undeniably new is the range and extent of Soviet involvement in areas very remote from her borders and a case can be made that it is not so much the will that has changed as the means. Even in the time of Lenin, there was a belief that the Soviet Union could derive profit from revolutionary movements but there were few ways of turning disaffection with capitalism and colonialism to advantage. Certainly there was a conscious turning away from interventionary instincts under Stalin, but Khrushchev returned to support Third World revolutionary movements with great vigour. Yet the means were still largely lacking, and it was not until the 1970s that the will and the means came together, with greatly increased military reach and allies who were prepared, for whatever reasons, to act in concert or under direction to further Soviet interests in the Third World. At the same time, a more pragmatic approach, which clearly has something to do with Brezhnev's style, allows the Soviet Union to support *regimes* which are by no means ideologically sympathetic so long as interests coincide. The cases of Syria and Iraq come at once to mind. This should not be taken to mean that the ideological imperative is dead, even if the ideology appears neither to fit the conditions of Third World societies nor to hold all that many attractions for Third World *elites*. Rather does it appear to be the case that 'what serves to enhance Soviet power internationally simultaneously increases the prospects of world revolution'.[1] One can be certain that the extension of Soviet influence – particularly in the military sphere – is part of that 'correlation of forces' that the Soviet Union wishes to move in a favourable direction. Furthermore, military power and influence can be used to spread ideology, and a clear line of pragmatism in the service of ideology can be traced back to the earliest days of the Revolution; there is nothing to suggest either a basic contradiction or even a serious argument in the Politburo, even if tactical differences are distantly heard. It must, after all, have been quite difficult to decide whether to back Somalia or Ethiopia in mid-1977.

It is the new means rather than the new methods or new objectives which are the subject of this chapter but the context is important for, unless it is possible to determine what it is that the Soviet Union is attempting to achieve, it will be hard to establish any kind of equation between means and ends and between costs, risks and benefits. To gain ground in the global struggle may satisfy as an overarching objective, but it is not specific enough to allow analysis of the military instruments. Some or all of the following objectives seem to apply in most Soviet Third World activity:

to gain control over raw materials vital to Western economies;
to demonstrate support for left-wing *regimes*;
to 'capture' Third World states for the Communist Bloc;
to keep Chinese influence out of the Third World;
to gain strategic advantage, through the acquisition of military facilities that might be useful in war;
to acquire footholds for use in peace as a means of extending influence;
to divert the attentions of Western powers away from Soviet borders;
to obtain useful economic concessions, as in fishing rights.

None of these are mutually exclusive; all can, to some extent, contribute to the correlation of forces even if their relative importance will vary from place to place and have varied over time. Nevertheless, although the list must have looked much the same since the death of Stalin, very few of these objectives began to be realised at all impressively until the latter part of the 1960s. What has made their realisation possible has been the growth of the military component of Soviet power. Although by no means all Soviet military procurement programmes should be explained by what happened over Cuba in 1962 (certainly naval building programmes should be attributed much more to the American production decision on missile-carrying nuclear submarines two years before the Cuban missile crisis), the fact remains that the lack of reach which was demonstrated most painfully to the Soviet Union in 1962 had, if possible, to be redressed if Russia was not to be outfaced by the United States in the Third World. The Soviet Union also began to realise, with something amounting to shock, that in competition with the West the other instruments of influence – political, cultural, diplomatic and economic – were not those which she could wield with any great success. Only the military instrument remained, and this has been refined over the past decade to the point where it is responsive and subtle in application whether through the supply of arms, through supportive military activity or through direct military intervention in many different guises. In the early 1960s, the Soviet Union lacked an ocean-going navy, sea-based air power, long-range transport aircraft and amphibious shipping. She could not maintain a fleet at sea and had few friendly ports of call. Even her mercantile marine was small and lacked the kind of heavy-lift equipment needed to off-load items like tanks in countries with minimal dockyard facilities. She had no specialised roll-on/roll-off shipping for rapid disembarkation of vehicles. By the end of the 1970s, all but one of these disadvantages has been remedied. The one that remains is the lack of sea-based airpower, but the Soviet Union has gone some way to make up for the lack of reconnaissance at sea by the extensive deployment of land-based maritime patrol aircraft and maritime reconnaissance satellites. Only in respect of sea-based strike aircraft does she remain totally deficient and likely to remain so (in making this judgement, FORGER aircraft are discounted, as being essential for the anti-submarine warfare (ASW) mission by providing air defence over anti-submarine forces).

ARMS, RAW MATERIALS AND MANPOWER

Forced by circumstances to concentrate on the military instrument as the means of extending influence, the Soviet Union has had the shrewdness to realise that, in the post-colonial era, Third World rulers of whatever political hue are hungry for military assistance, either to secure their *regimes* against internal or external threats (often very real) or simply because weapons are a potent symbol of national power and status. And it is precisely because these leaders feel themselves to be threatened that they are especially prone to grasp at offers of arms and support without realising the dependency that arms can create. Increasing wealth from raw materials has meant that many countries could afford to buy, so the door was open for the Soviet Union to extend her influence in the only way that she was good at.

Generally speaking, Russia has been hard put to it to offer hard currency or loans on attractive terms for development aid, and she has not needed to buy from the Third World the raw materials that is all that they have had to offer (with some notable exceptions like bauxite and phosphates). She has had a distinctly poor record in diplomacy, and has tended to show very little sensitivity to the needs, aspirations and essential dignity of Third World leaders. At least as arrogant and clumsy as the colonial powers at their worst, the Soviet Union has not found it easy to make friends; but to those who need weapons, military infrastructure, training, support and staff experience, she has been most liberal. And because the needs of her own relatively un-sophisticated military manpower are for the simple and robust, much of the equipment is rather better suited to the abilities of Third World soldiers, sailors and airmen than the comparable Western inventory. Her own requirements are very large so that the unit costs of weapons are usually low and she is able to build up enormous stockpiles of equipment withdrawn from service in front-line units as a result of generational replacement. A policy of retention against the un-expected (a policy not generally followed in Western nations) does therefore assist, in making it a simple matter to meet demands at extremely short notice. It has been reported that the average delivery time for American arms is three years; Soviet lead times, by way of contrast, are rarely more than 18 months. In 1977, for example, 85 per cent of orders placed with the Soviet Union were delivered within a year.[2] The fact that the arms are a generation old does not matter in many parts of the world, where the possession of 200 T-54 tanks can be very significant in a local power balance. The Soviet Union has another distinct advantage *vis-a-vis* the United States: she does not have to subject a decision to transfer arms to an independent body for approval. As Barry Blechman has noted: 'The nature of our democratic system is such that important foreign policy actions, including decisions to transfer arms, must be made with the support of the public and in close consultation with the Congress. This process takes time; time not needed by authoritarian regimes'.[3]

Despite the fact that the Soviet Union has gone a long way towards perfecting the interventionary instrument, a major constraint has remained the wish to avoid a direct clash with the forces of the United States or her allies. This has limited freedom of action and has led to a search for surrogates in order to reduce the risks of attribution. It seems likely also that the Soviet Union makes – and expects the West also to make – a distinction between what might be termed 'supportive' use of military means and 'substitutive' use; that is the distinction between helping others to fight better – by training, staff assistance, planning and logistic backing – and doing other people's fighting for them. In the former case, withdrawal of support can be rapid if the risks of involvement look like becoming too great for comfort; in the latter, there are real dangers, as with the United States in Vietnam, of an open-ended commitment arising and of direct confrontation. Well aware of these dangers, the Soviet Union has only very rarely committed her own forces to action in the Third World, preferring to remain behind the scenes. Obviously the case of Afghanistan is an exception to this rule but Afghanistan is contiguous to the Soviet Union and appears to have been treated by Moscow as if the Brezhnev Doctrine applied as forcefully there as in Eastern Europe. This makes Afghanistan a rather special case among Third World countries. Only in Egypt, between 1967 and 1972, did Russians man equipment which had been transferred to Egypt and engage in combat with Israeli aircraft, as pilots of combat aircraft and crews for surface-to-air missiles. So it must have been with a sense of relief that the Soviet Union found an ally willing and competent to perform the substitutive role when necessary. It has been the emergence of the Cubans in the Third World that has permitted a more thrusting policy of military intervention. Although it is traditional to cite the Cuban intervention in Angola as the first milestone, the signs of Cuban interest in Africa began many years before. Two Cuban tank battalions were sent to help Algeria against Morocco in 1963, although it so happened that the war was over before they could see action. From then until 1975, there were many Cubans in Africa, notably in Guinea, Congo (Brazzaville),

Somalia and (reportedly) Cameroon. However, it appears that the Cuban activity in Africa accelerated as a result of the economic upswing which began in Cuba in about 1970 which, together with Soviet assistance in transportation, enabled the Cuban Government to push ahead with a policy which was far from new but which had hitherto been difficult to put into effect.

The Soviet Union has relatively few vulnerabilities because she needs little from the outside world in terms of raw materials. Her external trade remains a very small proportion of GDP (about 4 per cent) but there remain some interests, particularly those in relation to technology transfers and strategic arms limitation, which she would perfer not to hazard. By using another Third World state, not only can the Soviet Union minimise the risks to such vulnerabilities as do exist, but she is well placed to cushion that state against threats of punitive sanctions arising from an aggressive foreign policy. In the case of Cuba, the Soviet Union can provide oil and buy about half the sugar crop at fixed prices as well as providing any less vital commodities that an embargo might affect. Any embargo against Cuba from the United States is effectively discounted in this way. The use of surrogates is increasing, with East Germany, South Yemen and Vietnam all, in one way or another, performing *roles* in the Third World on behalf of the Soviet Union. It should not be understood from this that these nations are being coerced, for there is an identity of interest in spreading Marxist power at the expense of the West and there is a subtle interaction whereby favoured *elites* find their positions strenghtened internally through Soviet support (so long as they do what is required of them) and, externally, countries which act for the Soviet Union find their position in the world greatly enhanced. Cuba would be only another poor Latin country in Central America if it were not for the attention paid to Fidel Castro because of his role in Africa. Nor should one suppose that these surrogates are mere puppets, although the Soviet leverage is clearly very great. There is a substantial quantity of evidence to show that interests have diverged: Eritrea was a case in point, where the Cuban view of what action to take was at odds with Soviet and Ethiopian wishes. Nevertheless, it would appear to be very unlikely that the Soviet position in the Third World would be as strong as it is without the help which she has obtained from surrogates.

THE DYNAMICS AND THE LIMITATIONS

Before looking more closely at the military instruments themselves, it is necessary to say something about the essential impermanence of military solutions in the Third World. With the exception of the French, Western powers long ago came to the conclusion that there was little that deployed military power could do to secure economic or even strategic interests if the country concerned became unfriendly. It may have come as something of a shock in Moscow to find that it is by no means easy to convert military dependency into a stable long-term relationship. So long as there is a threat to a Third World *regime* which can be countered with arms and military support, the dependency is likely to remain, but gratitude for past military assistance is not a noticeable characteristic of international relations. Furthermore, many Third World leaders are well aware that they have paid a stiff price in terms of their freedom of action by accepting Soviet military aid, and come to resent the burden. They know that they are serving Soviet ends and rarely believe that Soviet motives are altruistic, particularly if they have conceded useful military facilities as the price for aid. It is therefore not surprising that there have been almost as many failures as there have been successes in the Soviet drive to establish positions of enduring influence in the Third World; Egypt, Sudan, North Yemen, Somalia and, more recently, Guinea and even Angola serve to remind the Politburo that there is something lacking in their approach. But while the West may take some comfort from the fact that positions of influence which depend solely on military cement are unlikely to last, there does seem to be a similar awareness in Moscow; this has led, not to a solution to the problem (for, given the means that the Soviet Union has at her disposal, it is not a soluble problem) but to much greater care to re-insure positions in case of failure. So far as possible, doors are now left open for the re-establish-ment of good relations with a disaffected *regime* in the future. Sometimes, by backing both sides in a dispute as in the Horn of Africa, the Soviet Union manoeuvres herself into a classic 'no lose' position. She has also become aware of the need to continue the process of investment in a particular leadership rather than, as so often before, believing that the initial investment will suffice to bind the client for ever. As this process of continuous investment is mostly military in nature, the incremental costs are not great. The Soviet Union appears to have learnt what others have said; nobody can buy an African government – it can only be rented. By paying the rent regularly and on demand and, within limits, accepting rent increases payable in more and better military hardware without demur, Soviet influence will last longer and be much more difficult to shake off when the times comes. In a sense too, it is true that payment in military hardware lends itself particularly well to an instalment plan favouring the donor. As Minrod Novik has noted in his monograph 'On the Shores of Bab Al-Mandab':

> Such investments may yield benefits beyond the gratitude of the present leadership (the expression of which could be found in the granting of access to military facilities). The same military establishment that enjoys Soviet equipment and training often emerges not only as an important power base for the existing *elite* but as an eventual alternative to it, in which case the Soviets may find their influence further enhanced.[4]

Military equipment creates specific long-term dependencies on ammunition, spare-parts and technical support which may make it difficult for a *regime* to distance itself dramatically from the Soviet Union or even take an independent line on foreign or internal policy issues. The examples of Egypt and Somalia are clear cases where the termination of support has proved extremely costly, in terms of the reduction of military capability. Much of Egypt's very substantial hardware is of little use now that spares have dried up and that overhauls, particularly of aircraft, cannot take place in the Soviet Union. The more sophisticated the level of equipment provided, the more pronounced the importance of the continuing relationship for the target state. It is interesting to note that the breakdown of the average contract by value into weapons, support and infrastructure shows the Soviet Union normally providing these in the ratio 60:33:7 and the United States in the ratio 35:35:30. This indicates not only that the Soviet Union tends to transfer more actual hardware for a given sum but also that the recipients are likely to be more reliant on Soviet goodwill for such things as training support, construction and technical assistance which come under the 'infrastructure' heading.[5]

It would be quite wrong to think of Soviet military programmes as being cost-free even in economic terms, and it is significant that there has been a marked shift since 1974 towards much less advantageous credit terms and demands for payment to be made in hard currency. In earlier days, interest rates were low (at 2 to 2½ per cent) with a long repayment period of 8 to 10 years; prices were often discounted by as much as 40 per cent. All that has changed, although there remains the outstanding attraction for countries in a hurry that the Soviet Union can meet most requests very rapidly from stock: something that Western arms suppliers find difficult or impossible to match.[6]

Sometimes forgotten is the training given to Third World military personnel in the Soviet Union. It is estimated that some 3000 men may be in the Soviet Union at any one time and this clearly gives the Soviet Union an added opportunity of attempting some indoctrination. The counterpart to training courses in Russia for technicians and senior staff officers is the training carried out *in situ*. As many as 10 000 Soviet military advisers and technicians are assisting Third World countries to assimilate Soviet equipment. Their role and significance is well summarised by Leo Tansky:

> The rapid influx into the less-developed countries of large quantities of modern complex military equipment has demanded military skills that either are in short supply or nonexistent in these countries. This lack of skilled military manpower has posed more serious problems than a similar human resource gap in the economic sector because of the rapid rate at which military equipment has been delivered. The manpower base in these countries has been unable to supply in a short time enough men capable of being trained to command, operate and maintain the modernised military establishments. The acceptance of military personnel for training at Soviet military installations and the despatch of large numbers of Soviet military technicians to less developed countries subsequently have proved to be important elements of the Soviet military assistance program.[7]

Given such large transfusions of military-technical support, it is almost inevitable that the Soviet Union has been able to penetrate deeply into Third World military establishments, to gain intelligence and exercise a considerable degree of leverage over policies. This was particularly the case in Egypt between 1967 and 1972.

THE LONGER REACH

However it remains true that what has given the Soviet Union far greater reach, in a global sense, has been the growth of power at sea and the development of an effective long-range transport airforce; in order to gauge the extent of Soviet developments in these two fields, one must look beyond the military forces to the auxiliary and even totally 'civilian' air transport fleets and the mercantile marine.

It may be many years before we can distinguish satisfactorily between the chicken and the egg. There are those who see a consistent pattern (à la Gorshkov) in the construction of a deep-water navy for peace-time use. There are others who argue persuasively that very little would have been authorised for the Soviet Navy that does not have a specific war-related mission – whether to combat US strategic nuclear submarines or carrier task forces, or to interdict Western supply lines in war. Whatever the genesis, the fact remains that Soviet naval reach has increased quite dramatically over the past ten years. Even if the Soviet Union acquired that capability to influence events in distant waters in peace-time that the British were said to have acquired when they developed their Empire (in a fit of absence of mind), the most hardened anti-navalist in the Politburo would now have to admit that Admiral Gorshkov has delivered into their hands a very useful instrument. Many of the fleet units procured for anti-submarine warfare or to close-mark American carriers can, in a situation short of war, provide a credible naval presence in many parts of the world where their highly visible arrays of many different weapon systems gives them the appearance at least of a very business-like fleet.

Yet it remains true that Soviet naval reach is still less impressive than that of the United States. The Soviet Union is still short of a substantial amphibious capability in distant waters and has no strike aircraft deployed at sea.

While the presence of Soviet surface combatants far afield has undoubtedly increased, one would certainly doubt their ability to contest any waters, except contiguous seas, for any length of time but Soviet maritime presence is made very pervasive by fishing fleets, by intelligence-gathering ships, by survey vessels and the mercantile marine. Third World states tend not to make a distinction between combatant and non-combatant vessels and indeed, in the context of Soviet military penetration into the Third World, the *role* of the mercantile marine has been very important, for there is such a blurring of *role* that whether an urgent military cargo is carried in a naval vessel or in a merchant ship is a matter of convenience rather than a matter of principle; the direction of Soviet merchant vessels for state interests requires nothing more than a simple order. A number of roll-on/roll-off fast transports are about to enter the Soviet mercantile marine which have clear utility for moving military cargoes to Third World ports and many cargo ships have a heavy-lift capacity greatly in excess of what would be needed for normal commercial traffic.

It is extremely doubtful if one could ever quantify by tonnage the part played by the Soviet mercantile marine in shifting arms to the Third World but there can be little doubt that by far the greatest proportion of the total lift has gone by sea, even if the use of airlift appears more dramatic. The use of long-range transport aircraft for heavy cargoes remains essentially uneconomic, and overflying rights will always introduce an element of uncertainty into Soviet calculations. However the parallel development of Soviet long-range air transport has introduced a new element when time is short and when a rapid injection of arms or troops into an area of tension or crisis can pre-empt any possible Western response.

As with Soviet naval developments, it would seem wrong to attribute the procurement of a long-range air transport capability to a desire to intervene at a distance in the Third World. There are very good internal reasons why the Russian forces require transport aircraft to move men and *materiel* over the huge distances of the Soviet Union, especially from West to East but also from the central military districts to Eastern Europe in a crisis. Nevertheless the lift available is great and the long-haul range/payload characteristics are impressive, and they were demonstrated to the full in Ethiopia. The An-22 can lift 80 tonnes over 2700 nautical miles and the Il-76 can lift half that amount over the same distance. Given that the Soviet Union could muster at any moment not less than 50 Il-76s (of a total fleet of 80) and 30 An-22s (out of 50), a simultaneous lift of some 30 000 men on light scales is clearly feasible – say three divisions. This force can be supplemented at very short notice from *Aeroflot* with a further 1300 civil transport aircraft. By drawing on stockpiles of heavy equipment in Iraq, Libya, Aden or Vietnam, such a force could be in action within 24 to 48 hours anywhere in an arc stretching from Morocco, through the Sudan, the Horn and the Gulf to South-East Asia. The figure for the airlifted component of the arms shipments to Ethiopia of 61 000 tons is by no means excessive, given that the airlift continued at varying intensity for many weeks.

Nevertheless there are always likely to be problems in heavy reliance on airlift. Overflying is not something to be indulged in lightly and heavy air-transports are very vulnerable to attack from the ground or from the air, by even quite unsophisticated weapons. There are grounds for believing that the Ethiopian airlift was as much an exercise as a military operation. There was really no military need either to continue the airlift for as long nor to shift as much by air as they did, given that sea-lift was in a position to take over after about ten days. Granted that there may have been a need rapidly to draw down the Libyan stockpiles in the first instance, as some have suggested, what appeared subsequently to be the case was a deliberate exploration of many overflight patterns to test feasibility and political reactions. There were a number of reports that aircraft were flying empty, and even one that a complete parachute division was flown in to Addis Ababa and immediately flown back to Russia. All this is consistent with a desire to exercise the machinery of reinforcement to a maximum, in order to practise the generation of a large number of aircraft, crews and ground-handling equipment for a sustained period using as many *routes* through the Middle East area as possible. More recently, it appears that the Soviet Union moved some supplies to Vietnam with the concurrence of the Indian Government.

Not only therefore has the Soviet Union gained confidence that she can, if necessary, mount a very impressive long-range airlift to help an ally or intervene to secure an interest, but she has demonstrated to the United States and to the Third World that she is prepared to use this capability to help a friend in trouble. This says much about the credibility of Soviet commitments at a time when many are beginning to question not the comparable American ability but the American will to intervene with military power in the Third World.

To complete the picture, it is necessary to add that the Soviet Union remains reliant on ground refuelling and she has not, apparently, gone to the lengths of investing in in-flight refuelling for her transport aircraft. This is an alternative which the United States has decided to follow because of persistent uncertainties over staging rights in a period of political tension. It follows that the Soviet reach is distinctly limited with regard to very distant areas, unless she can complete a network of assured staging facilities.

To return for a moment to the use of Libyan stockpiles for the Ethiopian intervention, it now seems clear that what were once thought to be excessive sales of military equipment to certain countries such as Libya or Aden can be seen as a sensible effort to cut down Soviet reaction times and reduce the potential vulnerabilities inherent in overflying. By flying aircraft empty over, for example, Turkey using innocent flight plans, the possibility of interception and subsequent explanation is avoided completely. All that was left was to risk overflying Sudan or Uganda where the challenge was unlikely to be sustained, even if made. The haul in cargo could however be reduced to less than half by this means. We saw too the very early use of Adeni tanks in Ethiopia to stem the Somali invasion before the main lift began to arrive, and, because these tanks were manned by Adenis, none of the problems of training and assimilation arose. In short, a policy of stockpiling substantial quantities of arms in secure bases considerably enhances the Soviet ability to pass *materiel* to a client in a hurry and reduces the vulnerabilities that will continue to exist in respect of long-range transport aircraft. It is only necessary to contrast such a policy with the real difficulties faced by the United States in 1973 when she attempted to draw on NATO stockpiles for Israel's needs; the free and unfettered use of large amounts of military equipment is an essential element of rapid intervention. It is of course precisely the difficulty of moving heavy equipment over long distances which is causing the United States to invest in floating stockpiles for she, unlike the Soviet Union, appears unwilling (or, perhaps, unable) to find reliable and secure forward bases in which to stockpile equipment.

Hardware is but one part, albeit a very important part, of the story. Arms by themselves, even if they do create certain dependencies in the longer term, do not bind emerging *regimes* to the Soviet Union. Of greater concern for the West is the penetration of the fabric of the societies of Third World states by the Soviet Union and her allies.

THE SURROGATES

It is interesting to observe that there now appears to be, at least in Africa, a division of labour in the Eastern camp. The East Germans are becoming heavily involved with the state security apparatus and the intelligence services in, for example, Mozambique, Angola and Aden. The Hungarians are believed to be undertaking military engineering tasks in South Yemen and the Cubans, in addition to their military *role*, both substitutive and supportive, have brought in large numbers of personnel to strengthen the civilian infrastructure in many African countries. Cuban teachers, medical workers and civil engineers are present, and are much more acceptable to the host governments than Russians, and they seem likely to influence the continent in what the Soviet Union would regard as a favourable direction in the longer term than military advisers. However the *role* of Cuban forces has caught the imagination of the West and it remains the Cuban involvement which, in the strictly military sphere, has been by far the most significant element. The others have been brought in either because of Cuban overstretch or because they offer a particular set of skills that are useful to the Soviet Union in the Third World. That overstretch has become a problem for Cuba seems undeniable. There are clear limits to how much trained manpower a country of only ten million people can afford to export, and what casualties even a dictatorship can sustain without public discontent. Although to a quite marked extent Cuba has only been exporting unemployment at home, for jobs are in short supply and the rewards for overseas service are reputedly substantial, this only applies in the main to the relatively unskilled junior ranks and private soldiers fighting in Africa. Cuba also seems to have trained too many doctors and teachers but skilled technicians and senior ranks are less easily spared. Therefore we have seen the Soviet Union having to replace some of these categories in Cuba with Russians – notably in the case of pilots and air traffic controllers for Cuban air defences.

The costs, direct and indirect, to the Soviet Union are high. Subsidies, free arms shipments for Cuba and considerable logistic support were assessed in 1977 at a little over £500 million a year. But the advantages are clear: Cuban troops can use Soviet equipment with no additional training so that they can be flown in to pick up *materiel* ferried direct from Russia or a forward stockpile; Cubans are technically in advance of manpower skills of many Third World countries; and Cubans can be used to stiffen up local forces, to provide staff and communications personnel and, when necessary, engage in combat. In short, Cubans are essential to provide the nervous system without which many Third World armies are little more than a collection of poorly motivated and ill-disciplined individuals. It is also true that, at least in Angola and in Mozambique, language problems are much less serious, for the Cuban Spanish and the Portuguese spoken in both countries are close.

It is important to make a distinction between personnel answerable to the Cuban Ministry of Defence and those answerable to the Ministry of the Interior. The former are quite clearly part of the Revolutionary Armed Forces (MINFAR) while the latter, although sometimes uniformed, have a special responsibility for the training of militia forces as opposed to regular forces. This has led consistently to counting problems, with some authorities counting Construction Brigades as military and others as civilian. It seems likely that all Cubans can give some kind of military assistance in an emergency, as all have undergone military training at some time, but their primary roles are likely to remain distinct. It is also worth stressing that service in Africa is seen by the Cuban Government as having a socialising role in that it provides useful training, experience and 'hardening' for the next generation of Cubans.[8]

It is not easy to make a judgement either about Cuban *morale* in combat or their competence. There has been some evidence that Cubans were reluctant to engage in combat with UNITA forces in Angola and the South Africans have asserted that the Cubans did not fight well in clashes with South African troops in Angola during the fighting after Angolan independence (this was especially true at 'the Battle of Bridge 14', 9–12 December 1975). But as the major part played by the Cubans has not involved them in direct ground combat but as pilots, artillery crews, truck drivers and signallers, this has not greatly mattered.

Despite what Chinese leaders have been saying, it seems quite wrong to cast the Vietnamese as the 'Cubans of Asia'. There is a degree of altruism about Cubans or East Germans or even Adenis which does not seem to be present in the Vietnamese. Whereas the former do not have territorial ambitions of their own, Vietnam in marked contrast is intent on furthering her own influence in South-East Asia under a Russian umbrella and with Soviet diplomatic help, but for ends which do not appear to have much to do with World Revolution. Vietnam wants both Laos and Cambodia to pay tribute and she has used and is using military power to impose a *regime* on the latter which is friendly to Vietnam. While it is certainly true that this serves Soviet strategic interests *vis-à-vis* China, it is hardly the same thing as providing military missionaries for the Soviet Union in Africa or in the Middle East.

Mention of China in this context serves to underline the point that one of the more pressing reasons why the Soviet Union was drawn into the Third World in the 1960s was to either pre-empt or replace Chinese influence after the Sino-Soviet split. The contest was particularly clearly visible in Mozambique where the Chinese have, to quote a Chinese journalist 'been edged out by the Russians'.[9] What seems to have been particularly galling for the Chinese is the fact that their aid programmes were very much greater than Russian aid to Africa, amounting between 1970 and 1974 to 1.5 billion US dollars. Most Chinese military aid has gone to Pakistan and only a little to Tanzania. 'In contrast, the Soviets have given far less in economic aid but have focused on military aid *which is more visible and has more impact on unstable African governments*. Events have proved the wisdom of the Soviet choice'.[10] [emphasis added].

SUMMARY

From what has been written so far, it must be clear that it is hardly feasible to quantify an interventionary capability. Although there are clearly limits defined by air or sea lift, by the size of stockpiles of readily available equipment, by manpower and by distance, it is not easy to convert such data into useful planning figures. Trends can be detected but in the case of the Soviet Union and her allies (as with other powers) it is so easy to divert civil lift resources or to draw down stockpiles, or even to take risks by thinning out forces at home, that no tabulation can stand examination. Those trends are showing a development towards greater capabilities than before, and the experience gained in earlier interventions can be built upon to provide yet faster reaction times and more efficient staffwork in the future. And it seems increasingly probable that the Soviet Union will be emboldened by past success to take greater political risks in future, in terms of side-stepping overflying constraints. She has also added, with every forward move, to the staging bases available for a distant airlift and introduced greater flexibility of equipment supply by being able to draw from a larger number of stockpiles. Soviet maritime reach is increasing as more ports are open to Soviet naval vessels and as useful new amphibious shipping and specialised cargo vessels are brought into service. The demonstrative effects of the Ethiopian airlift and the invasion of Afghanistan are likely to exceed any theoretical capability possessed by the United States when Third World leaders weigh up their policies. The apparent lack of warning of the Ethiopian moves and the Afghan invasion is also unsettling. The Soviet Union has shown that she can intervene massively and at great speed in the Third World when Soviet interests are at stake – and the United States will not. That is a lesson which will give comfort to radical *regimes* and cause the more conservative to begin to doubt both the willingness and the ability of the United States to get to them first when they are threatened.

The global policies of the Soviet Union are characterised today by what amount to holding operations in those geographical areas of competition where unambiguous challenges would bring clear Western response, and a restless search for marginal gains wherever the West, for whatever reasons, is inhibited from responding to the challenge. In part this is a policy that the Soviet Union must adopt for ideological reasons and in part because she is a superpower with imperial longings facing another superpower that she would prefer to weaken and is not afraid to embarrass. A more careful calculation of the risks and costs of forward movement, and some willingness to withdraw from an exposed position if the alarm bells start to ring, add substance to the argument that Soviet concerns in the Third World are *relatively* low on the list of Soviet strategic priorities. But it is not easy for the Soviet Union to forego opportunities to foster instability and exacerbate tensions when the cost is low and Western or Chinese positions are weakened in the longer term. It is clearly legitimate from a Soviet perspective to give historical inevitability a little nudge in a favourable direction from time to time (and certainly history must not be allowed to go into reverse); but the more that the attainment of positions of real and lasting influence come to look like imperialism, the less willing are Third World leaders to accept a new master. And Soviet *rule* (as opposed to Soviet influence) is unlikely to have the quality of permanence unless backed by coercive imperial power. Many leaders, while finding it useful to seek Soviet military and diplomatic support at times, draw the line at mortgaging too much for that support. The dangers are clear; it is not always easy for them to escape from a dependency and, of all dependencies, the military one may be the most entangling for the reasons advanced here. Soviet military reach and readiness to use the military instrument have alike increased. If Third World leaders are tempted to sup with the devil, they will need very long spoons.

The hope for the Western World is that it ought to be possible to co-ordinate a strategy of economic support which would prove more alluring in the long run for there is noticeable disaffection in the poorer countries of the Third World over the amount of Soviet economic aid, much of which has nothing to do with the alleviation of distress and all to do with Soviet foreign policy and strategic interests. That aid has been based on 'carefully targeted, highly selective, and differentiated criteria'.[11] Indeed, Third World leaders were hardly encouraged by the Soviet attitudes to the Nairobi and Colombo conferences at which it became clear to them that the Soviet Union was ideologically opposed to the notion that poor countries should be helped out of the swamp by any Soviet economic assistance; Soviet writers have specifically disclaimed 'equal responsibility' with the capitalist powers. That may seem to track with the tenets of theoretical Marxism-Leninism but it cannot but present the West with opportunities to counter challenges based almost exclusively on Soviet military penetration.

An increasingly turbulent world offers unparallelled openings for Soviet military meddling and that is a situation that Western nations must learn to live with. Sometimes it may seem right to offer a military counter to such meddling, so that the prospective costs begin to look too high for what will usually, in Soviet eyes, be a marginal gain. Much more often it will be imprudent for the West to accept the implicit challenge on ground that the Soviet Union has chosen, for public support may not allow the challenge to be sustained. Far better to use the weapons that the West can use: the offer of trade and hard currency and development funds to counter Soviet military (and ephemeral) advantage.

NOTES

1. Hannes Adomeit, 'Ideology in the Soviet View of International Affairs', unpublished paper prepared for IISS Annual Conference, 1978.
2. *Government Business Worldwide Reports. Defense Business, 8/15* January 1979: *International Arms Trade; Arms Flows to LDCs; US–Soviet comparisons 1974–1977*, p.3.
3. Barry Blechman, in an address at the Woodrow Wilson International Center for Scholars, 21 May 1979, entitled "US–Soviet Progress in Conventional Arms Talks', reported in US International Communication Agency (ICA) Official Text, 23 May 1979, p.4.
4. Minrod Novik, Foreign Policy Research Institute (Philadelphia), Monograph No. 26, 1979, p.57.
5. *Government Business Worldwide Reports*, op.cit. p.3.
6. 'The Soviet Union and the Third World: A Watershed in Great Power Policy?' *US Congressional Research Service (86–221)*, 8 May 1977, p.71.
7. Leo Tanksy, 'Soviet Military Aid, Technical Assistance and Academic Training', in Raymond W. Duncan (ed.), *Soviet Policy in Developing Countries* (London, 1979) p.45.
8. For a fuller discussion of these points, see William Durch's article 'The Cuban Military in Africa and the Middle East: From Algeria to Angola', *Studies in Comparative Communism*, vol XI, nos 1 and 2, Spring/Summer 1978, pp.34–74
9. *Congressional Research Service*, op.cit., p.100.
10. *Ibid.*, p.99.
11. *Ibid.*, p.121.

3 Soviet Trade with the Third World

Brian Pockney

THE GENERAL POSITION

During the decade from 1969 to 1978, Soviet foreign trade turnover has increased from 20 milliard roubles per annum to 70 milliard roubles per annum and, whilst part of this increase can be attributed to the world-wide inflation in those years, a considerable part is the result of the Soviet Union increasing its participation in world trade. Within this impressive trebling of its total foreign trade with the rest of the world, the proportion with the Third World has remained remarkably consistent (see Table 3.1). In the decade under examination Soviet trade with the Third World fluctuated between 11 and 15 per cent of its total foreign trade. The average is 12.9 per cent and six of the ten years

TABLE 3.1 *Soviet trade with the Third World*

	% of total Soviet foreign trade	Turnover	Export	Import
		(in millions of roubles)		
1969	12.6	–	–	–
1970	13.1	–	–	–
1971	12.7	–	–	–
1972	12.6	3 358	2 008	1 350
1973	15.0	4 672	2 937	1 735
1974	14.4	5 772	3 388	2 384
1975	12.4	6 305	6 306	2 999
1976	11.4	6 545	3 740	2 805
1977	13.1	8 333	5 337	2 996
1978	12.1	8 557	5 726	2 831

are within 0.5 per cent of that average. That Soviet foreign trade has increased is not in itself surprising for, during the years of the 1960s and the 1970s, the USSR claims to have become the world's largest producer of many major commodities – oil, coal, iron, steel, iron ore, coke, mineral fertilisers, diesel and electric engines, tractors, timber, cement, woollen cloth, leather footwear, sugar, animal fats – and in numerous speeches and articles the aim of developing Soviet foreign trade rapidly has been proclaimed. The rapid growth of the Soviet merchant marine has also foreshadowed an expansion in Soviet foreign trade (see Appendix 1 to this chapter).

Thus it might appear that Soviet foreign trade has become an important part of world trade and an important factor in the trade of the Third World. However these developments need to be put into perspective. World trade generally has also greatly increased in these years even though in the Western world some of these years were the period of the most profound slump in the post-war period. The 1976 Report of the United Nations Conference on Trade and Development shows that whilst the trade of the USSR has expanded in physical and in monetary terms, as has the trade of most developing countries, the *proportion* of the world Import-Export market each group has taken has been *falling* for most of the years since 1960. The importance of this cannot be over-emphasised. Even with all the problems of oil prices, inflation, stagflation, and the biggest depression in the trade cycle since 1945, the developed market economies have been taking, together with OPEC countries, larger *shares* of an expanding world trade turnover (see Figures 3.1 and 3.2). The figures in Appendices 2,3,4 to this chapter indicate that, apart from the petroleum exporting countries, the share of *world exports* by developing countries has fallen even more than their share of *world imports*, for example Latin American exports have fallen from 10.9 to 4.3 per cent whilst imports fell only from 8.6 to 4.9 per cent. Africa's exports fell from 5.1 to 3.8 per cent whilst imports fell from 5.2 to 4.0 per cent. West Asia is an exception in that its export share has risen from 1.9 to 8.9 per cent and its import share from 2.2 to 3.9 per cent. As this region contains major oil exporters this is not surprising and South and South-East Asia revert to the main trend. Export share falls from 10.9 to 4.5 per cent and import share from 9.0 to 5.9 per cent. The same pattern can be seen in the figures of Appendices 2 and 3, where the developing countries are divided into Major Petroleum Exporters and Others. In general, it would appear that the poorer a country in 1974, the greater its proportionate loss in the world export market. The period under review was a time of maximum economic difficulty for most of the

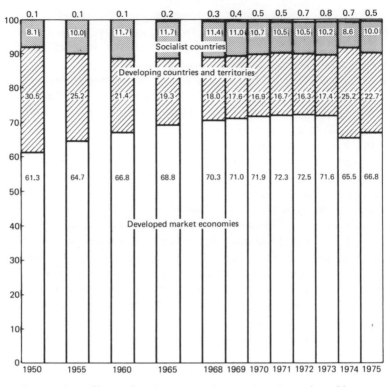

FIGURE 3.1   *Share of major economic groupings in total world exports*
                           (in percentages)

SOURCE   Proceedings of the United Nations Conference on Trade and
   Development, Nairobi, 1976 (New York: United Nations, 1977)
   table 1.9, p.37.

Third World countries and, whereas in 1950 many had been in balance
or earned a small surplus, by 1975 they were importing more than they
exported.

   It is against this background that Soviet trade with the Third World
has to be considered and whilst international figures covering large
groupings can give an indication of broad trends the scale of Soviet
trade can perhaps be seen in clearer perspective when it is realised that
Soviet trade with the city of West Berlin is greater in turnover, in
export or import, than with nearly all the countries in the Third World.
In Africa only Egypt and Algeria had greater trade with the Soviet
Union in 1976 and 1977 than West Berlin. Twenty-eight other African

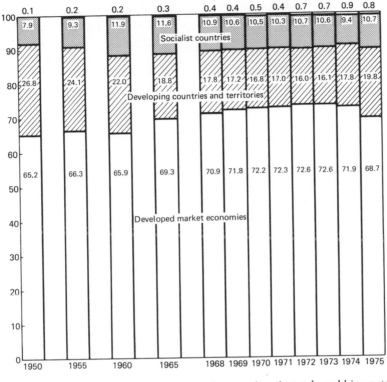

FIGURE 3.2   *Share of major economic groupings in total world imports*
(in percentages)

SOURCE   Proceedings of the United Nations Conference on Trade and
Development, Nairobi, 1976 (New York: United Nations, 1977)
table 1.10, p.39.

states had a smaller turnover and these included Angola, Ghana,
Kenya, Libya, Madagascar, Mali, and Nigeria. In Asia only Afghanistan, India, Syria, Iraq and Iran had a larger turnover (if we exclude
from our list of Asian countries Vietnam, China, North Korea,
Mongolia and Japan). West Berlin trade was larger in turnover than
that with Burma, Indonesia, Cyprus, Malaysia, Pakistan, Turkey or
Sri Lanka. And in South America only Brazil and Argentina could
show a bigger turnover whilst eleven other states had less trade with
the USSR than West Berlin.

One final example will serve to put into perspective the size and
scale of Soviet trade with the developing countries. Turnover with *all*

the developing countries in 1975 was 6305 million roubles. In that year, this was slightly more than the rouble turnover, in millions of roubles, with:

West Germany	2 777.3
France	1 296.5
Japan	1 922.4
	5 996.2

Why then examine this small part of world trade? The answer is to be sought, not in large volumes of trade or rapid growth in turnover, but in the nature of the trade between the USSR and the very large number of countries coming into the category called the Third World. Many of these are the ex-colonial territories of recent Empires, some are land-locked, some are rich in ores, others have an abundance of agricultural products whilst several have a strategic interest. The pattern of trade links that has developed throws light on certain problems of the Soviet economy as well as the desperate problems of the poor nations of the world.

AFRICA, ASIA AND LATIN AMERICA

If we divide the Third World into the three geographical areas of Africa, Asia and Latin America we find that in 1970, Africa and Asia had almost the same volume of trade in imports and exports and Latin America had an insignificant part of Soviet trade (see Figures 3.3 and 3.4). From 1970, trade with Africa was almost stable and exports to the continent fluctuated a little above and below 600 million roubles per annum. Imports from Africa rose but there was no dramatic change in the pattern. In Asia, both imports and exports rose at a steep rate and doubled by 1975. Soviet exports to Asia almost doubled again by 1978 but imports did not maintain a similar rate of growth.

Some of the most interesting developments are to be seen in Latin America. Soviet trade in the region has a pattern which is unique in its relations with any other regional groupings. Soviet imports from the region are always much greater than exports. In many years imports are three or four times greater than exports and in 1975 they were five times greater. If measured by *rate* of growth Latin America has been the region where a rapid expansion of Soviet trade has occurred but if we measure by *volume* then Asia was, and still is, the region of greatest interest.

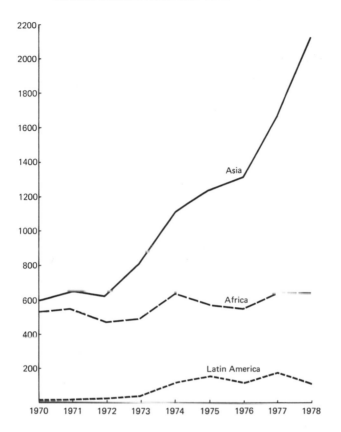

FIGURE 3.3   *Soviet exports to Asia, Africa and Latin America*
(millions of roubles) (calculated by addition)

SOURCE   Raw data from *Vneshnyaya Torgovlya.*

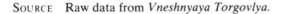

TRADE LINKS, CATEGORISED BY TURNOVER

Within these broad groupings it is possible to establish which countries
have the largest and most regular trade links with the USSR by a
ranking according to total turnover (see Table 3.2). Only Iraq in 1978
achieved a turnover in one year of 1000 million roubles. In the category
of 100–300 million roubles turnover per annum there is a lengthier list
but not all manage to retain a place continuously. The position of

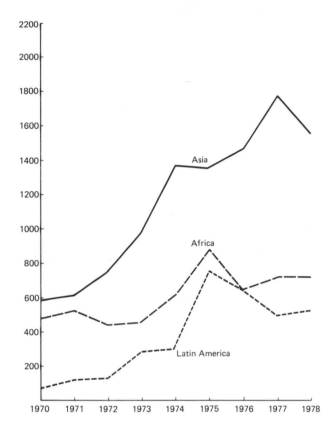

FIGURE 3.4   *Soviet imports from Asia, Africa and Latin America*
(millions of roubles) (calculated by addition)

SOURCE   Raw data from *Vneshnyaya Torgovlya.*

China is interesting in that it had recovered from the lowest ever figure
in modern times of 41.9 million roubles in 1970 and usually occupies a
position of second or third in the list of 'socialist developing countries'
after Mongolia (and since 1977 after Vietnam). Soviet trade with
North Korea reached a pinnacle in 1971 when turnover was 452.3
million roubles and then drifted downwards but since 1976 has shown
signs of a modest recovery. Substantial Soviet trade with Vietnam
could not be expected until the war ended but since then it has almost
doubled.

TABLE 3.2   *Trade links with USSR by turnover*

	1975	1976	1977	1978
500 million roubles or more				
Iraq	599.5	714.5	602.0	1,084.0
India	685.6	647.5	926.0	771.4
Iran	509.7	444.6	707.5	671.1
Egypt	710.3	530.6	492.4	345.5
'Communist Third World'				
Mongolia	480.4	614.5	676.5	716.9
300–500 million roubles				
Argentina	304.4	233.9	206.3	331.2
Brazil	396.1	445.5	314.0	165.1
'Communist Third World'				
Vietnam	206.5	296.1	404.0	457.8
China	338.2	300.5	248.5	338.7
North Korea	200.9	314.4	328.7	378.1
100–300 million roubles				
Syria	167.8	235.4	207.0	205.0
Afghanistan	132.2	154.3	190.1	215.0
Turkey	95.3	114.5	139.1	157.7
Malaysia	102.1	107.7	136.4	125.3
Algeria	247.0	190.3	162.8	139.6
Morocco	86.9	105.6	105.2	104.0
Nigeria	108.3	50.5	34.8	92.2
Ghana	57.0	81.2	116.9	114.2
Philippines	12.8	68.3	108.1	35.3

Of even greater interest than China, Vietnam and North Korea is the large turnover with Brazil. Until 1970 turnover with Brazil was insignificant and hovered around the 50–60 million roubles per annum level. By 1970 it had dropped to a pitiful 23.2 million roubles but after that it rose very rapidly (see Table 3.3). Only Iraq, Iran, Mongolia and Argentina can show such a rapid increase during the 1970s. The

TABLE 3.3   *Brazilian trade turnover with USSR (in millions of roubles)*

1970	1971	1972	1973	1974	1975	1976	1977
23.2	43.7	72.9	125.8	202.0	396.1	445.5	314.0

reasons for Brazil's rapid growth in trade as well as the very specific nature of it will be examined later. It suffices at this stage to show that it is fifth in the 'non-bloc' countries as measured by trade turnover, and ahead of several 'socialist' countries. Nigeria came into the third category (of 100–300 million roubles turnover) only once, in 1975, in all previous years it had fluctuated at much lower levels. Similarly, Ghana where trade with the USSR has gone through patterns very different from those of other African countries. Soviet trade with Ghana built up and was second only to Egypt in the African continent until 1965. Then it drifted downwards until 1972/73 when it began to climb sharply but by that time others had climbed higher up the ladder of Soviet trade with Africa.

Algeria's trade with the USSR was very small until 1965 when it began to climb (see Table 3.4). From 1965 to 1975 the climb was steady

TABLE 3.4   *Algerian trade turnover with the USSR (in millions of roubles)*

1965	1966	1967	1968	1969	1970	1971	1972	1973	1974	1975
17.3	22.2	43.0	53.6	107.3	118.3	121.9	114.5	116.8	171.7	247.0

without being dramatic and a peak appears to have been reached in 1975.

Thus Africa has one representative – Egypt – in the group of countries whose trade in this particular context could be considered substantial, none in the second category where trade figures are worthy of note and four – Nigeria, Ghana, Morocco and Algeria in the third category. Whatever other conclusions may be drawn it must surely be agreed that Soviet trade links with the great African continent are as yet in the very earliest stages of development. The number of countries in Africa with Soviet trade is considerable and the number has grown greatly in the 1970s, but apart from the countries mentioned, trade, as yet, is on a minimal scale.

With Asia the picture is different. India, Iraq and Iran are in the first category and are among the largest of the trading partners. In the second group there are no 'non-committed' Asian countries, only the strange bedfellows of Vietnam with its links with CMEA (Council for Mutual Economic Assistance), China with its pathological hostility to CMEA and Korea shuffling backwards and forwards between the two giant neighbours. In the third category Asia has Syria, Afghanistan, Turkey and Malaysia. The 1978 revolution changed the political complexion of Afghanistan and at the time of writing its trade pattern was bringing it closer and closer to the USSR. With a per capita GNP of only 81 US dollars per annum it is one of the poorest countries in the world but its trade showed a steady increase as seen in Table 3.5.

TABLE 3.5   *Afghanistani trade turnover with the USSR (in millions of roubles)*

1963	1964	1965	1966	1967	1968	1969	1970	1971	1972	1973	1974	1975
58.0	63.1	64.6	82.9	70.2	63.6	67.8	66.9	79.9	68.9	69.5	122.4	132.2

Trade with Turkey – a near neighbour, as is Afghanistan – was at an insignificant level until 1967 when, for the first time, it reached 50 million roubles and nearly trebled by 1973 (see Table 3.6). After that there was a downward drift until 1975 but since then the volume of trade has grown again.

TABLE 3.6   *Turkish trade turnover with the USSR (in millions of roubles)*

1963	1964	1965	1966	1967	1968	1969	1970	1971	1972	1973	1974	1975
14.2	17.2	32.0	41.6	50.4	54.7	79.0	83.3	102.0	144.7	132.8	129.1	95.3

Malaysia and Syria have very different geographical positions, very different resources and wholly dissimilar political systems. Malaysia has a per capita GNP of 572 dollars and Syria 397 dollars. She buys virtually nothing from the USSR and nearly all of the turnover figure consists of Soviet purchases. Whilst in some years Soviet purchases have fallen below 100 million roubles, they have often been above that level.

A similar position has developed with the Philippines. The first data on trade between the USSR and the Philippines appear only in 1975 when it was a humble 12.8 million roubles. Nearly all of this consisted of Soviet purchases in the Philippines and very minute sales of Soviet goods in return.

This was not the case with Syria. The turnover figures did not pass through the 50 million rouble level until 1968 and since then the flow of exports from the USSR to Syria has tended to exceed the flow in the other direction.

The pattern of Soviet trade with the developing countries has many variations both in volume and in geographical distribution. Over a span of 20 years only Egypt and India are regular trade partners with a turnover of any size. Brazil, Argentina, Iraq have a turnover of less than 100 million roubles per annum before 1970 and whilst trade increases with some countries, it declines with others. Even those countries showing an increase in total turnover must be viewed with caution, as the world-wide inflation of the seventh decade has had its distorting effects in this sector as elsewhere.

If we measure the changes in volume of Soviet trade with certain countries from the end of the eighth Five Year Plan in 1970 to the end of the ninth Five Year Plan in 1975 the result can be shown in Table 3.7. Whether or not the increase in the monetary turnover has compensated for inflation is more difficult to establish. Comparing 1970 and 1975 for the Asian countries the following picture emerges. Most countries show a considerable increase in trade – both in absolute terms and in percentages (see Table 3.8). For purposes of comparison Asia's 'Developed Capitalist Country' is shown. In 1975 its turnover was almost the same as India, Iraq, Iran and China combined. Soviet trade declined with a number of Asian countries in this period (see Table 3.9).

TABLE 3.7   *Changes in the volume of Soviet trade (millions of roubles)*

	1970	1975	
Brazil	23.2	396.1	i.e. + 372.9 (factor of 17)
Argentina	29.9	304.4	i.e. + 274.5 (factor of 10)
Iraq	63.5	599.5	i.e. + 536.0 (factor of 9)

None of the countries showing a decline in the years 1970/5 was a major trading partner (except Malaysia) and during these years its trade had shown big fluctuations as seen in Table 3.10.

By applying the same criteria to Africa, we find that from 1970 to 1975 most countries show a considerable increase in trade (see Table 3.11). In Africa six countries without trade relations in 1970 were trading in 1975, as shown in Table 3.12. Angola started trading in 1976. Countries showing a downturn in trade can be seen in Table 3.13. Whilst the percentage increases look most impressive, only Algeria, with an increase of 129 million roubles and Egypt with 104 million roubles showed an increase of 100 million roubles or more in turnover. In the first half of the 1970s the USSR was only just beginning to establish a trade network in Africa.

TABLE 3.8   *'Plus' Countries (Asia) (millions of roubles)*

	1970	1975	+	%
Afghanistan	66.9	132.2	65.3	98
Bangladesh	–	58.1	–	–
Burma	4.4	4.9	0.5	11
Vietnam	183.2	206.5	23.3	13
India	364.9	685.6	320.7	88
Iraq	63.5	599.5	536.0	844
Iran	231.2	509.7	278.5	120
Cyprus	9.3	16.8	7.5	81
China	41.9	200.9	159.0	380
North Korea	335.9	338.2	2.3	0.7
Lebanon	17.5	21.4	3.9	22
Mongolia	230.9	480.4	249.5	108
People's Dem. Rep. Yemen	4.5	13.9	9.4	208
Nepal	1.3	5.5	4.2	323
United Arab Emirates	–	1.9	–	–
Pakistan	60.4	60.7	0.3	0.5
Saudi Arabia	5.4	5.6	0.2	4
Singapore	8.4	14.5	6.1	73
Syria	59.1	167.8	108.7	184
Thailand	3.4	17.3	13.9	408
Turkey	83.3	95.3	12.0	14
Philippines	–	12.8	–	–
Sri Lanka	17.0	22.4	5.4	32
Japan	**652.3**	**1 992.4**	**1 270.1**	**195**

TABLE 3.9   *'Minus' Countries (Asia) (millions of roubles)*

	1970	1975	–	%
Indonesia	29.5	28.6	0.9	3
Jordan	6.4	4.0	2.4	38
Yemen Arab Republic	11.0	5.6	5.4	49
Cambodia	1.7	–		
Kuwait	10.0	3.5	6.5	65
Malaysia	112.6	102.1	10.5	9

TABLE 3.10   *Trade with Malaysia (millions of roubles)*

1970	112.6
1971	79.1
1972	59.4
1973	97.6
1974	188.7
1975	102.1

TABLE 3.11　*'Plus' Countries (Africa) (millions of roubles)*

	1970	1975	+	%
Algeria	118.3	247.0	128.7	109
Benin/Dahomey	0.7	3.0	2.3	–
Ivory Coast	1.9	32.7	30.8	1 621
Ghana	49.7	57.0	7.3	15
Guinea	14.2	34.1	19.9	140
Egypt	606.4	710.3	103.9	17
Cameroon	7.5	36.6	29.1	388
Kenya	1.8	3.3	1.5	83
Congo	1.5	4.2	2.7	180
Libya	12.9	18.8	5.9	46
Madagascar	0.6	1.1	0.5	83
Mali	6.4	6.6	0.2	3
Morocco	50.1	86.9	36.8	73
Nigeria	31.2	108.3	77.1	247
Senegal	1.2	3.2	2.0	166
Somalia Dem. Rep.	3.2	26.5	23.3	728
Sierra Leone	1.6	2.2	0.6	38
Tanzania	1.8	8.5	6.7	372
Tunisia	5.7	10.5	4.8	84
Uganda	3.9	6.1	2.2	56
Ethiopia	2.1	5.3	3.2	152

TABLE 3.12　*Six new African trading countries*

	1970	1975
Guinea Bissau	–	0.3
Zambia	–	7.5
Liberia	–	3.1
Rwanda	–	1.8
Central African Rep./Empire	–	0.1
Equatorial Guinea	–	2.0

TABLE 3.13　*'Minus' Countries (Africa) (millions of roubles)*

	1970	1975	–	%
Sudan	77.4	12.6	64.8	84
Togo	4.0	2.8	1.2	70

In Latin America the changes were of a similar nature. The percentage increases were enormous but the actual growth in turnover was much smaller (see Table 3.14). We can compare these figures against the turnover with the developed capitalist countries of Canada and the USA. A comparison with Latin America's member of CMEA, Cuba, again shows, as in Asia, that the volume of trade with the one socialist Third World country, or with the developed capitalist countries, is on a much greater scale than with all the other Third World countries combined. Of all the Third World countries in the Americas only Argentina with an increase of 275 million roubles, Brazil with 373 million and Peru with an increase of 118 million roubles have an increase of 100 million or more over five years. In the case of Peru it is doubtful if there is any significance in the magnitude of the figures as Table 3.15 shows.

TABLE 3.14   *'Plus' Countries (Latin America) (millions of roubles)*

	1970	1975	+	%
Argentina	29.9	304.4	274.5	918
Bolivia	3.1	12.6	9.5	306
Brazil	23.2	396.1	372.9	1 607
Venezuela	–	0.2		
Guyana	–	24.5		
Mexico	1.0	6.1	5.1	510
Panama	–	2.6		
Peru	0.3	118.5	118.2	39 400
S. Salvador	–	0.1		
Uruguay	1.8	15.0	13.2	733
Ecuador	0.8	13.5	12.7	1 588
Jamaica	–	11.2		
Canada	125.3	471.2	345.9	276
USA	160.9	1 599.5	1 438.6	894
Cuba	1 045.0	2 589.0	1 544.0	148

TABLE 3.15   *Trade with Peru (millions of roubles)*

1970	0.3
1971	0.2
1972	2.0
1973	19.7
1974	9.3
1975	118.5
1976	32.0
1977	46.8
1978	32.5

Three South American countries show a downturn in trade from 1970 to 1975 (see Table 3.16).

TABLE 3.16   *'Minus' Countries (Latin America) (millions of roubles)*

	1970	1975	–	%
Colombia	10.9	9.0	1.9	17
Costa Rica	6.2	0.5	5.7	91
Chile	0.8	–	–	–

ASIAN TRADING PARTNERS AND TRADING PATTERNS

It is in this great continent that the USSR's major Third World partners are to be found.

India

India was one of the earliest and when Nehru visited the USSR in 1955 he was the first of the non-bloc statesmen for nearly 10 years to visit the country, at the end of the desolate times of Stalinism. The Russian reception of him was rapturous and when Khrushchev and Bulganin reciprocated the visit and agreed to build the Bhilai steel works in India, a start was made to a partnership which has continued to develop for more than twenty years and has survived governmental changes in both countries. India has a licence to build Mig aircraft and its trade turnover of nearly 1 000 million roubles per annum makes it one of the most important of all the USSR's Third World partners. Its trade is approaching the level of Anglo-Soviet turnover and for a country with a low per capita GNP this represents a considerable part of its economic activity. In the first fourteen years of this partnership the USSR sold more to India than it bought (except for 1960 and 1967) but since 1969 the USSR has bought much more from India than it has sold and over the whole period shows a net deficit of 724.3 million roubles in the visible trade balance. In 1971 India and the USSR signed a Treaty of Peace, Friendship and Co-operation. In November 1973 Brezhnev signed a 15 year Agreement on the Further Development of Economic and Trade Collaboration between India and the USSR. Part of this agreement envisages that by 1980 trade will be 1.5 to 2 times the level of 1973 (that is 880–1170 million roubles turnover) and it seems likely this will be achieved. This would be the first time that the Soviet Union had generated a volume of trade with a developing country to the same level as that with one of the six major developed countries. By 1974/75 the Soviet Union took 12.6 per cent of India's exports and was her biggest single customer whilst it supplied India with 9 per cent of her imports and was the fourth largest supplier.

The USSR has helped build 40 major enterprises in India in metallurgical, oil prospecting, oil processing, heavy and power industries. From India the USSR buys 100 per cent of its imported mica and shellac, 90 per cent of its imported tea, 70 per cent of its spices, 20 per cent of the raw wool it imports. But India is not only an exporter of food and raw materials. She is an important industrial partner and regularly sells alumina, electric cable, rolled steel, steel cable, cotton cloth, electronic calculators etc. Currently India and the Soviet Union are engaged in joint explorations for oil as well as further expansion of the Bokara and Bhilai works. During the spring and summer of 1976, discussions were held and a protocol signed on 'extending the scope of bilateral links to cover co-operation on projects in third countries'. In the summer of 1976 this apparently referred to a joint supply of metallurgical equipment to Bulgaria, Yugoslavia and Cuba but it could be the harbinger of new developments and relations in the future. By autumn 1976, discussions were taking place on a Soviet-Indian Protocol under which India will supply coke-oven batteries for a steel works in Egypt at a cost of approximately 400 million rupees and will also supply similar equipment to Turkey. In an agreement of April/May 1979, India will supply rice to Vietnam in return for oil from the Soviet Union.

The economies of India and the USSR are closely linked in a number of ways. They have agreed on standardisation in automated information systems, establishment of a joint container stock for cargo shipping, joint work on laser technology. In early 1978 they had agreed on telecommunications co-operation and the establishment of a troposcatter communications system whereby the USSR is to provide the equipment and technology and India the antennae. The range of economic co-operation with India is unlike that with any other of the Third World countries and in certain respects is comparable with trade between two advanced and developed countries.

Iran

Iran is one of the Soviet Union's biggest partners in Asia and has a long common frontier. In 1957 the Soviet Union and Iran signed an agreement whereby Iranian goods to and from Europe could take the shorter route across the USSR and 20 000 tons were shipped in the first year. By 1977 the volume of transit traffic has grown to 2 million tons per annum and the frontier facilities had to be reconstructed to cope with the increased flow. With Iran the Soviet Union has concluded one of the more interesting trade deals of recent years. France, West Germany, Austria, Czechoslovakia, USSR and Iran concluded an agreement in 1975 whereby natural gas will be pumped from Iran to the USSR and then through the pipelines across Czechoslovakia to the final customers in Germany, Austria and France. The agreement is scheduled to run until 2001 and the Soviet Union will receive 150 million roubles per annum for transporting the gas. The USSR has supplied and installed the pipelines for transporting this gas. In addition to this multilateral project, the USSR regularly supplies a considerable range of industrial equipment for building enterprises in mining, iron and steel works, food processing factories, road building, and printing as well as a considerable number of cars, lorries, bulldozers and specialised vehicles. From Iran the USSR has regularly bought gas (about 10 million cubic metres per annum in recent years), cottonfibres and small quantities of lead and zinc, caviar, carpets and detergents.

With Iran, the Soviet Union has in most years had a substantial surplus of exports over imports (see Appendix 5 to this chapter). When this trade is examined from Tehran it assumes different proportions. In 1965 the USSR ranked tenth in the list of countries selling Iran 1.91 per cent of its total imports. By 1974/5 the USSR had moved to fifth place and provided 4.09 per cent of Iranian imports. The destinations of Iranian exports were world-wide and if oil materials and hydrocarbon solvents obtained from oil are *included* in the value of exports then in 1966 the USSR ranked fifteenth taking 1.27 per cent of Iran's exports. But if oil and its related products are *excluded*, then the USSR moves to third place and took 9.63 per cent of Iran's exports (West Germany took 14.25 per cent and USA 10.98 per cent). By 1974 the USSR had become Iran's biggest customer (when oil products are not counted) and took 16.29 per cent of Iran's exports (West Germany 16.02 per cent, USA 7.94 per cent).

Iraq

Iraq also occupies an important position in the galaxy of Soviet trade partners amongst developing countries. In recent years the trade turnover has climbed and Iraq is now amongst the biggest traders. The Soviet Union sells a wide range of products to Baghdad. Fifty to sixty per cent of its exports are machinery, equipment and transport equipment. This includes equipment for factories making tractors and agricultural machinery, electrical equipment, drilling machinery, bull-dozers, lorries, cars, aircraft, pipes, timber and other materials for a country set on the path of industrialisation. The pride of place in Soviet–Iraq joint construction projects goes to the complex of canals and the irrigation of land between the Tigris and the Euphrates utilising Lake Tartan. This is part of a programme over many years which has included a dam and hydro-electric station on the Tigris, a 65 km canal joining the Tigris to Lake Tartan, a canal from Tartan to the Euphrates and, now under construction, the Tartan–Tigris canal. It is claimed that when completed this will be one of the world's biggest irrigation reservoirs with a capacity of 85.4 cubic kilometres.

The list of Iraqi exports to the USSR is very simple and has very few items. The largest single item is crude oil. In most years dried figs are the second item and some cotton and shoes are likely to be the only other items listed. The oil purchases account for 90 per cent or more (by value) of all imports so Iraq exports have a very distinctive character. This feature is even more remarkable when the published statistics of the Iraq ministries are consulted, for according to these, not one drop of the oil has the USSR as its destination. Apparently the USSR buys the oil and sells it to various countries of Western Europe (see Appendix 5 to this chapter).

Syria

In this country the Soviet Union has achieved a spectacular set of constructions which should stand as a powerful advertisement to the underdeveloped countries of what Soviet aid and trade can mean. It is claimed that the Euphrates complex is the biggest in Syria and the Middle East. It includes a hydro-electric station of 800 000 kwts, a dam 58 metres high, 4.1 kilometres in length and a reservoir of 12 milliard cubic metres. The first stone was laid in March 1968. By 1974 the first 3 generators were operating and by 1976 another two were added. The project was completed in March 1978 and in addition to irrigating up to 640 000 hectares (1 536 000 acres) will provide about 90 per cent of Syria's requirements for electricity. As well as the construction of the complex the USSR has supplied some 2100 km of high voltage line across the whole country, equipment to modernise the railroads, and drill for oil. Soviet exports also include aircraft, lathes and building materials, including timber (50 per cent of Syria's needs). It is claimed that much of the material is delivered on favourable credit terms with a repayment time of 8 years. From Syria, the USSR buys wool, cotton, hides, oil, knitted goods, perfumery, carpets, towels, toothpaste and tobacco (see Appendix 5).[1]

Turkey

Trade and aid with Turkey have grown considerably in recent years. Until 1960, the fluctuations were marked but since that date annual protocols have been signed and turnover has increased tenfold. Aid agreements were signed in 1967, 1972, 1973, 1975 and 1977. Under these agreements 9 major projects have been completed and under the 1977 Agreement there is a perspective of 10 years of development. By 1976 the first stage of the construction of the Iskenderam Metallurgical Complex was completed and the first steel was produced in March 1977. This iron and steel works will be the biggest in Turkey and the Middle East with an initial capacity of 6 million tons per annum. Other projects in hand include an agreement to construct jointly a dam on the Arpa frontier river, the construction of a large hydrogen peroxide works and an extension to the Aliaga Refinery to enhance its capacity to 10 million tons. Turkey pays for these projects with its traditional exports and the Soviet Union buys

> 20 per cent of Turkey's exports of citrus fruits
> 15 per cent of Turkey's exports of nuts
> 15 per cent of Turkey's exports of raisins

as well as sheep, cattle, olives, tobacco and some textiles.

In 1978/79 USSR will buy 150 million dollars of goods from Turkey. The 1978/79 trade protocol provides for Turkey to import $138 million of goods including asbestos, petrol by-products, uric acid, drugs, ammonium sulphate, wood pulp, paper, ferrous alloys, metallurgical equipment, milling machines, 2 passenger planes, 3 helicopters.

There is an additional trade agreement whereby Turkey is to export an additional $52 million and will import crude oil – 3 million tons per annum in the first phase (see Appendix 5).

Pakistan

Trade turnover with Pakistan has been small but it is worth noting that in 1978 a new sea route from Odessa to Karachi was opened and the Soviet Union is involved in building a major new steel works for the Pakistanis. Three hundred Pakistan engineers had been sent in 1977 to the USSR for 'on the job' training. On completion the metallurgical combine will produce 1.1 million tons per annum which is about the level of current Pakistan demand. The Soviet loan for this project is approximately 470 million roubles and this will be repaid in cotton, carpets, clothing and shoes. The ore will have to be brought in by sea and a new port is being built at Kasem, but the Soviet Union is not involved in the construction of this nor is it financing its construction.

South-East Asia

From South-East Asia the USSR purchases 97 per cent of its rubber and latex imports and constitutes about 12 per cent of Malaysia's export trade and 7–8 per cent of Indonesia's.

With Singapore trade turnover is small but it is worth noting that since the first agreement of 2 April 1966 trade has increased sixfold. A joint shipping line – 'Sosiak Line' – has been formed and a branch of Moscow Narodny Bank opened. Since 1975 a joint Soviet–Singapore fishing company called Merrisko has been operating and it sells fish caught by Soviet fishing ships. From 1971 to 1977 the USSR spent nearly 30 million roubles at the ship repair yards of Singapore.

Trade relations with Indonesia have entered a new phase since 1976 and although still on a small scale there is likely to be a steady expansion in the next few years. In May 1976 the Indonesian Minister for Trade went to Moscow and expressed interest in Soviet skills in hydraulics, minerals and agriculture. Indonesia is buying textile machinery and mineral fertilisers and has now made agreements for the USSR to build 2 hydro-electric stations with a capacity of 800 mw, a plant to process low standard bauxite into aluminium. The capital required is 300 million dollars and the USSR offered easier terms than Europe or the USA.[2]

It was also in 1976 that a trade agreement with the Philippines was signed and the USSR began to purchase considerable quantities of sugar but sold very little in return (see Appendix 5).

AFRICAN TRADING PARTNERS AND TRADING PATTERNS

With the African countries there are certain distinctive features of Soviet aid and trade. Apart from Algeria and Egypt (and for a short time Ghana) Soviet trade with African countries has been on a very low level until the middle 1970s. During the 1960s the USSR had regular trade links with:

Algeria	Cameroon	Morocco	Sudan
Ghana	Kenya	Nigeria	Tanzania
Egypt	Congo	Senegal	Togo
Guinea	Libya	Somalia	Tunisia
Benin (Dahomey)	Mali	Sierra Leone	Ethiopia

Only in the 1970s did the USSR establish regular links with:

Angola	Liberia	Central African Empire
Ivory Coast	Malagasy	Equatorial Guinea
Guinea Bissau	Mozambique	Senegal
Zambia	Rwanda	

All the critical problems of the Third World are to be found in these countries – low GNP, low per capita incomes, poorly developed infrastructure, widespread illiteracy, a tendency to monoculture for export crops. At the 1976 United Nations Conference on Trade and Development at Nairobi (Fourth Session) most of them spoke vigorously of their economic problems – the fall in the prices of their export goods, the rise in the prices of their imports, the increase in their indebtedness, the difficulties of technology transfer; in this respect it must be noted that the outward turn in Soviet policy and attempts to develop trade have occurred in one of the most difficult periods of the post-war economy. Before examining some of the African countries there are certain features of general interest in Soviet trade with Africa. With many of the countries a fishing agreement has featured early in the mutual links. This usually takes the form of Soviet ships catching fish in local waters and landing them, and of training local people to become fishermen. Examples of this are:

GUINEA   Establishment of oceanographic centre at Conakry (13 May 1976).

MAURITANIA   Gift of a fishing trawler (3 May 1976).

MOZAMBIQUE   Fisheries research vessel in Maputo (FAO Programme).

SIERRA LEONE   Agreement for joint survey of fish resources. Aid to fishing industry.

LIBYA   Maritime Navigation Agreement signed (10 December 1976).

ZAIRE   Shipping agreement (10 December 1976).

ANGOLA   First meeting of Joint Fishing Commission. Mixed Fishing Company established (25 March 1977).

Another general feature is the search for mineral wealth. Statements by Soviet authors that this is to help build up an industrial base and to free the countries from dependence on monoculture have a measure of truth in them. It should also be noted that the trade arrangements help to guarantee the USSR's supplies of certain minerals for years to come. Examples of these agreements are:

CONGO   Extraction and Processing plant near Mfusti village – to produce 60 000 tonnes of polymetal ore each year. (29 June 1976).

ALGERIA   Agreement to train specialists in the petrochemical industry. (1 April 1976).

GUINEA   Agreement to construct aluminium plant in M'silah with an annual output of 140 000 tonnes. Supply of drilling rigs for oil and gas prospecting.

MOROCCO   Specialists to help develop fuel-shale industry and geological and aeromagnetic maps. (June 1976).

NIGERIA   Steel works of 1.3 million tonnes per annum to be built in first stage, later to be 5 million tonnes per annum.

MALI   Agreement on development of Kalama Goldfields. Complex to be commissioned by 1980.

BENIN   Protocol on geological co-operation. (11 November 1976).

LIBYA   Discussions on building of metallurgical works, developing gas industry. (22 November 1976).

MAURITANIA   Agreement to provide experts and equipment for survey work and to train geologists for Mauritania. (29 December 1976).

GUINEA   Agreement to help prospect for bauxite. (7 January 1977).
MALAGASY   Agreement on prospecting for minerals. (16 June 1977).

A third feature of interest is the extension of the *Aeroflot* network with the opening of regular airline services to many of the capitals of Africa. This is an indicator of future interest in the continent as significant as any other, for example:

Resumption of Moscow–Ghana route (9 July 1976);
Opening of Moscow–Bissau route (6 April 1976);
Opening of Moscow–Maputo route (4 July 1976) (Mozambique);
Flights to Angola to be increased from one per week (9 September 1976);
Opening of Moscow–Mauritania route (2 December 1976);
Agreement on establishment of a direct air link with Malagasy (18 March 1977).[3]

The Soviet Union claims that it now has more than twenty regular air routes to Africa.

Egypt

The first agreements were made in 1955 (although there is record of some trade even in the inter-war years) and after the events of 1956 the Soviet Union helped build the Aswan Dam.

For many years India and Egypt were the main Third World partners of the Soviet Union and whilst Indian trade has grown in recent years, Egypt has dropped to second or even third place since the disagreements of 1975.

Political relations between Egypt and the USSR have cooled, the military alliance appears to be at an end but nevertheless trade continues at a substantial level. President Sadat complained in June 1976 that the USSR was refusing to re-schedule Egyptian debts but the annual protocol was still signed and Egypt continued to supply cotton, yarn, citrus fruits, rice, textiles, leather footwear, alcoholic beverages and perfumery whilst the USSR sent machinery and spare parts, timber, chemicals, fertilisers, paper and 30 000 tons of frozen fish. It is worth noting that in addition to the Aswan Dam the USSR has supplied equipment for textile factories and other industries but since the rupture in relations Egypt is hardly ever mentioned in Soviet journals or books and detailed recent information is difficult to obtain. The statistics show that trade reached a peak in 1974–5 but since then has drifted downwards (see Appendix 5).

Algeria

With Algeria the outlook is different. From 1970 to 1975 turnover doubled and the underlying trend is of a steady growth in trade between the two countries with the USSR having a surplus of exports over imports for most of the years. It was in 1963 that the first agreements on Economic and Technical Co-operation as well as Trade and Payment Agreements were signed and nine years later (18 February 1972) a Long Term Agreement was signed. The USSR has helped in the construction of a steel smelting shop at El-Khadzhar which has a capacity of 410 000 tonnes of steel per annum. It was opened in May 1972 and is used mainly to make large diameter pipes for oil and gas transport (in Algeria). Co-operation between the two countries on this project continues and the second stage is now under construction. When completed it will be able to produce 1.8 to 2 million tonnes of steel per annum and for a time it will be the biggest steel works in Africa. The USSR claims that it has helped build 30 enterprises in Algeria plus two irrigation dams and amongst these can be counted Algeria's first enterprise for mercury (317 tons per day), a lead-zinc enrichment factory at El-Abede (2000 tons per day), a thermal power station and successful drilling for water in the Sahara which has irrigated 3000 hectares (7200 acres).

These and similar projects account for the predominance of machinery in Soviet exports together with certain raw materials vital for Algeria, for example 30 per cent of Algeria's requirements for asbestos are supplied by the USSR and 50 per cent of its timber requirements. In return the USSR buys traditional Algerian exports such as wine, cork, fruit juices, medicines and cork chips. The big jump in Algerian exports in 1975 was accounted for by a unique Soviet purchase of 983 000 tons of oil for 66 million roubles. In 1974 and 1976 there is no record that the USSR purchased oil in this country (see Appendix 5).

Morocco

Soviet trade with Morocco has been on a steady, if modest, level but in
the next decade it could grow dramatically. In January 1978, an
agreement was initialled to help finance the 2000 million dollar
Maskala phosphate mine project. The Moroccan News Agency
claimed that this would make Morocco 'the USSR's first partner in
Africa in the field of industrial co-operation'[4] and whilst others may
aspire to the role of first partner it is undoubtedly true that if this
project is brought to fruition it will be a major development in the
economy of Africa. At the same time an agreement was signed on
scientific and technical co-operation for 1978/9 in marine research,
geology, tea cultivation and land reclamation as well as the phosphate
industry. By March of 1978 Rabat radio was announcing that Morocco
would pay for the Soviet investment in the phosphate complex by an
annual delivery of 10 million tons of processed or raw sulphate. This
would be subject to review every five years and at present prices would
be worth $5000 million. Morocco and the Soviet Union also signed an
agreement for joint research on fishing and the fishing industry but
Soviet ships were not given permission to fish in Moroccan waters (see
Appendix 5).

Tropical Africa

In Tropical Africa the state emerging as the major trade partner by
1977/8 was Nigeria. The Soviet Union has been involved in helping
with approximately 200 projects in Tropical Africa of which 100 have
been completed, among them are an oil processing works in Ethiopia
with a capacity for processing 625 000 tonnes of crude oil per annum, a
cement factory in Mali (50 000 tonnes per annum), bauxite mining in
Guinea (2.5 million tonnes of bauxite per annum) and an ore-enriching
enterprise in Congo. But the most prestigious development has
recently been agreed in Nigeria. The USSR has agreed to help build a
steel works with an initial capacity of 1.3 million tonnes which in the
future will rise to 5 million tonnes and will then be Africa's largest steel
works. Some aid is being rendered in the building of small power
stations. A hydro-electric station with a capacity of 14 000 kwts. is
being built on the River Kivira in Tanzania and in Guinea a hydro-
electric scheme of 10 000 kwts. In Zambia and Guinea–Bissau thermal
power stations (diesel) are being constructed.

The extent of fishing agreements has already been noted. Another factor worthy of note for the present and for the future is that more than 8000 students from Tropical Africa have qualified in recent years in Soviet Institutes of Higher Education. The training of the 'technical intelligentsia' on this scale represents a considerable faith in the future of an Africa where the Russian language could, alongside English, be the means of transcontinental communication, as well as one of the languages for technology transfer in the last decade of this century.

LATIN AMERICAN TRADING PARTNERS AND TRADING PATTERNS

Brazil

Brazil is the USSR's biggest trading partner in South America. It is also one of the world's most rapidly changing and developing economies and since 1970 has become an important partner for the USSR. Brazil is one of the countries in the Third World where the USSR regularly buys more than it sells. In 1974 Soviet exports suddenly leaped from 9.3 to 90.0 million roubles but in the following year Soviet purchases surged from 112 million roubles to 302 million (see Appendix 5).

Soviet purchases are of interest. Of course coffee is a main item but the amount bought year by year fluctuates. A further examination of the table of Imports and Exports shows that only in 1960 did the USSR have a surplus of sales over purchases in Brazil and they also show that the graph of the purchases moves independently of the graph of sales, that is there are only a few years when both sales and purchases move up together or down together. Over the years from 1955 to 1978 the Soviet surplus with Brazil was 5.8 million roubles and its deficit 1067.9 that is a cumulative deficit of 1062.1 million roubles. With Argentina the comparable figures were + 6.7, − 1501.4 that is a cumulative deficit of 1494.7 million roubles.

In 1969 the USSR's main purchases in Brazil were cocoa beans, 17.4 million roubles, followed by cocoa oil, 10.4 million roubles, and coffee in third place at 7.3 million roubles. The only other sizeable purchases were rice, 3.9 million roubles, and cotton, 2.2 million roubles. That was the last year in which the Soviet Union bought rice in Brazil and apart from a nominal purchase of cotton in 1970, it was also the last year in which it bought that commodity (in which many Soviet writers claim they have a better productivity record than the USA). In 1970 they also bought no coffee but this commodity appears again in all subsequent years. Cocoa beans, 8.2 million roubles, and cocoa oil, 6.5 million roubles, were 70 per cent of the total shipping bill in 1970. A modest quantity – 879 tons – for 2.3 million roubles, of woollen yarn made up another 10 per cent and Brazil nut oil was the remaining substantial item. This item appears to have doubled in price from 1969 to 1970 for 6016 tons cost 773 000 roubles in one year and 6122 tons cost 1 818 000 roubles the next.

From 1971 to 1974 the commodities bought in Brazil were the same in most years with the greater part of the expenditure going on cocoa, coffee and woollen yarn, except in 1972 and 1973 when very large sums of money were spent on raw sugar – 34.8 million roubles in 1972 and 71.5 million roubles in 1973. In both years sugar was responsible for well over half the cost of the imports. None was bought in 1974 but in 1975 there was an immense expenditure of 84.1 million roubles on sugar. This was in spite of the rocketing increase in the price of sugar in 1975. Also in 1975 and 1976 there was a massive expenditure on maize and soya beans. 85 million and 54 million roubles were spent on maize in 1975 and 1976 whilst soya beans cost 64 millions and 248 millions in the same years. These expenditures dwarfed all other purchases in these years and were responsible for the cost of purchases in Brazil jumping from 112 million roubles in 1974 to 302.8 million in 1975 and 369.4 millions in 1976. The motivation for these purchases is not difficult to find. 1975 was a disastrous year in the USSR for the harvest. 140 million tons was the best estimate and this was far from adequate to feed the population, maintain the livestock and supply Eastern Europe with its grains.

Argentina

Purchases of maize and wheat in Argentina were also on a massive scale in these critical years of 1975 and 1976. Soviet purchases in Argentina are almost wholly agricultural primary products. Wool has been the major item in most years, followed by various flax and tung oils. Hides have also been purchased in quantity. But the dramatic increases in Soviet purchases in Argentina in the middle 1970s can be attributed largely to the massive purchases of wheat and maize in 1975 and 1976. In 1975 they spent 111 656 000 roubles on maize and 103 521 000 roubles on wheat. In 1976 expenditure on maize fell to 34 560 000 roubles but rose for wheat to 122 649 000 roubles. In the light of these figures one should hesitate to draw any firm conclusion about a dramatic long-term increase in Soviet trade in South America. The 1978 Soviet grains harvest was the largest ever in Russian history and it will be instructive to see the effects of this on foreign trade policy. In the case of Argentina it should be noted that some consumer goods were bought in 1975 and 1976 – clothes and wine – which is perhaps surprising in the light of Soviet problems with foreign currency. Argentina, like Brazil, always sells far more to the USSR than it purchases (except for 1956 and 1958) and the amounts bought by Argentina can only be described as derisory. With Brazil the trade bears the character of exchange of primary agricultural products against a primary extracted fuel but with Argentina the exchange is of primary agricultural product plus some processed and semi-processed against manufactured goods for industry and consumption with some fuel. In neither case is the pattern observed of bilateral (barter) type exchanges which is often associated with Soviet foreign trade policy. The prices of products change and fluctuate rapidly. Wool has changed its price from year to year as have coffee and cocoa. The forms and patterns of Soviet trade in these two countries are are not typical of the forms to be found in other countries.

When the problems of Soviet–Brazilian trade are considered from the viewpoint of Brazil there is an interesting perspective. Brazil has reserves of almost every non-ferrous metal, plus uranium and other strategic metals. The underground resources still remain largely uncharted and Brazil's imports of non-ferrous metals cost 500 million dollars per annum.[5] Brazil is importing machinery for heavy industry in large quantities from the USA and at first sight would appear to offer an ideal market for Soviet heavy industry exports. But Soviet policy appears to favour export of capital goods only when these are purchased by the state sector and there is no record of substantial sales in any part of the world of capital goods to the private sector. With consumer goods, for example cameras, cars, wines etc., there appears to be no such restriction and they are sold to private distributors as well as to state networks. Brazil is also an oil producer and the long-term perspective for Soviet oil sales cannot be too good unless in the developing Brazilian economy the consumption of oil rapidly outstrips the supply. Whilst Brazil and Argentina have served as major reserves of wheat and maize during the 1970s and otherwise have traded in their traditional products, it is worth noting that there was a similar surge in Soviet purchases in Argentina, but not Brazil, in 1965 and 1966.

Purchases of wheat leaped from 18 million to 65 and 96 millions and then returned to 21 millions of roubles.

Peru

One other country in Latin America is worthy of a more detailed examination. In 1969 diplomatic relations with Peru were established and a Trade Agreement signed. To 1975 trade turnover grew rapidly but then fell very quickly in 1976 (see Appendix 5). The USSR had a positive balance in only the one year of 1977. The main commodities involved were as seen in Table 3.17.

TABLE 3.17   *USSR imports from Peru*

	1971	1972	1973	1974	1975	1976	1977
Coffee (tons)	300	2 500	986	1 035	1 035	2 656	690
Thousand roubles (value)	205	1 341	570	997	897	4 271	1 489
Non-Ferrous Metals (tons)					6 018	6 144	
(Thousand roubles)					2 381	3 032	
Sugar (tons)			96 834	–	104 985	–	
(Thousand roubles)			14 856	–	85 852	–	
Concentrates of Non-Ferrous Metals in thousand roubles						9 615	11 203

Coffee was a stable item and the USSR had experienced annual fluctuations in its price but it was Soviet purchases of large quantities of sugar in 1973 and 1975 which caused the rapid escalation of total turnover. In passing it is worth noting that in 1961 to 1963 the USSR bought 12 800 tons of copper before trading between the two countries came to an abrupt halt.

Before concluding the survey of Latin America it is worth noting that when Brazil–Soviet trade is viewed from the Brazilian end, the USSR is twenty-sixth in the list of importers (by value) into the country but is ninth in the list of purchasers. The USSR plays a more important part in Argentina's structure of foreign trade but still is behind most of the South American countries and the 'developed capitalist countries' in value of purchases and sales. The authors V.N. Volkov and M.A. Khaldin write of Brazil 'The USSR buys many essential commodities in Brazil: (37 per cent of all the coffee imported into the USSR in 1971–75), cocoa beans. . . .Soviet–Brazilian trade is characterised by a significant excess of Soviet imports over exports. Its further development will depend largely on the readiness of Brazilian organisations and firms to increase their purchases of Soviet goods and to conduct trade on a balanced basis.'[6]

With Peru it should be observed that as well as the sudden flourishing in trade the USSR is helping Peru to build the Olmos project an irrigation and hydro-electric scheme which will involve construction of dams on both sides of the Andes cordillera. Exploratory work was completed by the summer of 1976. There are a number of other Peruvian–Soviet agreements covering the fishing industry and ferrous metallurgy as well as the Olmos project.[7]

The picture of Soviet trade with the Third World that emerges from this survey is complex. In South America the salient feature is Soviet purchases of wheat and sugar in years of poor harvest in the USSR. Without these purchases the turnover would be on a modest scale. In Africa only Egypt was a main partner for almost twenty years but in the second half of the seventies big changes are visible. Large scale important deals have been concluded with Nigeria and Morocco whilst Algeria appears to have established a regular trade pattern. In the shipping agreements, extension of scheduled airlines, and in large scale training of the 'technical intelligentsia' there is clearly scope for extending Soviet aid and trade in Africa in the next decade. Political conditions have been very unsettled, particularly South of the Equator and until there is greater stability it would be unwise to expect the trade indices to show signs of improvement. What is noticeable is that Soviet trade has not always followed Soviet political influence. With Angola trade fell heavily in 1978 and in the three years that trade has existed, shows the pattern as seen in Table 3.18. With Mozambique trade is on a very low level and with Ethiopia trade has grown. Whilst links have existed between Ethiopia and Moscow since Tsarist times it is only in recent years since the overthrow of the monarchy that sizeable trade has developed. With Somalia substantial trade began to develop in 1970 as can be seen from Table 3.19. As a result of the wars in the Horn of Africa in 1978 it will not be surprising if Soviet trade with Somalia falls to negligible levels.

TABLE 3.18   *Trading patterns with Angola, Mozambique and Ethiopia*

	1976	1977	1978
Angola			
Turnover	19.7	79.6	57.4
Export	5.3	69.2	47.8
Import	14.4	10.4	9.6
Mozambique			
Turnover	0	5.9	18.2
Export	0	5.9	17.4
Import	0	–	0.8
Ethiopia			
Turnover	4.3	23.9	68.5
Export	3.6	22.4	64.2
Import	0.7	1.5	4.3

Any broad conclusions about Soviet aid and trade with Africa must be tentative but it seems that whilst the USSR is able to render effective military aid it is not in a position, or perhaps not willing, to

TABLE 3.19   *Trade with Somalia*

	1969	1970	1971	1972	1973	1974	1975	1976	1977	1978
Turnover	1.9	3.2	7.3	14.6	12.6	18.8	26.5	23.4	23.0	No
Export	1.9	2.8	5.5	11.7	11.5	16.8	22.2	18.7	20.1	data
Import	0	0.4	1.8	2.9	1.1	2.0	4.3	4.7	2.9	published

render massive economic help. The claims of the 'Socialist Third World' are for many of the commodities and the skills that the African Third World needs and there were signs that the trade relations with some of the African states are likely to develop in a variety of ways. In the trade agreement with Ethiopia, the clause relating to payments stipulated that Ethiopia will pay in convertible foreign currency (that is western currencies). President Neto has been attempting to restore trade links with Western Europe, Mozambique has invited Portuguese technicians to return. Nearly all of the traditional links of the African states are with the developed capitalist countries and they are in no condition to disrupt these completely. Nor is the Soviet Union in a position to substitute immediately for the markets in and supplies from the developed capitalist countries.

It must also not be forgotten that, whilst overall the Soviet Union ranks as the world's second economic power, the Soviet economy is still in many respects one of the world's under-developed economies. This has several effects on the Third World. Some of the commodities the Third World can offer in exchange for capital machinery and equipment are commodities the USSR produces for itself, for example tea and cotton. Also the USSR is engaged in mighty efforts to obtain valuable raw materials from remote regions within its own borders, where the infrastructure is as under-developed as in any Third World country. It is relevant here to look at BAM – the Baikal–Amur railway project. Alone of the great powers the USSR is engaged in an active policy of building railways and the 3500 km length in eastern Siberia will give access to rich deposits of many valuable ores and fuels. The method of financing its construction is of interest. Japan is supplying essential machinery for the railway and for the extraction of deposits. From 1981, the Soviet Union will ship 5 million tonnes of coal per annum to Japan until the end of the century in payment for the equipment and machinery. In its form this is similar to the agreements made by the Soviet Union with several under-developed countries, for example India, Pakistan, Egypt, Morocco, Nigeria *et al.* but it indicates that the Soviet economy is not in a position to supply the requirements that many of the developing countries need.

The strain on the Soviet economy of supplying its own vast domestic market, the needs of Eastern Europe, the 'Socialist Third World', the earning of hard currency in Western Europe as well as the demands of the Third World can be seen by analysing one commodity. In recent years the USSR has modernised its motor industry and output per annum is now greater than ever before. But the demands of overseas trade for cars are so great that in spite of a bigger output year by year the number of new vehicles reaching the Soviet internal market is actually falling. This can be seen from Table 3.20 where it is shown that the incremental addition of cars reached a peak in 1975.

TABLE 3.20   *Incremental addition of new cars per annum*

	Annual output	Annual export	Output minus export	Net annual increment with a car life of 10 years	Net annual increment with a car life of 5 years
1960	138 822	30 200	108 622		
1961	148 914	32 800	116 114		
1962	165 945	39 700	126 245		
1963	173 122	35 700	137 422		
1964	185 159	44 500	140 659		
1965	201 175	48 600	152 575		43 953
1966	230 251	66 500	163 751		47 637
1967	251 441	68 900	182 541		56 296
1968	280 332	82 300	198 032		60 610
1969	293 558	73 800	219 758		79 099
1970	344 248	83 800	260 448	151 826	107 873
1971	529 041	149 700	379 341	263 096	215 590
1972	730 105	194 900	535 205	408 960	352 664
1973	916 700	237 500	679 200	541 778	481 168
1974	1 119 000	287 326	831 674	691 015	611 916
1975	1 201 000	295 616	905 384	752 809	644 936
1976	1 239 000	344 743	894 257	730 506	514 916
1977	1 274 000	361 993	912 007	729 466	376 802

NOTES
1. The 1976 and 1977 export figures exceed the 1970 total production figure.
2. From 1960–1977 the output figure has increased by 9 times.
    From 1960–1977 the export figure has increased by 12 times.
3. The figures for columns 4 and 5 are calculated in the following way:
    Assuming the life of an average car to be 10 years the net increments for 1970–1977 were:

1970	$260\ 448 - 108\ 622 = 151\ 826$
1971	$379\ 341 - 116\ 114 = 263\ 093$
1972	$535\ 205 - 126\ 245 = 408\ 960$
1973	$679\ 200 - 137\ 422 = 541\ 778$
1974	$831\ 674 - 140\ 659 = 691\ 015$
1975	$905\ 384 - 152\ 575 = 752\ 809$
1976	$894\ 257 - 163\ 751 = 730\ 506$
1977	$912\ 007 - 182\ 541 = 729\ 466$

4. Assuming the life of an average car to be 5 years the net increments for 1965–1977 were:

1965	$152\ 575 - 108\ 622 = 43\ 953$
1966	$163\ 751 - 116\ 114 = 47\ 637$
1967	$182\ 541 - 126\ 245 = 56\ 291$

1968	198 032 − 137 422 =	60 610
1969	219 758 − 140 659 =	79 099
1970	260 448 − 152 575 = 107 873	
1971	379 341 − 163 751 = 215 590	
1972	535 205 − 182 541 = 352 664	
1973	679 200 − 198 032 = 481 168	
1974	831 674 − 219 758 = 611 916	
1975	905 384 − 260 448 = 644 936	
1976	894 257 − 379 341 = 514 916	
1977	912 007 − 535 205 = 376 802	

In the August 1978 issue of the journal published by the USSR Ministry of Foreign Trade Tables A, B and C appeared. (Note: the tables are reproduced here as printed. The columns of figures do not add up to the totals given.)

TABLE A *Projects with Soviet help in developing countries*

Countries	Total per Agreements	of which completed	As at 1 Jan 1978 Industrial Enterprises per Agreements	of which completed
Afghanistan	118	71	38	17
India	72	52	50	36
Iraq	96	51	48	20
Iran	116	66	84	47
Peoples Dem. Rep. Yemen	25	10	5	3
Pakistan	13	7	5	1
Syria	48	23	18	9
Turkey	15	6	13	6
Sri Lanka	10	9	6	5
Algeria	100	55	31	25
Egypt	107	90	47	32
Guinea	30	21	10	7
Congo	15	9	3	2
Mali	14	12	1	1
Sudan	15	8	6	6
Ethiopia	21	4	5	2

Of a grand total of 1050 projects agreed upon less than half (42.6 per cent) are for industrial enterprises and if we re-order the ranking we find that the biggest recipient of Soviet aid (if measured by *number* of industrial enterprises) was Iran. With 84 industrial enterprises it is far ahead of India with 50 and Iraq with 48. The number agreed for Iran is

TABLE B   *Number of industrial enterprises built and under construction*
with Soviet help (by industries)

According to data of 1 Jan 1978

	per Agreements	Of which functioning
Electricity	88	49
Ferrous + Non-Ferrous Metallurgy	37	20
Coal, Gas + Oil Processing Industries	48	27
Chemical, Oil Processing + Petro-Chemicals	20	15
Engineering	51	42
Building Materials Industries	37	13
Light + Food Industries	152	72
Agriculture	149	73
Transport + Communication	96	61
Geology + Exploration	77	35
Education, Culture + Health	252	145

TABLE C   *Capacity of enterprises built with Soviet help to 1 Jan 1978*

	Unit of Measurement	Envisaged per Agreements	Functioning
Electric Power Stations	millions of kilowatt	11.92	5.69
Iron	millions of tons	17.90	7.54
Steel	millions of tons	19.64	6.76
Rolled	millions of tons	13.35	4.62
Iron Ore	millions of tons	14.00	9.20
Oil (Extraction)	millions of tons	65.32	59.82
Cement	thousands of tons	3 280	100
Elevators (Capacity)	thousands of tons	1 253	684
Housing	thousands sq metres	3 495	205
Railway line	kilometers	2 072	1 499
Roads	kilometres	2 085	2 085

almost as big as the total agreed for the three largest recipients in Africa, that is Egypt 47 and Algeria 31 and Guinean Republic 10.

However, this in itself is not a wholly satisfactory guide and it is useful to look at the final table which shows the actual capacity added and under construction in the developing world. That Soviet aid to the Third World has been and still is much smaller than the aid that flows from the Western World can be accepted but it misses the point that Soviet aid is channelled to what Soviet writers call a number of key industries, which will transform previously backward peasant economies into modern industrial societies capable of withstanding the demands of the multi-nationals. The iron and steel capacity which will be added under the agreements finalised by 1 January 1978 will be comparable with the total capacity of the United Kingdom's iron and steel industry. The volume of oil to be extracted is not insignificant, nor is the amount of iron ore and the length of railway line and roadway each exceeds 1000 miles.

But even these observations must be advanced with caution for Table B shows that Light and Food Industry with 152 enterprises headed the list of industrial projects. Of course it is most unlikely that they absorbed as much capital as the electricity generating or the iron and steel industries but in the absence of more detailed data the only firm conclusions to be drawn have to be based on the available data. Agricultural projects are the second largest group and if added together agriculture with 149 and light industry with 152 come to nearly one third of all the projects. The large number of educational, cultural and health projects totals almost one quarter of all the projects. These can range in importance from a small group of doctors and nurses to the full scale building and equipping of higher educational institutes.

THE NAIROBI CONFERENCE

The Soviet Union was a participant at the United Nations Conference on Trade and Development (Fourth Session) at Nairobi in 1976. The major powers considered the gathering important and Patolichev, Ministry for Foreign Trade, made a significant speech on behalf of the USSR. The documents of this Conference are full of the problems of the poorer developing countries and one of the favourite targets was the multi-national company. In their attacks on the multi-nationals the Third World representatives received support from Mr Patolichev. Algeria accused the Western countries of delaying tactics in implementing the integrated programme for commodities, financing of buffer stocks and principles of indexation. It was further alleged that none of the Tokyo Declaration (14 September 1973) had been honoured, that the problem of debt servicing had grown more difficult. He concluded with a rallying call to develop co-operation between the countries of the Third World and the socialist countries and in support of the Manila Declaration.

Many other countries made very similar declarations and lest it be thought that such statements were made only by 'radical' 'left-wing' governments it should be noted that nearly every one (except Chile) attacked the indifference or hostility of the Western governments and the activities of the multi-nationals. Burundi said very simply that since Bandung in 1955 Africa, Asia and Latin America had proposed reasonable solutions with little response from the wealthier nations. Argentina spoke of the 'disastrous consequences' which the economic crisis of the developed countries had had upon the Third World who had been forced to seek more costly sources of financing. Restrictive measures had blocked access to beef markets and Argentina had accumulated a deficit of more than 800 million dollars in two years. This was a paradox in a world where demand for food increased by 30 million tons per annum yet their efforts were being reduced to nothing. Argentina spoke of the control of the multi-national companies over the economies of the Third World, whilst Brazil stated: 'The moving and marketing of goods depended increasingly on decisions taken by multi-national corporations rather than on the classic instruments of commercial policy.'

When Patolichev spoke on the 11 May he opened by referring to the most serious crisis of capitalism since the 1930s 'causing unprecedented inflation and conjuring up the spectre of protectionism'. It was having a harmful effect on the developing countries and showed how dangerous it was for these countries to remain in the market economy system. His response to the Manila Declaration was hedged with some qualifications. He '. . . supported in principle everything in the Manila Declaration and Programme of Action that was directed against monopolies and everything that reflected the aspirations of the developing world to restructure the economic relations of inequality which characterised the capitalist economy. These aspirations would be realised neither by reverting to the open door policy for foreign capital nor by surrendering command posts in the national economy to multi-national corporations. The importance given to the public sector in industralisation showed that many developing countries were aware of these truths.'

Much of the remainder of his speech is routine but the sixth section discussed one of the most crucial problems. The instability of prices of raw materials and primary commodities and the markets for them as well as the effects of inflation and protectionist measures were discussed by all participants. The example of OPEC has started many similar thoughts elsewhere and the Soviet response reflects its midway position of being both a major world producer of primary products and a mighty industrial power importing raw materials. Patolichev's proposals are: 'An integrated programme for commodities could be based on a system of international stabilisation arrangements of a new type, in which all countries concerned, both importers and exporters, would participate. It would mean ensuring equitable and remunerative prices promoting the expansion of production by using advanced technology and taking account of changes in the relative prices of primary commodities and manufactured goods. The objective was to establish equitable terms of trade, eliminate price fluctuations and stabilise the export earnings of developing countries. The USSR was willing to co-operate with developing countries, on a bilateral or multi-lateral basis, in seeking solutions with a view to radically transforming the commodity market.'

Soviet trade officials are seriously concerned by the problems of price fluctuations and elsewhere in his speech Patolichev proposed 3 to 5 year agreements but he was also concerned by the role of the multi-nationals. In his opening remarks he had attacked them for the amount of profit they remitted to the metropolitan countries from the poorer states and towards the end he returned to the topic. 'His delegation was prepared to examine measures for achieving effective control over their activities. These companies were so firmly entrenched in the economy of developing countries that, unless there was appropriate control, they would be the only ones to benefit most from the stabilisation of raw material prices, expansion of exports of manufac-turers and increased co-operation activities.' Patolichev's speech concluded with a number of proposals for future action. Many of these are already operative in agreements with several countries (for example Long Term Agreement for two to three Five Year Plan Periods) and have been mentioned in this chapter.

He also proposed that there should be 'multi-lateral industrial co operation with the participation of enterprises from socialist countries, developing countries and developed capitalist countries'.

In this proposal there is probably the recognition that the task of reversing the trend of many Third World countries falling into deeper and deeper poverty is greater than can be solved by any one group of the industrialised countries and unless this trend is reversed the instability it can cause will be as great a menace to the world as the unchecked accumulation of nuclear weapons. No society or group of states is benefitting from the present system and there would be sense in a joint effort to finance capital exports, increase technology transfer, reschedule (or indeed abolish) debts and stabilise prices and quantities of primary commodities coming on the market. A speculative idea thrown out by Patolichev was that UNCTAD might be transformed into a world trade organisation with terms of reference extending to include matters within the competence of GATT.

The question neither posed nor answered by the Soviet delegation at Nairobi was whether the Soviet economy has yet reached a state of development and maturity which will enable it to satisfy a pent up demand on the home market, supply its own 'developing socialist countries' – Korea, Vietnam, Mongolia, Cuba, Romania (as it has now joined the Group of '77) and any others that may need to be classified this way, as well as the much larger number of poor Third World countries.

Even if the USSR were to double or treble its trade with the Third World every five years, it would be 1990 before this would show any significant change in the percentages of world trade amongst the major groups.

NOTES

1. *Vneshnyaya Torgovlya*, vol. 7 (1977) pp. 35 *et seq.*, vol. 10 (1977) pp. 26 *et seq.*, vol. 8 (1978) p. 12.
2. *USSR and the Third World* (London: Central Asian Research Centre).
3. See ibid. for details of these agreements.
4. Moroccan News Agency (31 Jan 1978).
5. *The Times* (8 Nov 1978).
6. *Vneshnyaya Torgovlya SSSR: Itogi i Perspektivy*, p. 162.
7. Ibid. pp. 162–3.

APPENDIX 1

Authentic detailed statistics on the Soviet Merchant Marine are not easily obtained from Soviet sources. The authors of *Vneshnyaya Torgovlya SSSR: Itogi devyatei pyatiletky i perspektivy*, ed. V.G. Pavlov, p.203 quote data from the Bremen Institute of Sea Transport Economics to show that by 1976 the Soviet merchant marine was the world's sixth largest fleet. The tanker fleet had 493 ships weighing 5.9 million tons and was 2.7 per cent of world tanker capacity (ninth in the world).

The dry cargo fleet had 2185 ships, 12.8 million tons, 5.8 per cent of world tonnage (sixth in the world).

Container ships of the Ro-Ro type (deadweight from 4000 to 20 000 tons) were built between 1971 and 1975 as well as carriers and 'combined' ships to carry liquid and dry cargoes.

G.A. Levikov in his book *Mezhdunarodnoe Morskoe Torgovoe Sudokhodstvo*, p.198 gives the following data:

Deadweight of the transport fleet (in tonnes)

1965	1970*	1975†
8 555 000	11 089 700	14 997 200

*1 January
†31 December

Levikov's figures do not agree with those of Pavlov. The latter states that on 1 January 1976 there were 2678 ships with a deadweight of 18.7 million tons constituting 4.3 per cent of the world's merchant marine. Subtle differences of definition may account for some of the difference.

APPENDIX 2

*Share of major economic and regional groupings in
total world exports, 1950, 1955, 1960, 1965 and 1968 to 1975
(in percentages)*

	1950	1955	1960	1965	1968	1969	1970	1971	1972	1973	1974	1975
Developed market economy countries	61.3	64.7	66.8	68.8	70.3	71.0	71.9	72.3	72.5	71.6	65.5	66.8
Developing countries and territories	30.5	25.2	21.4	19.3	18.0	17.6	16.9	16.7	16.3	17.4	25.2	22.7
Socialist countries												
E. Europe	6.8	8.5	10.1	10.6	10.5	10.2	9.9	9.7	9.7	9.3	7.9	9.2
of which USSR	–	3.7	4.3	4.4	4.4	4.3	4.1	4.0	3.7	3.8	3.3	3.9
Socialist countries												
Asia	1.3	1.5	1.6	1.1	0.9	0.8	0.8	0.8	0.8	0.9	0.7	0.8
Developing countries and territories												
Latin America	10.9	8.5	6.7	5.9	5.0	4.8	4.8	4.2	4.1	4.4	4.7	4.3
Africa	2.1	1.6	1.4	1.5	1.7	1.7	1.6	1.5	1.3	1.3	2.0	1.6
North African States and Madagascar associated with the EEC	1.1	1.1	0.9	0.7	0.8	0.8	0.7	0.6	0.6	0.6	0.6	0.6
Asia – West	1.9	3.1	3.2	3.3	3.4	3.2	2.8	3.7	3.7	3.9	9.8	8.9
Asia – South and South East	10.9	7.4	6.0	4.9	4.5	4.5	4.4	4.2	4.2	4.8	4.9	4.5
By major export and income category												
Major petroleum exporters	6.2	7.0	6.6	6.3	6.2	5.9	5.5	6.3	6.0	6.7	14.9	13.0
Other developing countries and territories	24.3	18.1	14.7	13.0	11.8	11.7	11.4	10.4	10.3	10.7	10.3	9.7
of which fast growing exporters of manufactures	3.7	2.7	2.2	2.1	2.3	2.4	2.3	2.4	2.6	2.9	2.7	2.5
Countries with a per capita GNP in 1974												
Over $400	11.5	8.4	6.5	5.7	5.1	5.1	5.1	4.5	4.4	4.6	4.5	4.3
$200–400	3.4	2.7	2.4	2.2	2.0	1.9	1.8	1.6	1.6	1.6	1.7	1.6
Under $200	5.6	4.4	3.6	2.9	2.5	2.3	2.2	1.9	1.7	1.6	1.4	1.3

Source   Proceedings of the United Nations Conference on Trade and Development, Nairobi, 1976 (New York: United Nations, 1977) table 1.9, p. 37.

APPENDIX 3

Share of major economic and regional groupings in
total world imports, 1950, 1955, 1960, 1965 and 1968 to 1975
(in percentages)

	1950	1955	1960	1965	1968	1969	1970	1971	1972	1973	1974	1975
Developed market economy countries	65.2	66.3	65.9	69.3	70.9	71.8	72.2	72.3	72.6	72.6	71.9	68.7
Developing countries	26.8	24.1	22.0	18.8	17.8	17.2	16.8	17.0	16.0	16.1	17.8	19.8
Socialist countries												
E. Europe	6.3	7.7	10.3	10.5	9.9	9.7	9.6	9.4	9.8	9.5	8.3	9.7
of which USSR	2.2	3.1	4.2	4.1	3.7	3.6	3.6	3.4	3.7	3.6	2.9	3.4
Socialist countries in Asia	1.6	1.6	1.6	1.1	1.0	0.9	0.9	0.9	0.9	1.1	1.1	1.2
Developing countries and territories												
Latin America	8.6	7.4	6.1	4.8	4.8	4.6	4.6	4.6	4.2	4.1	4.8	4.9
Africa	5.2	5.2	4.9	4.0	3.4	3.3	3.4	3.5	3.2	3.0	3.3	4.0
North African States and Madagascar	2.5	2.1	2.1	1.4	1.2	1.2	1.2	1.2	1.2	1.2	1.5	1.9
linked with EEC	1.0	1.1	0.8	0.8	0.7	0.7	0.7	0.7	0.7	0.6	0.6	0.6
Asia												
West	2.2	2.3	2.4	2.3	2.3	2.3	2.1	2.3	2.3	2.4	2.8	3.9
South and South East	9.0	7.5	7.2	6.2	5.9	5.7	5.4	5.2	5.0	5.2	5.5	5.6
By major export and income category												
Major petroleum exporters	4.1	4.3	4.5	3.6	3.4	3.4	3.3	3.5	3.6	3.7	4.2	6.0
Countries with a per capita GNP in 1974												
Over $400	9.6	8.1	6.6	5.3	5.2	5.1	5.2	5.3	4.9	4.7	5.5	5.4
$200–400	3.5	3.3	2.8	2.7	2.4	2.3	2.2	2.1	1.9	1.7	2.1	2.3
Under $200	5.2	4.6	4.6	4.0	3.1	2.9	2.5	2.4	2.1	1.9	1.9	2.1

SOURCE Proceedings of the United Nations Conference on Trade and Development, Nairobi, 1976 (New York: United Nations, 1977) table 1.10, p. 39.

APPENDIX 4

Value of exports in current prices 1950-75 (millions of US $ (f.o.b.))

	World	Developed market economy countries	Developing countries	Socialist countries, E. Europe	Socialist countries, Asia	Japan	Argentina	Brazil	Cuba
1950	60 700	37 200	18 500	4 140	790	820	1 167	1 347	667
1951	82 100	52 000	23 700	5 340	980	1 355	1 169	1 757	806
1952	80 700	52 700	20 900	6 070	950	1 273	688	1 409	694
1953	82 800	53 700	21 100	6 800	1 130	1 275	1 125	1 539	675
1954	86 000	55 200	22 100	7 400	1 200	1 629	1 027	1 562	563
1955	93 800	60 700	23 600	7 950	1 420	2 011	929	1 423	611
1956	104 000	68 900	24 900	8 440	1 700	2 501	944	1 482	695
1957	112 100	73 300	25 400	9 600	1 700	2 858	975	1 392	845
1958	108 200	71 200	24 700	10 130	1 970	2 877	994	1 243	763
1959	115 800	75 700	25 700	12 000	2 210	3 457	1 009	1 282	638
1960	128 300	85 700	27 400	13 000	2 040	4 055	1 079	1 269	618
1961	134 100	90 500	27 700	14 100	1 600	4 236	964	1 403	625
1962	141 600	95 100	28 800	15 800	1 680	4 916	1 216	1 214	521
1963	154 100	103 900	31 200	17 000	1 720	5 452	1 365	1 407	544
1964	172 800	117 600	34 200	18 700	1 870	6 673	1 411	1 430	714
1965	186 500	128 300	36 000	19 700	1 020	8 452	1 493	1 596	686
1966	204 300	141 700	38 600	21 200	2 290	9 776	1 593	1 741	593
1967	215 000	150 000	39 300	23 100	2 070	10 442	1 465	1 654	705
1968	239 800	168 600	43 100	25 200	2 080	12 972	1 368	1 881	651
1969	274 000	194 500	48 200	27 900	2 250	15 990	1 612	2 311	671
1970	312 400	224 700	52 900	31 000	2 380	19 318	1 773	2 739	1 046
1971	347 800	251 400	58 000	33 800	2 640	24 019	1 740	2 904	860
1972	411 500	298 300	67 100	40 000	3 210	28 591	1 941	3 991	835
1973	570 100	408 300	99 400	52 900	4 950	36 930	3 266	6 199	960
1974	829 600	543 200	209 400	65 500	5 950	55 536	3 931	7 952	1 830
1975	861 500	575 400	195 600	79 000	6 600	55 844	3 200	8 355	2 200

APPENDIX 4 *continued*

	Algeria	Egypt	Sudan	Ivory Coast	Iran	Iraq	Kuwait	Afghan- istan	India	USSR	South Korea
1950	333	513	103	89	60	140	195	42	1 178	—	—
1951	383	595	227	112	70	182	320	43	1 646	—	—
1952	415	431	153	108	82	278	438	45	1 299	—	—
1953	397	409	128	109	99	392	507	46	1 130	—	—
1954	401	413	116	156	183	489	564	47	1 193	—	—
1955	463	419	145	146	396	519	651	49	1 288	3 469	—
1956	429	409	192	151	561	478	675	51	1 317	3 612	—
1957	461	493	148	134	700	360	735	59	1 403	4 382	—
1958	488	478	125	150	726	566	930	46	1 222	4 298	—
1959	366	461	192	137	754	606	850	60	1 304	5 450	—
1960	560	568	132	151	815	654	1 000	50	1 331	5 564	—
1961	680	486	179	191	872	662	943	53	1 386	5 998	—
1962	800	398	228	193	917	692	1 051	59	1 403	7 030	—
1963	759	520	226	230	917	781	1 107	69	1 626	7 272	—
1964	727	537	197	302	1 254	840	1 218	71	1 705	7 683	—
1965	637	604	195	277	1 303	822	1 244	70	1 686	8 175	—
1966	621	604	203	311	1 309	934	1 342	65	1 836	8 841	—
1967	724	566	214	325	1 950	833	1 356	66	1 613	9 652	—
1968	830	622	233	425	1 881	1 041	1 437	70	1 761	10 634	455
1969	934	745	248	453	2 100	1 042	1 540	79	1 835	11 655	623
1970	974	762	293	469	2 150	740	1 600	82	2 026	12 800	835
1971	890	789	331	456	2 150	1 020	2 100	96	2 034	13 806	1 068
1972	1 120	825	360	553	3 800	950	2 300	92	2 415	15 361	1 624
1973	1 730	1 117	434	857	5 610	1 700	2 700	143	2 940	21 463	3 221
1974	4 135	1 516	350	1 210	21 120	6 520	8 900	214	3 906	27 405	4 460
1975	3 900	1 500	380	1 100	19 865	8 180	7 830	205	4 200	—	4 670

SOURCE Proceedings of the United Nations Conference on Trade and Development, Nairobi, 1976 (New York: United Nations 1977) pp. 2 et seq.

APPENDIX 5

Soviet trade with various countries (millions of roubles)

	India			Egypt			Iran		
	Soviet imports	Soviet exports	Surplus/deficit	Soviet imports	Soviet exports	Surplus/deficit	Soviet imports	Soviet exports	Surplus/deficit
1955									
1956	4.0	6.6	+ 2.6	13.8	9.9	− 3.9	17.2	20.2	+ 3.0
1957	16.5	36.4	+ 19.9	45.3	34.6	− 10.7	13.6	17.3	+ 3.7
1958	37.8	76.2	+ 38.4	99.8	74.0	− 25.8	16.7	28.5	+ 11.8
1959	45.8	117.0	+ 71.2	96.4	78.9	− 17.5	23.8	24.7	+ 0.9
1960	54.5	61.2	+ 6.7	83.4	79.2	− 4.2	16.9	16.2	− 0.7
1961	61.6	42.4	− 19.2	109.2	62.8	− 46.4	17.1	16.2	− 0.9
1962	60.2	85.9	+ 25.7	86.6	97.8	+ 11.2	16.5	16.3	− 0.2
1963	64.5	112.3	+ 47.8	65.7	93.0	+ 27.3	14.8	14.5	− 0.3
1964	85.3	199.7	+ 114.4	111.2	121.7	+ 10.5	16.0	21.4	+ 5.4
1965	140.3	208.6	+ 68.3	111.2	140.1	+ 28.9	18.9	19.6	+ 0.7
1966	169.4	193.5	+ 24.1	147.1	187.8	+ 40.7	16.3	13.8	− 2.5
1967	172.0	174.0	+ 2.0	135.0	178.8	+ 43.8	17.5	27.9	+ 10.4
1968	162.7	146.2	− 16.5	130.6	253.2	+ 122.6	27.5	56.7	+ 29.2
1969	164.6	165.0	+ 0.4	153.6	178.2	+ 24.6	36.1	79.3	+ 43.2
1970	199.3	154.2	− 45.1	205.3	214.4	+ 9.1	50.8	145.4	+ 94.6
1971	242.6	122.3	− 120.3	279.5	326.9	+ 47.4	62.2	169.0	+ 106.8
1972	255.8	116.3	− 139.5	300.7	343.2	+ 42.5	100.1	139.3	+ 39.2
1973	312.5	138.5	− 174.0	247.6	266.1	+ 18.5	134.0	95.5	− 38.5
1974	366.0	222.8	− 143.2	263.9	277.2	+ 13.3	139.6	137.3	− 2.3
1975	346.1	269.4	− 76.7	426.8	301.3	− 125.5	229.9	265.8	+ 35.9
1976	393.5	292.1	− 101.4	448.3	262.0	− 186.3	228.2	281.5	+ 53.3
1977	376.5	271.0	− 105.5	330.8	199.8	− 131.0	226.7	217.9	− 8.8
1978	565.2	360.8	− 204.4	289.1	203.3	− 85.8	283.4	424.1	+ 140.7
			+ 421.5			+ 440.4			+ 578.8
			− 1 145.8			− 637.1			− 54.2

APPENDIX 5 *continued*

Year	Singapore Export	Singapore Import	Singapore Balance	Malaysia Export	Malaysia Import	Malaysia Balance	Indonesia Export	Indonesia Import	Indonesia Balance
1955									
1956				—	19.6	− 19.6	0.1	3.3	− 3.2
1957				0.3	75.6	− 73.3	0.2	11.6	− 11.4
1958				0.6	43.9	− 43.3	5.1	17.8	− 12.7
1959				0.0	106.2	− 106.2	24.5	10.4	+ 14.1
1960				0.8	114.0	− 113.2	14.2	9.9	+ 4.3
1961				1.9	100.4	− 98.5	14.6	28.3	+ 13.7
1962				1.8	152.6	− 150.8	28.2	30.5	− 2.3
1963				2.0	144.9	− 142.9	52.7	34.8	+ 17.9
1964				2.8	120.4	− 117.6	44.9	26.8	+ 18.1
1965				3.0	63.8	− 60.8	42.0	23.2	+ 18.8
1966	2.6	0.0	+ 2.6	0.0	101.4	− 101.4	49.0	28.8	+ 20.2
1967	2.5	0.0	+ 2.5	0.0	113.0	− 113.0	4.3	27.7	− 23.4
1968	4.8	0.1	+ 4.7	0.1	86.9	− 86.8	4.7	21.9	− 17.2
1969	6.2	1.8	+ 4.4	0.1	90.4	− 90.3	4.7	17.2	− 12.5
1970	5.6	1.0	+ 4.6	1.5	109.6	− 108.1	3.2	21.4	− 18.2
1971	5.5	2.9	− 2.6	1.6	111.0	− 109.4	4.5	25.0	− 20.5
1972	4.4	3.7	+ 0.7	1.5	77.6	− 76.1	10.1	10.1	0.0
1973	4.4	4.6	− 0.2	1.0	58.4	− 57.4	2.6	6.8	− 4.2
1974	6.4	3.2	+ 3.2	0.9	96.7	− 96.8	2.7	4.2	− 1.5
1975	4.5	13.5	− 9.0	0.7	188.0	− 187.3	8.0	19.9	− 11.9
1976	3.8	10.7	− 6.9	0.8	101.3	− 100.5	7.7	20.9	− 13.2
1977	11.9	9.1	+ 2.8	4.2	103.5	− 99.3	4.4	27.9	− 23.5
1978	13.9	12.8	+ 1.1	8.6	127.8	− 119.2	7.6	24.1	− 8.5

Singapore Balance totals: +29.2 / −16.1 → +13.1

Malaysia Balance total: −2 307.0

Indonesia Balance totals: +107.1 / −184.2 → − 77.1

APPENDIX 5 *continued*

Year	Iraq Soviet imports	Iraq Soviet exports	Iraq Surplus/deficit	Turkey Soviet imports	Turkey Soviet exports	Turkey Surplus/deficit	Syria Soviet imports	Syria Soviet exports	Syria Surplus/deficit	Year
1955	0.3	0.0	− 0.3	4.6	6.7	+ 2.1	0.0	0.3	+ 0.3	1955
1956	–	–		5.9	5.4	− 0.5	–	–	–	1956
1957	–	–		4.9	8.1	+ 3.2	–	–	–	1957
1958	0.0	21.0	+ 21.0	10.3	8.5	− 1.8	–	–	–	1958
1959	2.1	21.0	+ 18.9	4.3	5.0	+ 0.7	–	–	–	1959
1960	3.1	18.2	+ 15.1	4.7	7.4	+ 2.7	7.0	9.9	+ 2.9	1960
1961	4.2	33.6	+ 29.4	4.4	5.2	+ 0.8	3.9	15.3	+ 11.4	1961
1962	3.4	46.8	+ 43.4	4.9	3.9	− 1.0	6.2	4.7	− 1.5	1962
1963	4.7	39.1	+ 34.4	6.4	7.8	+ 1.4	12.8	11.8	− 1.0	1963
1964	2.2	28.2	+ 26.0	8.3	8.9	+ 0.6	16.0	11.0	− 5.0	1964
1965	3.3	26.6	+ 23.3	17.0	15.0	− 2.0	16.7	11.4	− 5.3	1965
1966	2.9	32.3	+ 29.4	16.9	24.7	+ 7.8	18.3	20.4	+ 2.1	1966
1967	4.6	33.0	+ 28.4	25.1	25.3	+ 0.2	16.4	30.8	+ 14.4	1967
1968	3.7	45.7	+ 42.0	27.0	27.7	+ 0.7	18.8	37.9	+ 19.1	1968
1969	4.2	60.9	+ 56.7	26.9	52.1	+ 25.2	36.6	43.0	+ 9.4	1969
1970	4.1	59.4	+ 55.3	27.1	56.2	+ 29.1	17.3	41.8	+ 24.5	1970
1971	5.5	99.1	+ 93.6	33.6	68.4	+ 34.8	26.4	51.9	+ 25.5	1971
1972	61.6	90.1	+ 28.5	33.9	110.8	+ 76.9	53.7	58.6	+ 4.9	1972
1973	109.6	141.5	− 49.1	38.9	93.9	+ 55.0	46.7	72.1	+ 25.4	1973
1974	270.8	182.3	− 88.5	56.8	72.3	+ 15.5	102.3	70.1	− 32.2	1974
1975	325.4	274.1	− 51.3	57.1	38.2	− 18.9	68.8	99.0	+ 30.2	1975
1976	372.9	341.6	− 31.3	60.0	54.5	− 5.5	96.9	138.5	+ 41.6	1976
1977	321.0	281.0	− 40.0	65.7	73.4	+ 7.7	106.2	100.8	− 5.4	1977
1978										1978
			+545.4			+264.4			+211.7	
			−260.5			− 29.7			− 50.4	
			+284.9			+234.7			+161.3	

APPENDIX 5 *continued*

Year	Algeria Turnover	Export	Import	Surplus/deficit	Morocco Turnover	Export	Import	Surplus/deficit
1961	1.3	1.3	0.0	+ 1.3	7.7	3.0	4.7	− 1.7
1962	0.8	0.7	0.1	+ 0.6	10.5	5.1	5.4	− 0.3
1963	5.2	4.6	0.6	+ 4.0	17.9	8.8	9.1	− 0.3
1964	17.5	14.1	3.4	+ 10.7	13.2	7.3	5.9	+ 1.4
1965	17.3	13.9	3.4	+ 10.5	17.5	7.6	9.9	− 2.3
1966	22.2	16.9	5.3	+ 11.6	18.2	9.7	8.5	+ 1.2
1967	43.0	28.4	14.6	+ 13.8	36.3	18.0	18.3	− 0.3
1968	53.6	28.7	24.9	+ 3.8	33.8	17.3	16.5	+ 0.8
1969	107.3	51.9	55.4	− 3.5	49.5	33.4	16.1	+17.3
1970	118.3	62.5	55.8	+ 6.7	50.1	32.5	17.6	+14.9
1971	121.9	52.6	69.3	− 16.7	47.1	28.2	18.9	+ 9.3
1972	114.5	55.9	58.6	− 2.7	55.2	31.5	23.7	+ 7.8
1973	116.8	64.7	52.1	+ 12.6	54.4	28.3	26.1	+ 2.2
1974	171.8	110.3	61.4	+ 48.9	87.1	54.1	33.0	+21.1
1975	247.0	112.3	134.7	− 22.4	86.9	45.7	41.2	+ 4.5
1976	190.3	131.4	58.9	+ 72.5	105.6	55.3	50.3	+ 5.0
1977	162.8	123.4	39.4	+ 84.0	105.2	55.9	49.3	+ 6.6
1978								

	Algeria	Morocco
	+281.0	+92.1
	− 45.3	− 4.9
	+235.7	+87.2

APPENDIX 5   continued

Brazil (millions of roubles)

Year	Soviet imports	Soviet exports	Surplus/deficit
1955	1.7	0.0	- 1.7
1956	2.8	0.1	- 2.7
1957	2.0	0.0	- 2.0
1958	0.8	0.0	- 0.8
1959	4.3	0.9	- 3.4
1960	8.4	14.2	+ 5.8
1961	21.6	16.5	- 5.1
1962	32.2	27.1	- 5.1
1963	39.1	26.5	- 12.6
1964	33.4	21.6	- 11.8
1965	29.5	24.9	- 4.6
1966	27.5	24.9	- 2.6
1967	31.2	10.8	- 20.4
1968	25.2	12.4	- 12.8
1969	43.9	10.9	- 33.0
1970	20.8	2.4	- 18.4
1971	41.7	2.0	- 39.7
1972	65.8	7.1	- 58.7
1973	116.5	9.3	-107.2
1974	112.0	90.0	- 22.0
1975	302.8	93.3	-209.5
1976	369.4	76.1	-293.3
1977	209.6	104.4	-105.2
1978	130.2	34.9	- 95.3

Argentina (millions of roubles)

Year	Soviet imports	Soviet exports	Surplus/deficit
1955	25.3	21.6	- 3.7
1956	11.7	17.2	+ 5.6
1957	18.8	4.2	- 14.6
1958	14.4	15.5	+ 1.1
1959	25.1	15.1	- 10.0
1960	19.5	12.6	- 6.9
1961	17.9	9.5	- 8.4
1962	8.8	7.2	- 1.6
1963	16.6	0.8	- 15.8
1964	17.9	4.0	- 13.9
1965	64.8	18.3	- 46.5
1966	96.6	6.7	- 89.9
1967	20.8	4.3	- 16.5
1968	25.8	2.9	- 22.9
1969	23.0	6.1	- 16.9
1970	28.2	1.7	- 26.5
1971	30.4	1.9	- 28.5
1972	22.9	1.8	- 21.1
1973	72.2	4.5	- 67.7
1974	131.5	6.0	-125.5
1975	293.7	10.7	-283.0
1976	225.4	8.5	-216.9
1977	191.6	13.4	-178.2
1978	308.8	22.4	-286.4

Peru (millions of roubles)

Year	USSR exports	USSR imports	Turnover
1970	0.1	0.2	0.3
1971	0.0	0.2	0.2
1972	0.2	1.8	2.0
1973	4.3	15.4	19.7
1974	4.6	4.7	9.3
1975	28.3	90.2	118.5
1976	13.9	18.1	32.0
1977	26.4	20.4	46.8

SOURCE *Vneshnyaya Torgovlya.*

4. The Commercial Policies of the Communist Third World

Peter Wiles and Alan Smith

with contributions by Nicos Zafiris, Barry Lynch and Yukimasa Chudo

A. General

INTRODUCTION: PURPOSE OF THE STUDY

The Communist Third World is an area that defies precise definition. Our choice of countries to study has been determined in the main by analytical considerations, but has also been affected by the constraints of time and finance, the availability of scholars with the appropriate linguistic skills and the desire to avoid duplication with country studies being conducted elsewhere.

The principal question we have set out to investigate is the economic policy of the Soviet Union and/or Eastern European countries towards those developing countries that have proclaimed a Marxist–Leninist form of government, how it is modified by the countries concerned, and in particular what its effect is on (i) internal economic and social structure of those countries and (ii) the nature of the external economic relations of those countries with the Eastern bloc and the developed capitalist nations. We lay it down that these countries are substantially independent, especially in economic matters. They really can trade with whom they like, and their tempo of, say, agricultural collectivisation is also their own decision. *They, or rather their governments, are volunteers*, quite unlike Poland and Hungary.

For the purposes of economic analysis, we can reasonably distinguish between three major types of Communist economy:

GROUP 1   Those countries that are full members of the Council for Mutual Economic Assistance (CMEA); subdivided into: (a) The European 'core' – (Soviet Union, Bulgaria, Hungary, East Germany, Poland, Romania and Czechoslovakia); (b) Non-European members – Mongolia, Cuba and (since July 1978) Vietnam. We are including aspects of these three in our study, to illustrate one possible outcome of membership in the 'Communist Third World'.

GROUP 2   Countries that have been Communist a long time and are designated as Socialist in official Soviet/CMEA statistics, but are non-members of CMEA and currently beyond direct Soviet influence – Albania, China, North Korea and Yugoslavia. We have included aspects of Albania[1] and North Korea in our study, to illustrate yet other possible outcomes. There have been latterly almost overwhelming grounds for adding Romania to Group 2, but she is sufficiently studied elsewhere. If we may diverge for a moment into purely strategic/diplomatic matters, it need not be stressed how tolerable it would be for NATO, or 'The West', if all Group 3 countries took this road.

GROUP 3   Our major area of study is those developing countries that have proclaimed Marxist–Leninist forms of government but are not yet officially designated Socialist by the CMEA for purposes of statistical reporting, yet maintain or have maintained close relations with the USSR, and enjoy the informal Soviet appellation 'countries that have chosen the non-capitalist path'. Our target countries here are: Angola, Mozambique, South Yemen, and Ethiopia; to which we may now add Afghanistan, which went Communist too late for our project! There are also doubtful cases like Guyana, Congo-Brazzaville and Somalia.

It is basic to this study that the proclamation of Marxist–Leninism by the Group 3 countries is genuine. We reject the parallels, often urged, of Egypt about 1970 or Guinea about 1961. These countries were simply allied to the Soviet Union. They never proclaimed themselves to be Marxist–Leninist, persecuted religion, founded or encouraged Communist parties, put up innumerable pictures of Marx and Lenin etc. Their subsequent diplomatic turnabouts tell us much less about the future of, say, Mozambique than we can learn from Cuba.

Moreover USSR has learned a *little* tact from those early lessons.

A separate African Road to Socialism is more often talked about than, say the Polish (or indeed the Vietnamese) Road to Socialism. But, after all, the latter crop up often enough – and are subjected to this or that Soviet veto. Moreover, while Polish Communist policies or wishes are specific and definite, spring in fairly clear ways from local circumstances and traditions and form a permanent though developing body of more or less coherent doctrine, nothing of this sort can be claimed for any form of Afro-Marxism.[2] It is therefore much more probable that African countries will adopt Soviet ideology and – with due regard to stages – Soviet economic organisation than it is that Poland will. But those who say it does not matter that African leaders 'mouth Marxist–Leninist phrases' do Africa too little honour, and reveal themselves as virtual racists: it matters what people think and, even if they do not altogether mean it, what they say. On the other hand those who believe that an independent non-Soviet ideology or policy will emerge among the African countries we have selected, do Africa too much honour. They must specify exactly what its present beginnings are; exactly which African traditions, country by country, are in conflict with exactly which Soviet traditions; and how these particular countries will get out of the trap which they seem to be in. The African political culture is much shallower than the Polish or the Vietnamese. The case of Somalia is particularly instructive (Part B). All the above applies equally in our opinion to Yemen and Afghanistan.

It is true that most countries of Group 3 have gone Communist in very unorthodox ways. Their first-generation leaders began as hardly better Marxist–Leninists than, say, Castro. But that is also true of Lenin himself! And precisely Cuba was in its day the first Group 3 country.

The Russians too have difficulties with nomenclature and indeed concepts. The old distinction of a 'country of national democracy' (for example Guinea) has dropped out of the literature.[3] There is no official terminology any more, but our Group 3 does receive recognition in careful but unofficial phrasing. For instance Primakov (1979, our italics)[4] distinguishes them in the third and fourth paragraphs of his article:

Thus it is for example significant that the abolition of the colonial system, which culminated in the bankruptcy of the last colonial empire, the Portuguese, has led to the emergence of anti-imperialistic regimes in the former Portuguese colonies which *orient themselves to scientific socialism*. This is not least thanks to the circumstance that the victory of the national liberation revolutions in these countries was preceded by long years of stiff fighting in which cadres of revolutionaries grew up and became strong – cadres who saw the future of their countries in organic ties with the other components of the *world-revolutionary process* (revolutionärer Weltprozess): the socialist community of states and the international workers' movement.

The revolution has won in Ethiopia, and the revolutionary–democratic leadership has also chosen the path of deep-reaching transformations of society under socialist banners (literally Losungen). *The revolutionary* movement in Afghanistan has had a historic *victory. Revolutionary changes have deepened* in the People's Republic of Congo, in the Democratic Republic of Madagascar, in the P.D.R.Yemen, in the People's Republic of Benin, in Tanzania, Algeria, Libya etc.

But at the same time differently directed shifts of power have occurred in Pakistan, Sri Lanka and Bangladesh. A rejection of the socialist orientation is to be observed in Egypt, a turn to the right describes also a number of other under-developed countries (UDCs). What is the cause of these processes?

– and he continues for ten pages to describe the policies of multi-national corporations.

We feel here no need to analyse the place of the multi-national corporation in Soviet demonology. We only observe that Group 3, except for the P.D.R.Yemen, is correctly described above as places where the final (Soviet-type) Revolution has won. We agree with Primakov, and for our part we carefully explain why we think each of the Group 3 countries is Communist in Part B, and then proceed with our economic analysis. But a question we cannot answer is, is their state of socio-political closedness and economic openness meant to be transitional? In some longer-run sense of course it is: they must move through 'socialism' into 'Communism'. But short of this very long run there are many time intervals to consider. There appears to be no official Soviet doctrine on this point, since there is not, as we have seen, even any name for the group; everything is proceeding empirically, and there are many differences between countries.

It cannot be stressed enough that there is nothing unLeninist about the economic behaviour of 'Group 3', whether it is their own decision or USSR's. It is a virtually perfect copy of Lenin's own behaviour during the New Economic Policy (NEP, 1921–8), except that there are perhaps rather more state farms but rather less nationalisation in other sectors, with big foreign capitalist enterprises being particularly tolerated. However if the NEP cannot give us an exact parallel to the kind of tolerance extended by Angola or South Yemen to multi-national corporations the USSR of the so-called *détente* is itself slightly more welcoming than during the NEP. On the other hand social and political arrangements were more tolerant under the NEP than in Group 3 today (or USSR today).

It is an empirical fact that no great social or political risk attends the Communist country that opens up its economy. No harm *has* been done to either Group 3 or to USSR itself – today or in the NEP. Certainly extremes of hostility prevent trade, but trade does not greatly 'corrupt' culture or affect the grip of the security police. Whatever Lenin once thought on this question during the NEP, he was wrong at the time. Today, now that USSR is a military superpower and has a whole empire of Communist satellites, she and they have every reason to be self-confident.

Of course a major reason for the general Group 3 policy is that USSR and Eastern Europe simply cannot supply all that the group wants to buy, or use all it wants to sell. The Third World generally does not like Communist machinery, because it is not very good. Its members, even in Group 3, are particularly oriented to the markets of their ex-colonial masters, by language, custom, personal knowledge and industrial standardisation. They are at least largely independent, especially in comparison with CMEA members; and must be expected to choose what is in their own opinion their best interest, even against Soviet advice. However that advice has become in recent years fairly clear: the Soviet Africanists and Orientalists are of opinion that Group 3 should remain attached to the capitalist world market.[5]

And here again we need feel no surprise. If Poland may borrow as much as she can from Chase Manhattan, and keep an uncollectivised peasantry; if Hungary may run a half-market economy in her socialist sector, and buy 37 per cent of all imports and 34 per cent of her machinery imports from capitalist countries, and set up co-operation agreements for multi-nationals on Hungarian soil, why is Mozambique out of line in re-admitting Portuguese workers?

In short, Group 3 countries have not necessarily more political independence than CMEA members because of their economic policies. These are very similar to other Third World policies, and not evidence one way or the other. Group 3 are doing what all very poor left-wing countries objectively must do, and there is plenty of Communist precedent for it. Their political independence must be judged separately, by their political actions at home and abroad. If to say this is bad Marxism so be it – the Communist 'superstructure' was always independent of its 'base'. Moreover gross differences in the ultimate economic order are surely less likely than political defections to Group 2, that is refusal to join CMEA but retention of a Soviet-type economy.

SOVIET/CMEA POLICY TOWARDS GROUP 3: JOINT PLANNING

A recurrent theme in Soviet long-term policy toward the economic relations between socialist-states over the past sixty years has been their unification under a joint economic plan. Compare on this Article 96 of the 8th Party Congress of 1919, reiterated by Bukharin and Preobrazhenski (1921) and Khrushchev (1962).[6] Khrushchev aroused vehement opposition in Romania, and the issue was again put into cold storage until recently. The Soviet economists Alampiev, Bogomolov and Shiryaev[7] referred to 'the final result – integration of all the socialist national economies in one international economy regulated under a common plan', but added that 'this goes beyond the framework of the forseeable future'.

Assuming therefore that in the short run no such far-reaching integration is on the agenda on pragmatic grounds, the following questions would appear to remain concerning the external relations of the target countries.

(i) Will the countries of Group 3 (assuming no grand political reversal on their part)
   (a) Remain largely independent both of one another and the other Communist states, that is join Group 2 (with or without directing a greater proportion of their trade towards other Communist states generally), or
   (b) Eventually become members of CMEA – and if so, how integrated will they become with other members:
(ii) Point (b) above also raises the question of the future relation of the non-European members of CMEA – how integrated will they become with the European 'core'?

Although some of the evidence is conflicting, we feel that we can make a reasonable preliminary attempt to answer some of these questions, encompassing a period of perhaps the next ten to fifteen years, using both qualitative and quantitative evidence.

It is clear that there has been renewed pressure in the 1970s to establish joint planning procedures within the CMEA which could ultimately form the basis of a joint plan. Although the Soviet Union (and in particular Gosplan) appear to be the main movers of these proposals, progress towards this goal has been cautious and has carefully avoided any reference to direct supranationality. Furthermore, Soviet preoccupations with the difficulties in establishing joint-planning procedures within the CMEA over a ten to fifteen year period make its extension beyond CMEA over that time period unlikely, although this need not preclude the possibility of other countries following the example of Cuba and Vietnam and becoming full members of the organisation.

Therefore the critical questions in this regard would appear to be (i)(b) and (ii) above. Soviet attitudes to these questions appear to envisage a two-tier approach both to the time horizon over which integration will take place and to the countries that will be included – but are sufficiently open-ended to permit variations in the pattern. Thus during earlier (abortive) attempts to introduce joint planning, Soviet economists argued that the European CMEA members would enter the stage of communism under the direction of the CMEA before the Asian countries. This was echoed by Khrushchev who spoke of 'the need to . . . go in for planning at the level of the CMEA and *afterwards* at the level of the socialist world system as a whole' (our italics).

Currently it is argued[8] that the first stage of integration will cover roughly the next three five-year plan periods (this is up to 1990) and appears to apply to the existing CMEA countries only, whilst 'the second stage will be marked by a higher degree of economic and organisational unification of the national economies of the *socialist* countries in an international economic complex. From plan co-ordination the countries will go on to the formulation in one form or another of a common plan, for advancing the world socialist division of labour'.

The role of non-CMEA countries in this process is left deliberately open:

the stages of integration may be considered not only in terms of the

development of economic ties between the countries which have
now announced their intention to participate in it. Some stages in
the advance of integration may also be connected with the involvement of new countries into the integrating community. Because the
integrating community is not a closed one, other countries accepting
its tasks and purposes may later join in. *However, it is not possible at
the present time to anticipate such stages . . . with various modes of
inclusion of individual countries in the integrating community* (our
italics).

How then will this process affect the trade patterns of those developing countries that are (or may become) members of CMEA and can we
predict which countries will become members?

The three main proposals to establish joint planning activity in
CMEA (enacted since 1974) are:

(a) The long-term target programmes – basically an attempt to
    integrate members' perspective plans on a sectoral basis (which
    could considerably affect investment programmes);
(b) The Agreed Plan of Multilateral Integration measures for 1976–80
    (that is improved integration of five-year plans including specific
    joint investment proposals and measures to raise the living standards
    of the developing CMEA countries, especially Mongolia);
(c) The inclusion of special sections in members' annual, five-year and
    perspective plans to ensure the national allocation of resources for
    CMEA agreements and projects.

SOVIET/CMEA POLICY: LEVELLING UP

It seems wrong to us, perhaps particularly if we are Marxists, to try to
integrate the poor with the rich. But, on reflection, there is nothing
impossible in it, any more than there is in the fact that they engage in
classical trade with each other. Nor is there anything undesirable from
the economic as opposed to the political viewpoint. Trade should, of
course, continue to be based on comparative cost – and even under
Communism this is more or less the case. Provided that this is so, co-
operative projects can be rationally based on the trade that will result
from them; and rational, even fair, supranational plans can be agreed
upon, embracing eventually the whole economy. Only migration must
be strictly controlled, for that takes place on the basis of absolute

advantage and will go from poor to rich in all skill grades. Indeed all of these points apply, *mutatis mutandis*, to capitalism.

Such integration does not necessarily raise the productivity or real income of the poor country to that of the rich one, but rather tends to enable both to grow equally. It is only the ultimate form of integration – annexation or federation – that tends to the strict equalisation of incomes. For the unified state must permit migration; and being a welfare state, it pays out unitary social services, sets unitary health and schooling standards, levies unitary progresssive income taxes and even encourages or enforces unitary wage-scales. Such is the Central Asian case, and that of the Old South in the United States. But it follows that no rich state in the modern world will be willing to annex a poor one! All such collocations inside one boundary are inheritances of the past, when the state was not responsible for economic welfare and so for equality.

Annexation, then, implies *levelling up*.[9] This process is in no way implied by the original CMEA founding document, the brief communique of Jan. 1949[10] – which does not even mention socialism! In 1958 the very authoritative Stepanyan[11] argued that European CMEA members would enter the stage of Full Communism, under the direction of the CMEA, before Asian Communist countries. This implies levelling up at least in Europe. But the geographical distinction was abandoned by Khrushchev in 1959 (Pravda, 28 Jan.) when he said that all Communist countries would reach Full Communism at about the same time.[12] This was a very bold statement indeed, when we consider that the split with China was as yet by no means *chose jugée*. To level China up would take more resources than USSR disposes of.

Not surprisingly, then, levelling up is present only in very shadowy form in the Charter of 16 May 1960: Art 1 on 'Purposes and Principles' lists 'the raising of the level of industrialisation in the industrially less-developed countries'.[13] It is equally absent in Satyukov, Pravda 27 Oct. 1961.[14] But then comes, rather surprisingly, the CMEA's own super-official Resolution, 'The Basic Principles of the International Socialist Division of Labour'.[15] This is absolutely explicit, and at some length, that levelling up will take place; moreover it is at this very meeting that Mongolia was admitted. This country then has received a most definite promise that it will be levelled up. No doubt the rapid *volte-face* is due to the definitive character of the Sino-Soviet split at this date.

It was at this same meeting that Khrushchev proposed supranational planning, thus antagonising the Romanians who saw in it the suppression of their sovereignty. That he raised this issue at the same time is, we have shown, no coincidence.

However, there is a good deal of confusion about levelling up among Soviet experts. It is sometimes presented as just a purely factual statement about Communist countries. Indeed it is a quite true statement, doing them much credit, for it means that the very poorest do not stagnate, as in the rest of the Third World. Levelling up is of course by no means unknown under capitalism: it is normal, as under Communism, for medium-level countries to outgrow rich ones. But it is certain that the EEC has no coherent policy on this at all, and no very poor members. Indeed under capitalism the very poor grow very slowly whether in or outside the EEC, but this is not so under Communism. Thus an early reference is by Morozov.[16] He quotes the sentence from the 1960 Charter above and adds:

> In the process of realizing this goal countries with less developed economies are quickly raising their national products to the level of the leading states of the socialist camp, the level of economic development of all the countries of socialism is rising and becoming more even. (p.11)

He is so little concerned with levelling up as a CMEA commitment that he quotes as instances Mongolia, and also North Vietnam, which was not yet a member.[17] Yet his book is entitled 'CMEA, Alliance of Equals'. He is thus confused as to the role of CMEA, but not as to the effects of Communism.

Nevertheless two years before he published levelling up had become a firm policy commitment. It remained so in August 1971, with the Comprehensive Programme sec. 2. But this only refers to Mongolia, a mere 1.4 million people – and indeed what else was there to refer to? For let us remember that by that time Bulgaria and Romania had more or less levelled themselves up, while Abania had ceased to attend (Dec. 1961).

But in July 1972 Cuba joined. Ptichkin's article on this (1972)[18] stresses the levelling-up-as-policy commitment to Mongolia and surely extends it to Cuba, though not *totidem verbis*. His article on Vietnam's accession in May 1978[19] makes only one feeble mention of levelling up.

Currently Mongolia and Cuba are participating in all sections of the integration proposals and have included special sections in their national plans (which Romania has refused to do). The nature of their participation does appear to differ from that of Eastern European countries in that:

(a) Their trade relations with CMEA countries are more highly concentrated with the USSR.
(b) As predominantly suppliers of raw materials and food products they will be net recipients of CMEA investment resources in the first instance (like USSR!).

A further indication of Soviet/CMEA policy may be found in these countries' trade structures. For geopolitical reasons Mongolia's extra-bloc trade is negligible, whereas Cuban imports from the industrial West still compose 33 per cent of all imports (or three times the value of imports from Eastern Europe excluding the USSR).

Historically Mongolia and Cuba are very different. Mongolia is USSR's oldest satellite: she only collectivised her nomad agriculture in 1955–9, but long before had got into step with history by going through the Great Purge in 1937–8, at the same time as USSR (as indeed did Catalonia). This again shows the primacy of politics over economics. With a population of only 1.4 million, and very many Soviet advisers, she is best described as a very poor autonomous oblast' in Siberia. She was admitted to CMEA in June 1962, when the restriction to Europe was erased from the statutes. This was also the height of Khrushchev's campaign for supranational planning: he included Mongolia in the countries that should reach Full Communism simultaneously with USSR (above). After all, so few people could be lifted to the Soviet level without great expense. A small but important consideration, moreover, was surely to maximise unrest in Inner Mongolia. The 1.9 million Mongols in this Chinese province are indeed two to three times as rich as the Han people in general,[20] but this leaves them very far below Outer Mongolia. At the moment this does not matter, since Peking (and Moscow?) forbid contact. But the gap must in the end become a very awkward matter indeed for Peking.

In 1962 Cuba still harboured Che Guevara, with his unorthodox ideas about centralisation, bonuses and money. The country was not yet trusted as properly Communist – indeed it did not have a duly constituted Party. Cuba, then, was a member of many subordinate agencies of CMEA for some time before she formally joined the Council itself, in 1972. By this time Brezhnev was in power and Full Communism was off the menu. Consequently Cuba's admission constituted no promise rapidly to raise her real income to East European levels. But it was a guarantee of economic aid and indirectly but very certainly – military security for ever. We may instance the sugar/oil/African-adventure deal which seems to have followed: as the price of oil rose (even inside CMEA) after Yom Kippur 1973, the USSR paid even more for sugar, and Cuban troops played a role in Africa that would have been very dangerous for Soviet troops.

We were initially much puzzled by the admission of Vietnam (June, 1978), but we should not have been. Already in May 1977 she had joined the two CMEA banks IIB and IBEC. Moreover on considera-tion the Cuban precedent is most convincing. Both countries are indeed poor and distant, but there is no longer a promise of rapid economic equalisation. Cuba abandoned Guevarism in 1970; Vietnam unified her currency and brought the South under the Northern economic management in May 1978. Both countries, again, are threatened by hostile, neighbouring great powers; and since these powers are enemies of USSR both are of great strategic value. Both have made a business of exporting their own citizens, on a scale quite unknown in other Communist countries. Both have sent their troops abroad, in an exportation of revolution that clearly owes more to native thrust than to Soviet initiative. It has been rumoured that Vietnam consciously imitated Cuba in all these matters.[21] It is certain that Cubo-Vietnamese relations have been very cordial ever since Cuba was the first to recognise the South Vietnamese PRG in 1972, and Fidel Castro visited the 'liberated' portion of South Vietnamese territory in September 1973.[22] He was the first foreign Communist leader to do so.

Vietnam, rather like Cuba, went through an experimental period. She could not, like Cuba, consciously imitate the Chinese, but turned right instead. In 1977 she joined the IMF and the World Bank, and is indeed the only CMEA member to be in the latter (see Table 4.2). Clearly she had been taking a far more pragmatical and open-minded line before plumping for CMEA: one thinks of the sale of oil rights to European companies, and of the very liberal foreign investment law. Nay more, even after joining she showed far greater sensitivity to her neighbours than ever Cuba did. Thus she tried to obscure the military and diplomatic threat implied by her joining CMEA. From 2 to 28 July 1978 the Deputy Foreign Minister Phan Hien visited Japan, Singa-pore, Australia, New Zealand, Malaysia and Thailand (that is, not Indonesia). He assured them of Vietnam's continuing independence, and her desire for close economic and cultural relations with the countries visited.[23] Even Soviet propaganda against the Association of South-East Asian Nations (ASEAN) eased up considerably.[24] Indeed until the Boat People crisis it looked as if CMEA membership would be compatible with openness to multi-nationals – and for this there is good Hungarian precedent. But now it is less certain.

An important reason for the admission of both these countries to CMEA is clearly the wish of USSR to impose some of their aid burden on the other members, nearly all of which enjoy higher consumption levels than herself. Rumours that, for instance, Czechoslovakia opposed the entry of Vietnam are extremely plausible, though they cannot be confirmed. If CMEA membership is no longer a guarantee of total levelling up, it still promises a good deal of aid.

The cases of Cuba and Vietnam indicate that a rough uniformity of economic practice may be a condition of entry.[25] And yet more than uniformity is surely required: there must be an assurance of irreversibility. For like too many other white men Russians do not take Africans seriously, and do not believe in their commitment to this or that ideology. Admission to CMEA, so long delayed in the Cuban case, is an accolade. It will be noted that, relying on the interventions of Soviet arms, East German police, and so on, we are more convinced of the irreversibility of Communism in Group 3 than, evidently, is USSR. But then we are only academics and bear no state responsibility!

In the long run, however, we would expect the countries that become members of CMEA to join the integration proposals, and their investment plans to be affected accordingly. To the extent that this would limit convertible currency earnings, this would result in a reduction in their trade with the West. We at present expect that this would only affect South-East Asian countries, but further research is required to substantiate this assumption.

Finally, we do not feel that at the moment there is any clear indication of an attempt to introduce the African countries or Yemen directly into this process (although Angola and Ethiopia currently have observer status at CMEA). The logic of economic systems, Marxian analysis (to which their leaders subscribe), historical and cultural factors and factor endowments all point in this direction. Thus, it would appear that the African countries may adopt a 'New Economic Policy' (NEP) type economy with substantial foreign capitalist investment, if required. As the Soviet Union is attempting to integrate CMEA through joint-planning activity and is eschewing market-type solutions this would limit participation in CMEA to specific (isolated) projects. A preliminary analysis of trade patterns would appear to confirm this.

Furthermore, a revealing indication of Soviet intentions in this area may be that the payment agreements concluded in 1976 with Angola and Mozambique stipulate that payments between the countries will be made in convertible currencies (not transferable roubles). This would appear to be a strong confirmation of our hypothesis.

TRADE PATTERNS OF GROUP 3

Meanwhile the *trade patterns of Group 3* states have not altered much since Communisation. This is very different from the early experience of Eastern Europe, but not at all irrational. First and foremost, in the period of *détente* capitalism is quite willing to finance or at least trade with Group 3. Indeed the sort of goods that such countries will want is certain to be compatible with CoCom, and it was precisely the beginnings of CoCom that caused Stalin to cut off East–West trade.

It follows that an essential part of Soviet policy towards the Communist Third World is the *divorce of aid from trade*. The difficulty with trade is that the Soviet Union, and indeed CMEA, can export almost nothing that advanced capitalist countries cannot export better. This is because Communist agriculture is, of its nature, very unproductive and Communist research and development (R and D) is little better. So agricultural exports are simply unavailable and industrial exports, though certainly available, are inferior. Moreover it is remote from Soviet or CMEA tradition to import tropical products, the traditional luxury food exports of the Third World; and the indirect tax on such commodities is spectacularly high, even in comparison with that on other consumer goods. As to the Third World's new and competing exports of consumer-goods manufactures, these are kept out by administrative devices typical of the Soviet-type economy, but surprisingly similar to the quotas whereby advanced capitalist countries do the same thing.

No wonder then, that Third World-CMEA trade lags. It should be possible to concentrate such opportunities for expansion as the Soviet-type system allows on Cuba and Vietnam, and after them on Group 3; but although this has to some extent happened, still the imports from Group 3 countries have not risen a great deal (see Table 4.1). But aid is much easier to concentrate. Financial capital to lend abroad (that is savings surplus to domestic requirements) is, to the great credit of the Soviet System, almost as difficult to find as exports, domestic requirements being kept high by the large planned volume of investment.

However the concentration of the small sum available on a few countries does raise its importance a great deal.[26] More than 83 per cent of aid committed by Communist countries to the Third World in 1954–72 was concentrated on fifteen countries.

Of course, there must be *some* exportable commodity to back up financial aid, unless the latter is to be convertible. That commodity is, in the Soviet and CMEA case, machinery (for after all bad machinery is better than none) and arms. We have little accurate idea of the volume of arms deliveries by any country in the world, still less of the method of payments; there is always some secrecy but our preliminary estimates indicate that hard currency earnings from such sources are not insignificant for the USSR, follow political opportunities rather than commercial relations and need not depend on the recipient's potential if sympathetic states with large hard-currency balances can be called upon to support them.

In this way the ordinary rule, that aid follows trade, high volumes of the one going with the other, is broken. We give here, for reasons partly of space, imports without exports. But it should also be remembered that exports, including as they do arms deliveries and the rent of military bases, are really unknown.

TABLE 4.1   *Soviet imports from 'Group 3' countries (million transferable roubles)*

	1970	1973	1975	1976	1977	1978
from						
Afghanistan†	30.9	34.4	64.3	66.8	76.5	75.7
Angola	–	–	–	14.4*	10.4*	0.8*
Ethiopia	0.8	2.2	2.1	0.7	1.5	4.3
Mozambique	–	–	–	–	–	0.8
Somalia	0.4	1.1	4.3	4.7	2.9	n.a.
P.D.R. Yemen	0.2	0.1	0.1	–	2.0	2.5
Total	32.3	37.8	70.8	86.6	93.3	82.1
As a % of all						
Soviet imports	0.3%	0.2%	0.3%	0.3%	0.3%	0.2%

SOURCE   *Vneshnyaya Torgovlya SSSR*, various years.
* Composed entirely of natural coffee.
† Imports from Afghanistan are composed of wool, cotton and food products.

Few details are available for imports from Group 3 countries from East European sources, which presumably indicates negligible volumes of trade. Poland and Romania commenced importing from

Angola in 1976; Polish imports reached $8 million in 1976 and $16 million in 1977, Romanian imports were $1.5 million in 1976 and fell back to zero in 1977.

INTERNATIONAL ECONOMIC BODIES

A country's commercial policy is above all illustrated by the *international economic bodies* to which it belongs. Table 4.2 shows only serious grant- or loan-making bodies, and covers a wide span of left-wing countries to make comparison possible. We have recognised as

TABLE 4.2　*Membership of international organisations*
(dates of joining unless otherwise stated)

	CMEA	World Bank[c, i]	IMF	Regional
Angola	never	never	never	never Lomé[m]
Mozambique	never	never	never	never Lomé[m]
Ethiopia	never	always[d]	always[d]	always Lomé[m]
PDR Yemen	never	71/72	1 Jan.71	
Afghanistan	never	always[d]	always[d]	ADB Dec.66 [j]
Somalia	never	always[d]	always[d]	always Lomé[m]
Congo Brazzaville	never	always[d]	always[d]	always Lomé[m]
Mongolia	June 62 [n]	never	never	never ADB[j]
Albania	? Feb.47–Dec.61	never	never	–
Vietnam	June 78	77/8 [a, i]	c. 1 Aug.76[a]	ABD Feb.77 [j]
South Vietnam	never	up to 74/5 incl.	up to Aug.75 incl.[f]	ABD Dec.66 [j]
Laos	never	always[d]	always[d]	ADB Dec.66 [j]
Cambodia	never	1970/71[i]	c. Apr.70	ADB Dec.66 [j]
North Korea	never	never	never	never ADB
Cuba	July 72 [h]	up to c. 1 Nov.60 [c]	up to c. 1 June 63[g]	
Romania	Jan.47	72/3[b, i]	15 Dec.72	–
Poland	Jan.47	up to Feb/Mar 50	up to c. 1 Mar.50	–
Czechoslovakia	Jan.47	up to 1 Jan.54[c]	up to 1 Jan.55	–
Hungary, Bulgaria	Jan.47	never	never	–
Yugoslavia	Feb.47–[l] July 48	? always[d]	? always[d]	–
China	never	never	never	never ADB[j]

NOTES TO TABLE

[a.]　Probably acceded on a successor-state basis, in view of South Vietnamese membership (UN Mission p.55); but note intermissions.

b. Not International Development Association (IDA).
c. Earlier years from International Financial Statistics (IFS) monthly.
d. Before 1969/70.
e. From IFS.
f. As printed in IFS. Taken literally, this means that the new 'independent' Communist government of South Vietnam was a member for one year.
g. First moment of vacation of directorate.
h. Long previous membership of subordinate agencies.
i. Joined in fiscal year 1 July–30 June: from annual report.
j. Foundation Day was 19 Dec.1966. Data on the Asian Development Bank (ADB) from Huang.[27]
k. But an application or invitation was mooted in 1978: see text.
l. But an application or invitation was mooted in 1961–2.[28] and a formal association has been in force since 1965.
m. The Lomé convention is treated as essentially African. Of Portuguese ex-colonies, only Guinea-Bissau belongs. The two conventions are dated Feb.1975 and Oct.1979. (Euroforum, Brussels, 16/1979).
n. See text above.

regional bodies which are 'serious' in the sense meant only the Asian Development Bank and the Lomé Convention. There are therefore no 'serious' European bodies, except of course the EEC and the CMEA itself. UN regional bodies clearly do not qualify.

When Communism began to spread from USSR the new Communist countries, rich or poor, observed the Stalinist principle of belonging only to CMEA. China and North Korea have avoided even that. Yugoslavia and Albania left CMEA, the one to become part of the comity of nations, the other to cut herself off more and more. Within CMEA, Czechoslovakia, Poland and Cuba even abandoned the World Bank and the IMF. But since about 1970 new joiners have carefully maintained their outside links – as well they may, since beggars cannot be choosers. Also Romania has struck out on her own.

B. Country Studies
Mozambique by Nicos Zafiris

BACKGROUND TO THE ECONOMY AND INTERNATIONAL TRADE

Mozambique is the largest of the former Portuguese dependencies in

Africa in terms of population. It also had, before independence, the second largest Portuguese colonial community but remained basically a poor country. Per capita GNP for 1970 has recently been estimated at US $594 per annum,[29] which makes Mozambique a 'less developed country' by any standards, although not among the very poorest in Africa. Agriculture occupies the vast majority of the population and accounts for the greatest part of GNP, the main products being cashew nuts, cotton, vegetable oils, sugar and timber. There is considerable potential, as about 66 per cent of the cultivable area is at present unoccupied. The country is, on the other hand, poor in minerals, coal being the main resource. Oil, iron ore, manganese and gold have recently been discovered but exploitation is not yet significant. The main industrial activity is processing of food and primary products, but there is also some textile production. Fishing is fairly well developed due to the country's long coastline. Geographical factors are also responsible for Mozambique's great significance as a freight transit link for neighbouring Rhodesia and South Africa, through the ports of Maputo and Beira, while tourism from those two countries has also been an important factor in Mozambique's economy.

Dependence on South Africa and Rhodesia has, in fact, been a striking feature of the Mozambican economy for a number of decades, and future relations with the two countries will clearly be of decisive importance for the pace and character of the country's economic development.

The economic significance of the presence, before independence, of European farmers, businessmen, administrators and skilled workers has been rivalled, until very recently, by the economy's ability to export a large portion of its black labour force to the South African and Rhodesian mines. The number of Mozambican workers reached a maximum in 1976 of about 180 000 in South Africa and 80 000 in Rhodesia. The South African connection has been particularly important, as the Mozambicans were mainly employed in the gold mines and over half of their wages were paid in gold to the government of Mozambique at the 'official' price of US $42 per ounce. The government was then able to sell the gold in the free market at a considerable profit, while paying the workers in local currency. The net value of the 'gold deal' to the government exceeded US $100 million annually, in the few years before and immediately after independence and the arrangement was the country's biggest foreign exchange earner until its discontinuation by South Africa in 1978.[30]

The emergence of the liberation movement in 1960 resulted in a belated effort by the colonial government to build up the country's infrastructure. Thus, even before independence, the economy was characterised by a fair degree of state ownership and direction. Transport, communications and municipal services were state-owned and the state also co-operated with big capital in other fields and with peasant farmers in agricultural co-operatives. Frelimo's victory marked, of course, a significant extension of the role of the state in the economy.

Mozambique is heavily dependent on foreign trade (around 30 per cent of GNP) but her long standing deficit on visible trade has recently deteriorated further. Exports are concentrated on a few products, that is cashew nuts, cotton, tea, fish, sugar and vegetable oils, which have generally been insufficient to pay for the much more diversified imports of industrial equipment, crude oil, textiles and, more recently, food. Surpluses on invisibles (mainly freight transit) and gold sales helped to achieve a balance on current account until 1975. The overall balance of payments position has markedly deteriorated since independence, due to the exodus of the Europeans and consequent disruption in agriculture and industry, and to organisational changes in both agriculture and industry. Other influences have included floods in 1976 and 1977, which destroyed a considerable part of the main crops and led to food shortages, the closure of the Rhodesian border in 1976 and the consequent loss of freight transit earnings, Rhodesian air raids and other hostilities (whose cost is currently being put at $350 million per year); in addition there is the seemingly indefinite settlement of many Mozambican workers in Rhodesia, with almost total discontinuation of remittances, and a growing influx of refugees from Rhodesia (currently estimated at 100 000). The termination of the gold deal with South Africa and the ensuing loss of gold sales and workers' remittances was accentuated by losses on capital account due to the granting of some transfer facilities to outgoing Europeans following independence. According to one estimate a payments deficit of US $25 million in 1975 has increased to something like US $225 million by 1978.[31] The position now appears to have become critical and international aid is urgently needed. Some has been received, from Western as well as CMEA sources, and more is being sought by the government.

Foreign trade has been heavily concentrated on a small number of partner countries namely Portugal, the Republic of South Africa, the United States, Japan, West Germany, the United Kingdom and France, who have accounted for over 66 per cent of total trade in

recent years.[32] A significant feature of Mozambique's trading pattern
has been the very small amount of trade with other African countries
(with the sole exception of South Africa), a result of the isolation to
which Portugal and its colonies had been condemned by the rest of
Africa before independence. Since independence and in 1977 in
particular, Mozambique has started to import relatively small amounts
of transport and other equipment from the Soviet Union, while
steadily moving towards a position of heavy dependence on the USSR
for arms. In at least one instance, arms were obtained for cashew nuts
on a barter basis. Of the remaining CMEA countries, Romania and
Bulgaria and more recently East Germany, have begun to record
substantial exports to Mozambique but without a corresponding flow
of imports.[33] All in all then, the country remains open to the international economy but there is some evidence of a slight movement of
its trading pattern towards the CMEA group. Trade policy in the next
few years is likely to be dominated by immediate requirements,
particularly the need to reduce food imports through an effective
restoration of normal productivity in agriculture.

THE POLITICAL ECONOMY OF SOCIALIST INDEPENDENCE

Given the predominantly rural character of the Mozambican
economy, Frelimo was fundamentally a peasant nationalist movement
in origin. Its adoption of Marxism was probably evolutionary and the
early orientation was Maoist. During most of the war, independence
remained the primary objective while Chinese views seem to have taken
precedence over Soviet ones. The early measures taken by the new
government in the economic sphere represent a mixture of attitudes
and considerations, but there can be little doubt that a serious Marxist
socialist programme has by now been embarked upon. A shift away
from the Chinese model can also be observed but some of the policies
are perhaps best explained in terms of simple pragmatism.

The main economic reforms can be briefly summarised: nationalisation of the land and establishment of a multiple system of agricultural
organisation including state farms, co-operatives, 'communal villages'
as well as individual farming;[34] takeover of many Portuguese and other
foreign industrial assets, but with negotiations initiated in most cases
with a view to some compensation; nationalisation of health, educational and legal services; and simplification of the tax system and
increase in overall taxation through a progressive income tax and

higher consumption tax on luxuries. Socialisation has thus stopped short of complete abolition of private enterprise, and stratification and material incentives are permitted in the socialised sector. But there have also been attempts to get production moving through moral exhortation and compulsion. Decentralisation seems to be aimed for, especially as attitudes to socialisation tend to vary from one part of the country to the other.

On balance, then, Mozambique can be said to be following a NEP (i.e. Leninist) type of economic strategy, with a smattering of Maoist-style measures and a good deal of pragmatism in international economic relations. The latter is particularly evident in connection with South Africa, while at the same time the attitude to Rhodesia is uncompromising, and new trading partners are primarily sought among the politically friendly East Europeans. It is probably too early to say to what extent the sum total of the domestic and foreign policies followed amounts to some coherent version of the broad Marxist approach. There is no evidence yet of any urgent desire to introduce Soviet-type comprehensive planning on any scale. 'Decentralisation' rather than 'planning' is being spoken of and Chinese-type mass mobilisation methods have been experimented with. One conclusion, however, can safely be drawn: Chinese ideological influence, although very strong during the war of independence, is declining. Chinese opposition to the MPLA in Angola (see below) during that country's civil war seems to have been the decisive factor which turned Mozambique's feeling away from China. Significantly, the Chinese were absent, alone among Communist countries, from the third Frelimo Congress in February 1977.

Internal political change may offer a clearer guide to the government's ultimate intentions than economic measures taken under the pressure of circumstances. Frelimo is now an unambiguously communist movement, its espousal of Marxism having come early in the movement's history. Since independence, the organisation has been developing from a 'liberation front' into a 'vanguard' party of the typical communist one-party structure. The consequences for religion and culture have been very clear and, on the whole, repressive in favour of straightforward official Marxist–Leninist ideology. The establishment of the state apparatus as a close but subordinate parallel of the single party has been proceeding along standard communist lines. The country is, of course, officially designated as a 'people's republic'. The system is thus developing into a politically 'closed' one. The slogans adopted by the third Congress are, perhaps significantly, reminiscent of what might be expected of an Eastern European communist party in, for example, attacking 'liberalism', emphasising the party's role in 'directing the masses', its need for 'strong organisation and iron discipline' and the desire to 'create a new man'.

The crucial factor will probably turn out to be the strength of the links with the Soviet Union, consolidated recently in the form of a twenty year treaty of friendship and co-operation, signed between the two countries in the spring of 1977. As we have seen, the USSR is now practically the sole supplier of arms and the main supplier of technical assistance. But while leaning towards the Soviet position in the dispute with China, Mozambique has not finally swung behind the Soviet Union and she has also denied the USSR naval facilities in the country.[35] The attitude is then somewhat eclectic, and extends to relations with other countries such as Yugoslavia, so that the possibility of an independent–Socialist (Group 2) type of development may not be altogether ruled out. Some goodwill, coupled again with pragmatism, has also been manifested towards Portugal, for example in the form of negotiations for compensation on account of property taken over, as well as welcoming back skilled Portuguese settlers, old and new, and a recent agreement for technical co-operation.[36] The tense state of relations with Rhodesia since 1976 has been counterbalanced by increasing links with Tanzania, with which the establishment of a free trade zone has recently been announced and, despite some shift of trade towards the communist camp, the overall trading pattern is not dramatically different from what it was before independence.

Angola by Nicos Zafiris

BACKGROUND TO THE ECONOMY AND INTERNATIONAL TRADE

Angola is the largest of the former Portuguese dependencies in area, and the second largest in terms of population. Before independence, it also had the biggest Portuguese settler community, of whom the great majority fled the country with the collapse of colonial rule. Per capita GNP is estimated at US $736 for 1970,[37] a figure which puts Angola ahead of Mozambique as well as many other countries in Africa, but the country must still be regarded as 'less developed'.

The country is mainly agricultural, the principal products being coffee, sisal, corn, cotton, rice, sugar and palm oil; but it is also endowed with considerable albeit largely unexploited mineral wealth, mainly oil, diamonds, copper, iron ore, manganese, lead, tin, silver and gold. Angola is an important maritime centre, with two well-developed ports in Luanda and Lobito, and a transit route for Zambian and Zairean minerals. There is moderate industrial development in the form of food processing, production of soft drinks and beer, cotton and tobacco processing, cement, tyres, plastics, soap, papers, cans and oil refining. But the economic future of the country lies largely in its ability to exploit fully its mineral wealth and, most of all, its potentially significant oil reserves.

Mainly due to exports of oil, coffee and diamonds, Angola has for years enjoyed a considerable trade surplus which, before independence, made a significant contribution to the metropolitan Portuguese budget Imports are more diverse, comprising mainly industrial and transport equipment but also some foodstuffs and consumer durables.

Of the main partner nations, trade with Portugal accounted in 1974 for 27 per cent of Angola's exports, taking second place to the US which received 38 per cent. Canada, West Germany and Spain were the only other significant importers of Angolan goods. Portugal retained, however, in 1974 its leading position as the principal exporter to Angola, followed by West Germany, the United States, South Africa, the United Kingdom, France and Japan. A marked decline in foreign trade could be observed in 1975 and 1976 (the years of the civil war), but by 1976 the US had gone vastly ahead of Portugal and all other countries as the leading importer nation and had also narrowly passed Portugal as the leading exporting country, with West Germany running a close third The same year marked the beginning of trade with the Soviet Union: by 1977, according to Soviet statistics, Soviet exports to Angola, composed mainly of motor vehicles and aircraft, amounted to 69 million roubles while Soviet imports, composed entirely of coffee, reached 10.4 million roubles.[38]

Recently Angola has entered into trade, aid and co-operation agreements with a variety of CMEA members in addition to Western countries, notably Portugal, Brazil, Belgium and Italy, and is making efforts to normalise relations with Zaire.

Despite data limitations, it can thus be observed that, while the overall trade pattern does not appear to have changed dramatically in relation to the immediate pre-independence period, the East Europeans are making increasing inroads into Angolan trade to a greater extent, it would seem, than in Mozambique. The decline of trade with the old colonial power is particularly marked. Still, the evidence does not justify any inference that Angola is becoming significantly integrated in any international socialist division of labour. Like Mozambique, she remains, on the whole, open to the world economy.

THE POLITICAL ECONOMY OF SOCIALIST INDEPENDENCE

Angola's economic institutions are undergoing transition to a more stable form of socialist economy, coming firmly under state direction. Following independence and the end of the civil war, the state took over the most important enterprises including banking and insurance which had already been nationalised by the colonial government. Negotiations for compensation, on account of foreign assets taken over, are under way in some cases while foreign capitalist participation is continuing in key areas, notably oil (an agreement with the Gulf Oil Company to resume production and exports) and diamonds (negotiations are in hand with the former Portuguese and other Western interests within the Diamang Group). There is also, however, an agreement for the Soviet Union and Cuba to manage the state fishing industry. Finally, agriculture is still largely uncollectivised, following some peasant resistance to collectivisation plans. A massive drive is under way to restore agricultural production which was badly disrupted by the civil war and has been further depleted by the exodus of white and black refugees. Emergency steps have included the organisation of city dwellers in teams to help with the coffee harvests.

The political dimension of recent developments in Angola has been very intricate and has included a number of novel features. Angola's struggle for independence was shared by three movements, namely the Marxist and eventually pro-Soviet MPLA, the 'liberal' FNLA and the 'populist' UNITA. The last two finally came to depend on the West (including South Africa) but also on China for support, while the MPLA was able to benefit from the direct intervention of Cuban troops in its favour.

Although the conduct of the civil war necessarily added a dimension of pragmatism to the policies of the MPLA leadership (and it may be fair to say that they were bound to rely on those who gave them support), this should not cast any doubts on the organisation's basic

Marxist–Leninist character. It is not clear whether the Soviet/Cuban intervention was wholeheartedly welcomed in view of the heavy dependence which would inevitably follow it, and the decision to utilise the 'Katangese gendarmes', in particular, must have been taken with reluctance. Since the end of the war, the signs have been that the government is anxious to reduce dependence on Cubans, of whom thousands are still in the country, and also to contain the activities of the Katangese who seem to have found a permanent home in Angola.

The government's main efforts in the field of external security must be seen in conjunction with its efforts in the domain of economic relations in general. The government thus seems at present to be gratefully accepting Soviet military aid and the Soviet link has now been formalised in the form of the 1976 twenty year treaty of friendship and co-operation. At the same time, the overall policy appears to be one of normalisation and extension of economic relations with other, particularly neighbouring, countries. Relations with Portugal are also characterised by willingness to continue co-operation and certainly to obtain Portuguese technical assistance. Portuguese with skills who fled the country are being invited back.

But the clearest manifestation of MPLA pragmatism has been in the dealings with the Gulf Oil Company, which has been responsible for the oil operations in Cabinda. The MPLA had come to an agreement with Gulf before independence, and the agreement has been re-activated since, and is now operative after an unsuccessful attempt by the Cubans to run the oil industry themselves. Experts from a number of other countries have been called in to help put back in operation the other mines (including diamonds). The government's attitude towards multi-national corporations in general seems to be, in the words of a Minister, 'not to proceed with nationalisation except for those enter-prises which have been abandoned by their owners'.[39]

As in the case of Mozambique it is in the strictly political area that we find the clearest expression of attachment to Marxism–Leninism. The state apparatus is being reorganised along typical one-party lines. But unlike Mozambique, we see in Angola a considerable amount of infighting within the movement which culminated in the abortive coup in 1977 by the N. Alves group. In denouncing internal opposition as 'factionalism' the MPLA appears to have adopted one more char-acteristic feature of communist party behaviour. Yet, in a sense, the plotters seem to have represented a more 'purist' element within the movement, and their defeat may be interpreted as evidence of the relative predominance of more pragmatic and flexible attitudes. That may be regarded, ultimately, as the success of the NEP-like strategy which Angola, like Mozambique, has been pursuing.

Ethiopia by Barry Lynch

BACKGROUND

If judged by GDP per capita, Ethiopia is one of the least developed countries in Africa. In 1970, GDP per capita was approximately US \$190.[40] As is characteristic of countries in the early stages of economic development, primary production is of overwhelming importance, with 45 per cent of production taking place at subsistence level. The level of general education is low, with 95 per cent illiteracy. There has been a shortage of skilled labour of all kinds and an abundance of unskilled workers, which is disguised in agricultural unemployment.

Ethiopia recognised the need for development planning late in the 1950s with the introduction of the first development plan (1958–73). Agriculture was recognised as the mainstay of the economy, and agricultural land the main national asset. Nearly 80 per cent of the population relies on it for a living but the country is barely self-sufficient in food, the modern agricultural sector accounting for only 7 per cent of total agricultural production.

Manufacturing constitutes only 5.3 per cent of GNP. This is mainly due to the failure to discover raw materials which could become the basis of industrial development, the smallness of the domestic market and the lack of comparative advantage which would allow it to build up export oriented industries.

As a result, manufacturing is basically import-substituting and is only viable with heavy protection.

In foreign trade, there has been a persistent trade deficit. This deficit has been financed by a capital inflow where long-term loans, particularly in the form of development aid, have been more important than private foreign investments, while technical assistance has accounted for a considerable proportion of this inflow.

DOMESTIC POLICY

The new military government initiated a series of economic and social reforms in 1974. On 20 December Ethiopia was declared a socialist country. Within two months, one hundred companies had been nationalised or partially taken over. In March 1975, rural land became the 'collective property of the state'. In the Land Reform Proclamation, the landlord–tenant relationship was abolished and each peasant given the right to farm up to ten hectares of land. The use of hired labour was prohibited. In addition, Peasants' Associations were organised, each of which could farm up to 800 hectares communally. Later, in July, urban land was nationalised, and houses and businesses were seized by the state.

On 21 April 1975 the National Democratic Revolution Programme was announced, which was designed to strengthen the economy and raise the standard of living by consolidating the gains of the revolutions, namely the destruction of the monarchy; the proclamation of socialism; the nationalisation of rural and urban land and the means of production and distribution; labour law reform and the creation of farmers' co-operatives. The stated objective of the programme was to pave the way to the creation of a People's Democratic Republic through the leadership of a single party of the proletariat and other progressive parties and institutions. The political and social structures of Ethiopia can thus be seen to be broadly based on Marxist–Leninist principles. Whether they prove durable will depend upon the ability of the ruling group to gain wide popular support through the establishment of a Marxist party at all levels of society.

US support for Ethiopia continued after the revolution, but military aid was suspended in November 1974 following the execution of followers of the former Emperor. By March 1975, the United States once again agreed to provide Ethiopia with arms, partially to check the Soviet buildup in Somalia, but while Ethiopia had requested US $30 million of military aid the United States provided only $7 million, and was not therefore seen as a reliable source of arms.

Marxist ideology and the socialist restructuring of Ethiopia did not immediately lead to a shift to military dependence on the Soviet bloc. In late 1976, this anomaly began to disappear. In response to the inadequate offer of aid from the United States, Ethiopia approached the Soviet Union for military and economic aid. By February 1977, Ethiopia's dependence on the US for arms ended with the commitment of arms deliveries from Eastern Europe. The Soviet Union agreed to equip the Ethiopian army in its struggle with the Somalis and has continued its military support. Since 1977 it has sold nearly US $1000 million worth of arms to Ethiopia on commercial terms.

In spite of receiving military aid from the Soviet bloc, most of Ethiopia's economic assistance continues to come from the West and China, despite severely strained relations with both. Out of US $117 million in loans listed in the 1979 budget, more than 75 per cent comes from the West, especially the World Bank and the EEC. Trade with the West has also continued since the revolution. Up to 1974, both imports and exports to developed capitalist countries were declining as a proportion of total imports and exports. In 1974 and 1975, this decline increased but in 1976 such trade rose to pre-revolutionary levels. Throughout the period, however, it was not the centrally planned economies which benefited from this decline, but rather the developing market and Middle Eastern economies. Thus the period 1974–6 appears to be characterised by 'free-market' Marxism–Leninism.

We feel that Ethiopia can be classified as a Group 3 country. Its commitment to Marxism–Leninism does appear to be genuine even though not all of its policies support this. For instance, Ethiopia does persecute religion but so far has not encouraged the formation of a communist party. Ethiopia, however, is designated as a socialist country by CMEA and has observer status within it.

Somalia by Barry Lynch

BACKGROUND

Somalia is classified as one of the least developed countries in Africa. Its per capita GDP is low – approximately US $220 in 1970[41] and it has a limited natural resource base. Of its population of about 3.4 million in 1977, 75 per cent are rural and, of this, 35 per cent are nomadic herdsmen. It is a very homogenous population, however. Almost all belong to the Somali ethnic group which has a strong sense of cultural identity despite internal (clan) distinctions. There is heavy emphasis on livestock activities which reflects the fact that most of the country is arid and only suitable for grazing. Only 9 per cent of GNP is derived from manufacturing.

Somalia became an independent country in 1960, being formed from the former British Somaliland and Italian Somalia. In 1969 a left-wing military *coup d'état* brought the Supreme Revolutionary Council to power, which later disbanded itself in favour of a 'scientific socialist' party, the Somali Revolutionary Party, with strong Islamic commitments. The Somali Democratic Republic thus became a single-party state.

'Scientific socialism' is interpreted as a pragmatic adaptation to local conditions of Marxist–Leninist principles. It is an attempt to blend the official ideology of the state and the party – Marxism–Leninism – with the beliefs of the state religion – Islam. It specifically rejects the atheistic basis of Marxism. The basis of 'scientific socialism' is said to be found in the ideology of Islam and the Koran, with its emphasis on equality, justice and social progress. In general, it puts great emphasis on self-reliance, that is, a more efficient use of domestic resources, popular participation and public control and ownership of the essential means of production. Thus after the *coup*, schools, banks, electricity and transport services and land were nationalised. The policy was to develop the economy along basically socialist lines although private enterprise was encouraged on a small scale.

Even before the 1969 *coup*, Somalia had close relations with the Soviet Union. The first agreement on economic assistance was concluded shortly after Somali independence in 1961. By November 1963, Somalia was accepting military aid and, by 1967, military advisers. This aid was increased after 1969 until by 1976, with the signing of a treaty of friendship with the USSR, the Soviet Union had established a military presence in Somalia, including a naval base at Berbera.

Although Somalia's military aid came from the Soviet Union, some economic aid came from China, the Arab states and the West. China assisted in rural development and road construction. In 1974, Somalia became a member of the Arab League but it received little aid.

Somalia traded primarily with the West, although, after independence, imports and exports from and to the developed market economies declined. The bulk of this trade was conducted with Italy, one of the former colonial powers. On the export side, declining trade with the capitalist countries was taken up by greater exports to the Middle East and, to a more limited extent, the Communist countries. On the import side, however, the latter steadily gained a larger proportion of the total. The external economy of Somalia was still very open nonetheless, and relied on Communism for only 11 per cent of its exports and 21 per cent of its imports.

Following the Ogaden war, the future path of development of Somalia remains uncertain. It is unlikely however that it will follow the path of development of those countries that we have classified as Group 3. Internally its commitment to Marxism–Leninism may not be as strong as that of the other African states, and its external relations will necessarily be affected by the fact that it has fought a war with another socialist country enjoying Soviet assistance.

People's Democratic Republic of Yemen (PDRY) by Yukimasa Chudo

'SCIENTIFIC SOCIALISM' IN THE ARAB WORLD

South Yemen (People's Democratic Republic of Yemen) had a population of two million in 1978. In 1970, income per head was US $287.[42] Political leadership in the struggle for independence had been contested between the Front for the Liberation of Occupied South Yemen (FLOSY), basically an urban organisation, and the National Liberation Front (NLF), organised among indoctrinated peasants and tribesmen from the hinterland, the latter obtaining the upper hand in the struggle.

Since Yemen has historically constituted an inseparable economic, political and cultural unit, it seems sensible to view it as a divided country like Germany or Korea. Reunification, by aggressive means, with the North is a ruling obsession in the PDRY government. So South Yemen's foreign policy should be observed not only through its narrow ideological consideration but sometimes through its strong commitments to reunification and, more widely, to the Arab cause.

Although the NLF declared its commitment to 'scientific socialism' in its First Congress in 1965, the interpretation of the phrase had been the focus of internal conflict between the moderates and the leftists, the former stressing the national and Arab character of the party, the latter its class character.

After independence, the inability of the NLF's policies to overcome the economic malaise of the country, together with intermittent outbreaks of military confrontation with North Yemen, forced the leadership more and more toward a need for help from the socialist countries, resulting in an ideological split between pro-Chinese and pro-Soviet factions. The current supremacy of the pro-Soviet faction is not unrelated to the evolution of international relations around the area, and the consequent increase of Soviet interest in it. Little substantial economic and military support came from the Eastern bloc until the mid-1970s, when the region became an important point for Soviet strategists due to the reopening of the Canal, the existence of pro-Soviet *regimes* in the Horn of Africa and the increasing strategic importance of the Indian Ocean. After the loss of Asmara in Somalia, Aden became the main staging post for Soviet political and military activities in the region. At the height of the Ethiopian–Somali war, Aden was the main staging post for Soviet reinforcements to Ethiopia and still is for its military commitments in the Horn of Africa, despite the PDRY's reluctance to support the enemies of its Arab 'brothers' in Eritrea. Furthermore, the presence of substantial numbers of Soviet, East German, Cuban and Ethiopian troops could and did play a decisive role in the delicate political development of the country.

After the succession to power of the pro-Soviet Abdel Fattah Ismail, the PDRY officially became a one-party state under the Yemeni Socialist Party, based on 'scientific socialism' and 'proletarian internationalism', in mid-October 1978. Nevertheless even this pro-Soviet *regime* continues Islam as the state religion and its leaders take care to be seen in the mosques.[43]

Although PDRY stands firm in its verbal commitment to proletarian internationalism, the new *regime* has shown that it would like to withdraw, to some extent, from the neighbouring conflicts in the Horn and Oman. It seems that the present *regime* intends to concentrate on its own internal development into a Marxist–Leninist state but to soft pedal, to attract aid from wealthy conservative Arab states, in spite of its deepening political and military commitments in its Soviet-type internal development. This pragmatism and its range of manoeuvre is being put to the test now in its confrontation with the North.

IN SEARCH OF A STABLE DEVELOPMENT FUND

The population of the PDRY on attaining independence in 1967 was estimated to be between 1.2 and 1.4 million, of whom between 450–500 000 were urban dwellers. They were mainly engaged in service-orientated activities in Aden (the Government and the British military base absorbed a substantial portion of employment) and Aden Port and associated activities (import and transit trade, free zone activities largely catering to visiting ships, passenger traffic, bunkering and refining activities). This 'modern' sector is sharply contrasted with the 'traditional' sector where the remainder of the population was rural, mostly agricultural (450–600 000) and *bedouin* (120–150 000). This part of the economy was believed to be one of the poorest in the world. With hardly any agricultural or mineral resources to exploit, the Adeni economy was the main source of South Yemen's income, with its strategic position in the network of global international trade.

So, after independence, the main sources of income – the Aden Port, the British base and British subsidies – were lost. The closure of the Canal resulted in a loss of some £25 million per year. In addition to the loss of substantial income from the British military and civilian personnel stationed in the country, aid from Britain after independence was reduced to £12 million from an anticipated £60 million. The economy was virtually in a state of collapse. The PDRY anticipated a great deal of aid from the socialist countries but this proved to be unfounded. The Soviet Union offered some £600 000 in aid in the two years after independence, albeit in the form of military aid. China's aid was also of a military nature and although the PDRY received all forms of aid from most of the other socialist countries including Romania and North Korea, they could not recover their losses. Between 1966 and 1968, the country had an estimated negative growth rate of 10–15 per cent.

The government had no choice but to resort to austerity measures. To consolidate the organisational basis of the austerity measures, helped by the victory of the 'leftists' in the NLF, the Adeni government nationalised eight banks, shipping, trading and insurance companies with nominal compensation, to be integrated into the Public Sector Economic Corporation. But the BP refinery, the largest foreign owned enterprise in the country, was not nationalised because, with no oil in its territory, the PDRY would have been unable to obtain crude oil for refining (which is essential for its domestic consumption and bunkering activities). A series of socialist economic measures followed. Private enterprises were banned from importing most foodstuffs, cigarettes and vehicles (November 1969), privately owned buildings were taken over except for one dwelling for each family (August 1972). Socialist education was encouraged to consolidate these economic policies ideologically.

In spite of such socialist measures in addition to the Three Year Plan (1971–4), the *regime* could not increase production because it could not enhance the will to work, and a mass exodus of the people caused a labour shortage. Consequently the State Economic Corporation was disbanded in 1973 and incentive bonuses for meeting targets were introduced.

As much of the development fund since independence was raised abroad, most of the deficit in the balance on goods and services was covered by aid from the socialist countries. An interesting feature here is that China and the Soviet Union occupied almost the same share up until 1975. Another important contribution to the balance of payments was remittances from workers and merchants working abroad. Although this has been the biggest hard currency earner, the disincentive effect on families living on remittances poses a major dilemma for the regime. All in all, despite all efforts at economy and efforts to attract foreign aid, the PDRY had to manage to survive with an annual per capita income of less than US $300 at 1970 prices.

But the political climate of the region has begun to develop in favour of the PDRY, to reduce the burden of its financial difficulties. The reopening of the Suez Canal gave back the PDRY some of its strategic importance. It also put a huge amount of oil money in the hands of its conservative Arab 'brother' countries to the north.

Although the opening of the Canal itself failed to produce the large revenue of the pre-1967 period, the PDRY's strategic importance for the political ambitions of the socialist countries, especially those led by the Soviet Union, was attractive enough to make them almost double the aid disbursement in 1976, getting far ahead of China for the first time since independence. After their political set backs in Somalia and Egypt and especially after Aden's strong commitment on the side of Soviet-led forces in the Horn of Africa, this trend is all the more evident, culminating in a US $36 million aid commitment in February 1979, after the establishment of a pro-Soviet regime in the country. GDR and Czechoslovakia are following this line and Cuba is also sending sugar. There is a strong possibility that radical oil producing countries might extend their aid.

As for financial aid, from the oil-rich conservative countries of the Peninsula, Kuwait has been making continuous contributions to the country. The Kuwaiti fund alone represents more than 20 per cent of the PDRY's outstanding debt in 1977. In contrast Saudi money is more political in nature. Although Saudi Arabia extended an offer of US$35 million through the Saudi Fund for Economic Development in 1977, assured by Rubai Ali's moderate policy, political development since the execution of Rubai Ali brought the relations of both countries back to confrontation. However, Saudi Arabia wants to use money for the PDRY to secure political stability of the whole Peninsula, as the PDRY wants to use the moderation of its foreign policy to acquire the money for its socialist economic development. So the final outcome will depend on the balance of power in the region, especially after the fall of the Shah and the Egyptian–Israeli peace treaty.

Helped by the favourable impact of increased foreign currency transfer through workers' remittances and foreign aid, the PDRY has embarked on a plan to diversify its economic base. Modernisation of the port facilities, fishing, related industries and infrastructure investment dominate the scene. Hand in hand with the emphasis on the socialist transformation of the internal economy, imports from industrial Western countries have more than quadrupled between 1973 and 1977, whereas imports from the East have less than doubled. Western technical experts are being invited and foreign bunkering companies are more and more tolerated. (The BP refinery was transferred to the PDRY in May 1977 and the UK government-owned communication company Cable and Wireless nationalised in 1979, both by mutual consent).

The PDRY, having firmly committed itself politically to 'scientific socialism', seems now to be concentrating on economic reconstruction through pragmatic manoeuvring at different levels in inter-Arab and East–West politics. While mainly depending on the Soviet-led socialist allies for its economic, political and military support, it will also try to attract oil funds, even by refraining from any revolutionary commitment in the Peninsula for the time being. The Soviet bloc, for its part, will try to make Aden commit itself more in its role as a strong military post in the area, but at the same time seems to encourage Aden's moderation for oil money which might enhance Aden's creditworthiness for Moscow's arms trade. Radical oil countries are also in line with this design. Imports from the West will continue to grow. The private sector[44] and western companies will also continue to play an important role in its pragmatic task of 'socialist transformation'.

NOTES

1. Albania never formally resigned or was expelled from CMEA. She is treated as a member in Czechoslovak and Polish, but a non-member in Soviet, trade statistics. North Korea is an 'observer', along with Angola, Laos and Ethiopia. Yugoslavia is a 'participant' according to a 1965 agreement with CMEA. The analytical significance of observer status

remains obscure and requires further study.

2. On this very vague concept cf. Colin Legum in *Problems of Communism* (January-February 1978).

3. We can speak thus confidently on the assurance of Prof. Hans Bräker 'National (*natsional'naya*) democracy' was of course always junior to 'People's (*narodnaya*) democracy'. That word meant the East European satellites and Mongolia, all of which have now 'founded socialism'.

4. Yevgeni Primakov, *Gesellschaftswissenschaften* (East Berlin, 3/1979).

5. Stephen Clarkson, *The Soviet Theory of Development: India* (Toronto, 1978). Ian Jeffreys, 'The Stalinist Economic System as a Model for Underdeveloped Countries', PhD thesis 1974, in LSE library.

6. N.I. Bukharin and E. Preobrazhenski, *The ABC of Communism* (London, 1921). Also Penguin edn (London 1969) pp. 446–7. N.S. Khrushchev in *World Marxist Review* (September 1962).

7. P. Alampiev, O. Bogomolov, and Yu. Shiryaev, *A New Approach to Economic Integration* (Moscow, 1973).

8. Ibid., p. 84.

9. The Russian is usually something like '*sblizhenie i uravnivanie ekonomicheskogo razvitia*'.

10. Michael Kaser, *Comecon* (Oxford, 1965) (2nd edn) pp. 11–12.

11. Ts. A. Stepanyan in *Voprosy Filosofii* 10/1958

12. S. Yowev in the *Bulletin* of the Institute for the Study of the USSR (Munich, 1960).

13. Kaser, *Comecon*, pp. 182 et seq.

14. And in a less authoritative place: Titarenko in *Politicheskoye Samoobrazovanie* (March 1962).

15. For example in *Neues Deutschland* (17 June 1962).

16. V.I. Morozov, *SEV, Soyuz Ravnykh* (CMEA, Alliance of Equals) (Moscow, 1964).

17. Note that he speaks of a 'camp' (*lager*). 'Camp', President Tito is said to have said, 'that means to us a concentration camp'. Nowadays the approved Soviet word is 'commonwealth' (*sodruzhestvo*).

18. N. Ptichkin in *Vneshnyaya Torgovlya*, 9/1972.

19. Ibid., 10/1978.

20. Observations of Peter Wiles, September 1979 (incl. Chinese official statements at various levels) The total population of Inner Mongolia is 19 mn. The total number of Mongols in all Chinese provinces is 3.0 mn.

21. *Far Eastern Economic Review*, 22 June 1979, p. 7. But there are substantial differences. Cuba was infinitely more humane, allowing rather free emigration of its bourgeoisie and selling only its few prisoners to USA for a properly arranged prior ransom. Vietnam takes their money for a place on a leaky boat – money she could take anyway by passing a law against private gold and currency holdings. That is, for Cuba the currency was the main thing, for Vietnam it is the expulsion. Again the Vietnamese Communists have always been much more orthodox than Castro.

22. Yearbook on International Communist Affairs (Hoover Institute, 1974), p. 567.

23. Hans Bräker, *Die Aufnahme Vietnams in den R.G.W.*, Bundesinstitut

fur Ostwissenschaftliche und Internationale Studien (Cologne, 7–1979). pp. 31–2.

24. Ibid., pp. 41–3.

25. When Hungary, once in, made great changes (1968), nothing of course could be done except invade again – and this was not done. Anyway, Hungary continues to use the command system for CMEA trade. In much more important ways Romania remains 'in' but is no longer 'of' CMEA.

26. Deepak Nayyar (ed.), *Economic Relations between Socialist Countries and the Third World* (London, 1977). pp. 3–4; *UN Statistical Yearbook 1973*, p. 715.

27. Po-Wen Huang, *The Asian Development Bank* (New York, 1975).

28. Kaser, *Comecon*, p. 100.

29. I.B. Kravis, A.W. Heston and R. Summers, 'The Real GDP per capita of more than 100 countries', *Economic Journal*, 1978. Using a Fisher's Ideal purchasing power parity if the authors are to be believed – and we incline to believe them – all previous dollar estimates of income per head at the poorer end of the Third World must be multiplied by about 2.5. Much the main reason is that the purchasing power of, say, the rupee (India is their basic country) over Indian non-tradables has been hopelessly under-estimated by taking the rate of exchange, or by failing sufficiently to adjust it; and, per contra, the purchasing power of the dollar over US non-tradables hopelessly over-estimated by the same process. India's reversion drags up all other poor countries with her. The rank order of countries is not much affected: neither are the actual values of the US–Western Europe comparisons.

30. *Africa Research Bulletin*, vol. 15 (1978) nos. 1, 3 and 6.

31. Estimate provided by the Government of Mozambique to the UN Review Mission 1977.

32. United Nations, *Yearbook of International Trade Statistics*, 1976 and 1977.

33. BBC, Summary of World Broadcasts, ME/W/1032 22 May 1979.

34. There has of late been a shift away from the development of state farms, which were generally established on land abandoned by the Portuguese and conceived in the context of a mechanisation programme due to shortages of skilled labour.

35. T.H. Henriksen, 'Marxism and Mozambique', *African Affairs*, vol. 77 (1978) no. 309.

36. BBC, Summary of World Broadcasts, ME/W/1032 17 April 1979.

37. See note 29.

38. *Vneshnyaya Torgovlya SSSR*, 1977.

39. E. dos Santos, speech of 14 February 1976.

40. See note 29.

41. See note 29.

42. See note 29.

43. *New York Times*, 27 May 1979.

44. The private sector is tolerated in the field of retail trade 'on condition that it observes the fixed price and supply regulations', (BBC, Summary of World Broadcasts, ME/W/1012/A1/10). Private investment is confined to the construction of individual housing for family use.

Part II Regional Aspects

5 The Soviet Union in the Middle East: Great Power in Search of a Leading Role

Karen Dawisha

THE BACKGROUND

The Soviet invasion of Afghanistan has been interpreted by many Western commentators as the first stage in a new era of Russian activism in the Middle East and the Persian Gulf. The Russians, it is argued, have sought ever since Tsarist times to secure warm water ports in this region not only for trading purposes but also in order to solve the perennial problems caused by trying to support and supply widely dispersed fleet areas. The naval disasters of the Russo-Japanese war in 1904–5 are used to illustrate the long-standing strategic importance to the Russians of the Mediterranean and the Suez Canal. While it is not entirely without justification that some analysts continue to explain Moscow's policy in the Middle East largely in terms of these strategic interests, nevertheless to focus exclusively on Russia's geo-strategic requirements would only produce a myopic distortion of the intricate web of interactions and influences which serve to delimit Soviet power and determine Soviet policy.

It is certainly true that in the inter-war period, Soviet policy toward the Middle East was ill-considered, largely formulated by the Communist International, and almost entirely determined by the current state of Soviet relations with the colonial mother-countries in Europe.[1] Economically, too, the Soviet Union had few direct interests to protect or promote in the Middle East. These considerations, combined both with Moscow's limited capability to influence events in the region and the colonial status of most of the Arab states, at least up until the

1940s, goes far to indicate why the Soviets did not become interested in expanding their relations in this area until the post-war period.

The breakup of wartime alliances and the growth of irredentist and nationalist movements in the Middle East resulted in Soviet support for a variety of anti-Western activities, ranging from the foundation of the state of Israel to the 1948 Iraqi demonstrations against the Portsmouth Treaty and the 1952 'Black Saturday' riots in Cairo against British activities in the Canal Zone. Yet following the Arab defeat in the 1948 Palestine war, the Middle East remained relatively calm until the mid-fifties; and, despite isolated outbursts, the relations between the West and the Middle Eastern states were fairly stable, thus denying the Soviets an opening to the area. In Moscow, too, the rigid 'two-camp' doctrine enunciated by Zhdanov in 1947, while not precluding the growth of progressive forces in the Middle East, neither envisaged nor encouraged such an occurrence.

Not until after Khrushchev came to power was Soviet policy gradually reorientated to take account of the benefits which might be gained from more active support of the nascent movements for non-alignment in the Middle East and other states of the Third World. Equally, only at about that time did Arab leaders emerge who were eager to encourage a greater Soviet *role* in the area as a panacea for problems associated with post-independence economic and political development. Since then, the Middle East has been a focus for global rivalries, with influence over events trying to be *maintained* by the West, and *attained* by the Soviet Union.

Despite the fact that the Soviet Union is now in many ways a recognised power in the area, nevertheless Soviet policy has not been without setbacks, and successes have not always been achieved without substantial and sometimes disproportionate costs. In examining Soviet policy in the Middle East, therefore, it is instructive to keep several questions in mind. Given that Soviet policy has placed high priority on the Middle East for a quarter of a century, what benefits have the two sides reaped now that the honeymoon is well and truly over? What has been the cost to Moscow of its Middle East policy? To what extent have Soviet objectives and capabilities changed and under what influences? And finally, how does Moscow balance not only short-term expedients with long-term goals, but also specific regional aims with overarching global interests?

SUEZ AND AFTER

Three main influences have interacted to shape the Soviet Union's objectives towards the Middle East since 1955: Soviet views of Western intentions, attitudes toward the national liberation movements, and shifts in Soviet capabilities. The establishment of the Baghdad Pact as a component in the Western policy of containment was perceived by Soviet decision-makers as a major threat to their security. As a result, beginning with the Czech arms deal to Egypt in 1955, Moscow made public its willingness to commit resources (primarily military) to counter-act this threat. The single-minded pursuit of this strategic objective dominated Soviet policy until well after the Suez crisis, during which the Soviets extended full diplomatic support for Nasser's nationalisation of the Canal Company. Yet despite the dramatic series of notes despatched to Israel and the Western powers threatening a Soviet missile strike on European cities,[2] the failure of the Soviets to intervene decisively during the crisis demonstrated both their own cautiousness (and preoccupation with the Hungarian uprising) and their very real lack of military capability at that time. The weakness of their navy and their inability to airlift large numbers of troops and supply them in foreign countries were two of the factors which, when combined with their lack of economic leverage in the area, explain both their low profile during the Suez crisis and their subsequent concern to prevent similar uncontrolled crises from breaking out.

This initial domination of strategic considerations also resulted in the Soviet support of any Arab government willing to pursue an anti-Western foreign policy, irrespective of the ideological disposition or domestic programme of its leaders, and despite the frequent persecution of local communists. Khrushchev himself stated in 1957 that 'many Arabs . . . are very remote from Communist ideas. In Egypt, for instance, many Communists are held in prison . . . Is Nasser a Communist? Certainly not. But nevertheless we support Nasser. We do not want to turn him into a Communist and he does not want to turn us into nationalists.'[3]

The period from 1958 to 1967 witnessed a departure from the near-monopoly which the strategic-military objective had exerted. The 1958 revolution in Iraq, which replaced the monarchy with a republican and leftist *regime* under Abd al-Karim Qassem, led to that country's withdrawal from the Baghdad Pact and an end to Western hopes of establishing an Arab-centred security system. Advances in missile technology, improvements in Soviet economic capabilities, and the strenghtening of quasi-socialist trends in Iraq, Syria, Egypt, Yemen, Algeria and other Arab states also contributed to this re-evaluation. These factors, plus growing pressure from within the international communist movement (and particularly from the Chinese), led the Soviets to pay more attention to the domestic policies of its Arab clients and to invest more aid in effecting the economic transformation of these countries, total figures for which are presented in Table 5.1.

TABLE 5.1   *Communist economic credits and grants extended to less developed countries (million US $) 1954–76*

	Total	USSR	East Europe	China
Total*	27 127	13 487	9 361	4 279
Africa	5 249	1 800	1 249	2 200
Algeria	1 331	715	524	92
South Asia	4 509	3 010	746	753
Middle East	9 241	5 868	2 898	475
Egypt	3 141	2 211	796	134
Iraq	1 163	699	419	45
North Yemen	221	98	17	106
South Yemen	116	39	21	56
Syria	1 306	467	778	61

*excluding Cuba and Vietnam.

SOURCES: UN, *Statistical Yearbooks,* and US, CIA, *Communist Aid to the Less Developed Countries of the Free World 1976,* ER 77-10296 (August 1977).

It was during the 1958–61 period, when the union between Egypt and Syria was functioning, that Moscow found it most difficult to reconcile its various objectives. On the one hand, the United Arab Republic under Nasser was firmly anti-Western and committed to non-alignment and social progress. On the other hand, first the Egyptian Communist Party, and then its much stronger Syrian sister organisation, were ruthlessly suppressed. This coincided with a short-lived period of communist ascendancy in Iraq, and as a result, in the rift which developed between Nasser and Qassem, the Soviets supported the Iraqi *regime.* Khrushchev and Nasser exchanged the first in a long series of public polemics which were to characterise and periodically disrupt relations between the two countries for the next two decades. With the decline in communist prospects in Baghdad, the promulgation of radical nationalisation measures by Nasser, the breakup of the

U.A.R. in the autumn of 1961, and the successful conclusion of the Algerian war of independence, Soviet relations with the Arab world settled down in the early 1960s.

For almost three years after Khrushchev's fall from power in 1964, Soviet objectives remained stable. Only after the Arab defeat in the June 1967 war did the Soviet leadership re-examine its policy. Israel's pre-emptive strike and the subsequent and overwhelming Arab defeat had a dramatic effect on the domestic and international politics of the Middle East. The Arab world went through a radical phase as popular revulsion against the defeated blamed the corruption of the *ancien regime*. By the end of 1969, radical and militant leaderships were in power in Syria, Iraq, Egypt, Libya, Sudan, North Yemen, Algeria and the People's Democratic Republic of Yemen (PDRY). Soviet military advisers in their thousands were sent to Egypt and Syria to help rebuild the shattered armies. The position of the communist parties in these radical states also was strengthened and in Egypt, where the Egyptian Communist Party had voluntarily disbanded itself in 1965, communists now gained such a position of strength within the ruling Arab Socialist Union that Soviet writers began referring to the ASU's transformation into a 'vanguard party' capable of carrying out the revolution 'from above'.[4]

RELATIONS WITH EGYPT

Soviet objectives were upgraded not just because of the radicalisation of Arab politics. After 1967, the Soviets correctly assessed the increased vulnerability of the defeated Arab *regimes* who were now more willing to accept greater Soviet participation in the economic and military reconstruction of their countries. The severance of diplomatic relations between many of the Arab states and the USA on the one hand, and between Israel and most of the socialist states on the other, polarised the international politics of the region and increased Arab dependence on the Soviet Union. At the same time, the dramatic increase in the size of the Soviet navy and the Soviet difficulty in supplying Vietnam following the disruption of its Chinese routes to Hanoi resulted in a greater Soviet willingness to incur costs in the establishment of a military presence in the Middle East. The securing of military facilities in Egypt, as the only state other than Israel with coastal access to both the Mediterranean and Indian Ocean fleet areas, assumed a particularly high priority. Having lost its submarine base in

Vlone, Albania in 1961, the Soviets lacked the logistic ability to support forces deployed at sea until after the 1967 build-up in Egypt. From then until 1973, the annual number of Soviet ship days in the Mediterranean increased dramatically (as indicated in Table 5.2). This increase was achieved both by sending more ships into the area (the number of surface combatants annually transitting the Turkish Straits increased from 39 in 1964 to 126 in 1973[5]) and by stationing them there for longer periods (the average surface combatant deployment from the Black Sea to the Mediterranean rose from 41 days in 1966 to 86 days in 1968[6]). The absence of aircraft carriers from the Soviet navy until July 1976 made it dependent on land-based support. This was provided until 1972 by Soviet-piloted aircraft operating from seven

TABLE 5.2   *Soviet naval presence in the Mediterranean: 1964–76*

	Annual ship days	Average daily strength
1964	1 500	5
1965	2 800	8
1966	4 400	12
1967	8 100	22
1968	11 000	30
1969	15 000	41
1970	16 500	45
1971	19 000	52
1972	18 000	49
1973	20 600	56
1974	20 200	55
1975	20 000	55
1976	18 600	50

SOURCE: Robert G. Weinland, 'Land Support for Naval Forces: Egypt and the Soviet Escadra 1962–1976', *Survival*, vol.20, no.2, 1978, p.74.

Egyptian airfields. The increase in the average duration of deployment also necessitated, and indeed was partly a result of, the provision of repair and resupply facilities at the Egyptian ports of Alexandria, Port Said, Mersa Matruh and Sollum. With the closure of the Suez Canal during the Six-Day war, the Soviet naval presence in the Indian Ocean became especially dependent upon the maintenance of base facilities not only in Egypt but also in South Yemen, the Horn of Africa and Iraq. Yet the facilities enjoyed by the Russians in Egypt were un-rivalled while they lasted.

. Within months of Sadat coming to power following Nasser's death in 1970, it became apparent that the new Egyptian President's own political objectives and orientations did not coincide with the Soviets'. Sadat certainly did not share Nasser's views about the common features of Soviet and Egyptian socialism. In particular he did not support the growth of communist influence within the ASU, and his dismissal, in 1971, of Ali Sabri and other leftists from that organisation ended Soviet hopes of establishing a vanguard party. Sadat also made it clear at a very early stage that the Soviets could not always rely on Egypt, either as an unquestioning ally or as a vehicle for spreading communist influence throughout Africa. This point was clearly made when Sadat helped Sudan's President Numeiri defeat an attempted communist *coup* in 1971.

The Soviet interest in maintaining influence in Egypt was such that, after 1971, Moscow was constantly being put on the defensive in its relations with Cairo, with the costs of those relations gradually out-stripping the benefits Following the downfall of the Ali Sabri group, Moscow and Cairo agreed to conclude a Treaty of Friendship and Cooperation under which Egypt was tied more closely to the Soviet Union while Moscow was contractually committed to increasing Egypt's military potential. Sadat made it clear from the outset that the only reason why he 'insisted on concluding a treaty' was to build up his army for 'the battle'.[7]

Sadat's announcement that 1971 was to be the 'year of decision' in the Arab–Israeli war led both to an increase in Egyptian demands for offensive weapons and to a clash between Egyptian and Soviet priorities. By this time, Soviet leaders were preoccupied with the Indo-Pakistan war, East–West relations, and the possibility of signing a peace treaty ending the Indochina war. The last thing they wanted was to be dragged into an ill timed Arab attack on Israel which would jeopardise *détente*. And when Sadat sought reassurance during his April 1972 visit to Moscow, that the Soviet Union would not make any agreements with Nixon about the Middle East, Brezhnev evidently cautioned restraint and warned (on this occasion and three other times prior to the October war) not to attack Israel within her pre-1967 borders.[8] As a result of this meeting, and Brezhnev's subsequent failure to supply Sadat either with a comprehensive account of the May 1972 Nixon–Brezhnev summit or with a statement of Soviet intentions relating especially to the supply of offensive weapons, Sadat decided that the stationing of approximately 15 000 Soviet military experts in Egypt had in fact become an impediment to the pursuit of his objectives, and he therefore decided to expel them. By 17 July, the numbers of Soviet personnel had been reduced to under 1000 and most of the advanced weaponry (including MiG-21s, MiG-25s, SU-11 interceptors and TU-16 reconnaissance aircraft, as well as the advanced SAM missile batteries) also had been withdrawn.[9]

Despite Sadat's actions, the Soviet side did everything to heal the breach. Such was the extent of Soviet interests and investments in Egypt that costs in loss of prestige and control caused by the expulsion still did not outweigh the benefits of maintaining relations. Although Soviet naval access to Egypt ports was not affected by the expulsion, Egypt did take control of all Soviet military facilities, thus substantially limiting the air cover available to the Soviet fleet. As a result, until the aircraft carrier *Kiev* was deployed and some alternative facilities were found in neighbouring countries, well after 1975, the number of Soviet surface combatants transitting the Straits declined by 40 per cent, from 126 in 1973 to 79 in 1975.[10]

In the economic and military aid fields too, the Soviets were heavily committed to Egypt. In the two decades following the Czech arms deal, 23 per cent of all Soviet arms exports had been to Egypt (41 per cent to the Middle East as a whole, with most of the remainder going to South and South-East Asia).[11] Moreover, from 1954–71, 16 per cent of all the capital commitments by socialist states to less developed countries went to Egypt, and in 1972 this figure actually increased to 21 per cent. Looking at the Soviet estimates alone, Egypt accounted for nearly 30 per cent of all Soviet aid to the Third World, a figure which rises to around 43 per cent for the 1954–71 period if Soviet credits to South Asia are excluded. Taking the period from 1954–76, the decline in the proportion of Soviet aid to Egypt, as shown in Table 5.1, was due not only to the disruption of relations but also to the dramatic increase in aid to Africa and other Middle Eastern states after 1972.[12] When one adds to these considerations the fact that, prior to the rise of the oil-rich states after 1973, Egypt was the clear and undisputed leader of the Arab world, it is not difficult to understand why the Soviets were willing to do almost anything, including the resumption of weapons supplies necessary for an attack on Israel, to keep Egypt from turning to the West. As a result, in October 1971 during Egyptian Premier Aziz Sidqi's visit to Moscow, Kosygin made it clear where Soviet priorities lay: 'The Soviet Union has one foreign policy, one political line in Middle East affairs. This is a line of all-out support for the Arab peoples and progressive *regimes* in the Arab countries in their struggle against Israel's aggression.'[13] Arms supplies were resumed on a massive scale and by April 1973, Sadat was able to declare: 'The Russians are providing us now with everything that is possible for them to supply'.[14]

By supporting, even if only tacitly, the Arab decision to launch a strike against Israel, the Soviets obviously calculated that their influence in the Middle East would have declined without such support. Equally, the level of Arab preparedness was thought to have so improved from the 1967 experience that total defeat could be avoided. Although the Soviets clearly knew that Israel's own nuclear capability plus American guarantees would preclude a total Israeli defeat, there might (provided the crisis could be contained within acceptable limits) be limited territorial gain made by the Arabs, in addition to breaking the diplomatic stalemate and enhancing Soviet influence in the Middle East as a whole, without jeopardising *détente*.

Events proved, however, that the Soviets had miscalculated in several key respects. Although the Arab armies did well in the first days of the 1973 war, on 15 October the tide began to turn decisively in Israel's favour. By 24 October, the Egyptian Third Army was surrounded and in risk of being annihilated. The Soviet leadership was faced with the prospect of an unacceptable level of defeat for their Arab client, and as a result Brezhnev informed Nixon that if the United States did not agree to a joint expeditionary force to stop Israeli violations of the ceasefire, 'we should be faced with the necessity urgently to consider the question of taking appropriate steps unilaterally'.[15] The American response was to put all American forces, including those in charge of strategic nuclear weapons, on a 'Defense Condition Three' alert, while at the same time increasing their pressure on the Israelis to lift the seige, which they ultimately did.

Although the crisis de-escalated after 26 October, superpower behaviour during the war, and in the months following, illustrated that while there was a mutual interest in developing *détente* as a set of mechanisms for managing and containing crises, nevertheless both sides were pursuing policies which, far from strengthening the substantive basis of cooperation, actually made future crisis more, and not less, probable. This was not because of any lack of genuine interest in improving East–West relations, but rather because at that time the two states assigned a higher priority to promoting their own interests and protecting their own regional clients, including those in the Middle East. Thus, the Soviet support for the Arab oil boycott led Nixon to postpone the introduction of a bill into Congress in November 1973 which would have given the USSR most favoured nation status.

Equally, Kissinger's step-by-step diplomacy was notable not only for the two disengagement agreements it produced, but also for the Soviet exclusion from the bargaining process which resulted.

Kissinger's successes would not have been possible without Sadat's decision, following the October war, to find an opening (or *infitah*) to the West for the solution both of the Arab–Israeli conflict and of Egypt's economic problems. The Soviet Union consistently opposed Sadat's separate initiatives, maintaining that Israel should withdraw to its pre-1967 borders, the legitimate rights of the Palestinians to establish their own state should be recognised, and all states in the region, including Israel, should exist within universally recognised and 'reliably guaranteed' boundaries.[16] Yet apart from curtailing aid and supporting the other Arab states in their opposition to the Sadat initiative (actions which only strengthened Sadat in his resolve and led him to abrogate the Soviet–Egyptian Friendship Treaty in 1976), the Soviet Union was ultimately powerless to prevent the signature of the Egyptian–Israeli peace treaty in 1979.

The loss of Egypt, and the changes in the international system after the October war, had a substantial impact on Soviet policy. In the first place, there were the economic implications of the break. At the time of the abrogation, it was officially announced in Cairo that Egypt's military and non-military debt to the Soviet Union stood at $7000 million (out of a total debt of $14 100 million).[17] Sadat's announcement in October 1977 that Egypt's repayment of the Soviet debt would be suspended for a ten-year period had the effect of further reinforcing the Soviet trend of decreasing the amount of credits extended to Arab states, putting their trade on a more mutually advantageous basis and insisting that arms should be paid for in hard currency on delivery. The number of projects being built with Soviet aid did indeed decline, combined with a tendency to insist that the Soviet Union would no longer so readily absorb those goods which would have been unsellable on Western markets. There was a concomitant increase in the import of oil, gas, phosphates and other raw materials.

The Soviet import of oil from the Middle East grew steadily throughout the 1970s, particularly from Iraq, where Soviet geological assistance in the exploitation of the Rumailah oilfields was repaid with an assured supply of oil, averaging at approximately 5.5 million tons of crude oil per annum.[18] Official Western estimates calculated that Soviet domestic oil production would peak in the 1980s, creating a possible situation in which oil would fall from 35 per cent of total energy production in 1975 to 17 per cent in 2000.[19] Although nuclear energy as a proportion of total energy production was increasing faster in the Soviet Union than it was in the West, nevertheless it was thought that the Soviet Union could experience serious energy shortfalls, particularly if the new Siberian deposits did not come into production at a rapid enough rate to maintain acceptable 'reserves-to-production' ratios or if the East European states (whom the Soviets had been trying to wean off Soviet supplies and on to Iranian oil and gas before the revolution there) put political pressure on Moscow to supply them at below-world prices. Irrespective of the precise level of future Soviet oil production, it is clear that economic considerations and objectives have increased in Soviet calculations, not just because of the economic advantages which accrue to the USSR but also due to Soviet awareness that oil was the West's 'Achilles heel'. By importing oil, the Soviet Union denied this commodity to Western states, thus further straining their economies. Moreover, the export of oil to the Soviet Union allowed nationalised Arab oil companies to diversify their trading links, thereby weakening the political influence previously exercised by the multi-nationals.

As the Middle East increased in its economic importance, so too was its strategic centrality enhanced. The opening of the Suez Canal in 1976, and the improvement in Soviet military capabilities, especially in the fields of aircraft carriers and rapid troop transport, both helped to offset further losses of Egyptian facilities. In May 1975, Egypt curtailed Soviet naval facilities in Alexandria by stipulating that Soviet ships henceforth would have to give advance notice of arrival and departure. Then, in May 1976, with the abrogation of the Treaty, Sadat gave the Soviet Union one month to close down its remaining support facilities. Western intelligence reported that the USSR had been successful in obtaining limited base and port access in Aden to service the Indian Ocean contingent, with the possibility of quite substantial opportunities in the Horn of Africa.[20] Nevertheless, the situation in the Mediterranean was affected heavily by the loss of Egyptian bases, and the Soviets were largely unsuccessful in finding replacements, a situation which led Vice-Admiral James Watkins, the Commander of the US Sixth Fleet, to comment early in 1979 that the Soviet naval strength in the Mediterranean would be increased if it were able to use facilities in the Middle East countries instead of protecting the navy by flying 'out of the Crimea as they do now'.[21] The Soviet leadership had been particularly interested in the Syrian ports of Latakia and Tartous as part of a general shift from Egypt to the Levant, but the Syrian intervention in the Lebanon and the total rift between the two Ba'athist *regimes* in Damascus and Baghdad made progress on that front very difficult.

SYRIA AND LEBANON

When the Syrians first intervened in Lebanon, it was on the side of the Christian and right-wing forces. As it happened, Prime Minister Kosygin was in Damascus on the very day (1 June 1976) the invasion began. The Soviet leader reportedly told Assad that while the Soviet Union approved of Syrian actions in the Lebanon, Assad should not expect any public declaration of support because of the Soviet commitment to the Palestinians.[22] The Soviet stand, and the continued supply to arms to the Syrians, was thought to be based on strategic considerations arising out of Kosygin's attempts both to obtain port facilities and to form a united front between Syria, Algeria, Libya, South Yemen and Iraq to isolate Egypt. When both these efforts failed, Brezhnev sent two letters to Assad in July, appealing 'to the Syrian leader to end military operations against the resistance and the Lebanese national movements', since not to do so would allow 'the imperialists and their collaborators to bring the Arab people, the area's progressive movements and the Arab states with progressive regimes under their control'. One of the Brezhnev letters was leaked, according to Assad, by the Soviet leaders themselves, to show the tough stance they purportedly would take against any state suppressing the Palestinian cause.[23] The Syrians' response was to reject this criticism and to refuse permission for the Soviet fleet even to call at Syrian ports (this situation remained in force until June 1978).[24] Soviet arms supplies subsequently were curtailed, but were never entirely cut off. Moscow's reluctance to condemn completely Syria's moves against the Palestinians underlined only too well the precedence which strategic interests took over ideological consideration in the formulation of policy.

By April 1977, when both Assad and Arafat visited Moscow, the Soviets publicly were supporting the Syrian role which by then had changed to prevent either the Christians or the leftists from gaining an overwhelming victory. Arms deliveries were restored to their previous high levels and, until the Israeli invasion of South Lebanon in March 1978, the Soviet leaders considered the Syrian presence there to be a stabilising force. However, following the Israeli invasion, there was a heightened risk that a local skirmish in Lebanon might spill over, sparking off a new Middle East conflict. The fact that such skirmishes had increased, and not decreased, after Sadat's visit to Jerusalem in November 1977 was interpreted by Soviet commentators as proof that Israel was prepared to use the changed balance of power further to improve its military position along Syria's borders.[25] This, plus the effect on Syria's defence policy of Egypt's withdrawal from any unified Arab strategy, created a fundamental problem for both the Syrian and Soviet leaders, and it was clearly a problem to which they had differing solutions.

The Syrian view that the military balance between Israel and her Arab neighbours had shifted in Israel's favour following Camp David was the subject of Assad's visit to Moscow in October 1978. The joint *communique* referred to 'decisions' which had been taken to redress the imbalance,[26] and the Syrian Minister of Information subsequently confirmed that Assad was given to believe that the Soviet Union would build up Syria's military potential to match Israel.[27] In November, when a high-level military delegation led by Syria's Chief of Staff, Hikmat Shihabi, flew to Moscow to finalise details of the arms transfers, they were surprised to discover that the Soviet leaders had completely changed their minds and were no longer prepared to supply the most advanced items on the Syrian shopping list, including not only the MiG-27s but also T72 tanks and advanced missile systems with integrated radar. Shihabi broke off negotiations and returned to Damascus after completing only three of the scheduled six day visit.[28]

The Soviet attitude was all the more mystifying to the Syrians in view of the dramatic reconciliation between Iraq and Syria which had resulted from the Baghdad summit convened earlier in the month. The participants had allocated £925 million per year to Syria for the re-establishment of the strategic balance with Israel, so it was certainly not lack of finance which was the cause of the breakdown in talks.[29] To the Syrians, it appeared that the Soviet Union was protecting its Great Power interests by *not* introducing weapons which might lead to a new war. The dispute reached its worst point when Assad recalled his ambassador to the Soviet Union and cancelled a trip to Moscow he was to have made with Iraq's Vice-President Saddam Hussein. Only after Hussein's personal intervention on Syria's behalf did relations begin to improve, and the visit by Prime Minister Tlas in January achieved a renewed Soviet pledge to provide advanced weaponry, although there was still uncertainty over the supply of MiG-27s.[30]

The sudden Soviet reluctance to serve as the arms-supplier to Syria was thought to signal a major shift in Soviet strategy towards the Middle East. At a time when Soviet–American *détente* was at a crossroads, and when the alignment of forces in the Middle East was even more contradictory than usual, the need for caution and an evaluation of the costs and benefits of various courses of action had never been higher. On the one hand, Syria was an important ally and it was becoming more important. It now had close relations with Jordan, Saudi Arabia and Iraq. The *rapprochement* with Baghdad had also eliminated some of the divisions within the Palestinian movement, and Syria's influence over the PLO and its armed wing increased. Although Syria's continued presence in the Lebanon constituted a severe drain on the morale of the Syrian army and on the nation's economy, nevertheless Syria was also in a position to exercise a key role in any political settlement in that country. For these reasons the Soviet Union needed to maximise its influence over the Damascus *regime*. However, the Syrians were not dependent on the Soviet Union for anything except weapons. Ever since the October war, Syria, like Egypt, had been pursuing its own Open Door policy. In 1977, non-military imports from the Soviet Union totalling £48.3 millions were substantially behind the £60.5 millions spent on American-made products.[31] By the end of 1978, West Germany had surpassed both of these figures to become Syria's largest trading partner.[32] As a result, it appeared that for the Soviets the only way to maintain, much less extend, their influence was to continue supplying arms.

It was recognised that the introduction of sophisticated weaponry could conceivably exacerabate the situation in the Middle East and undermine other fundamental Soviet objectives. The Syrians argued that a military build-up was necessary, not so much for future offensive operations but to act as a deterrent against an Israeli strike. According to Syrian officials, however, the Russians maintained that a prerequisite for supplies was a strong defence alliance between Syria, Jordan and Iraq, with a joint command and an increased Jordanian combat commitment. Otherwise, if sophisticated weaponry were to be introduced into Syria before a common strategy was agreed, there would be an open invitation for Israel to launch a pre-emptive strike. Soviet leaders were particularly worried because they calculated that Israel's hostility toward Syria was such that should a strike take place, Israel would repeat its past behaviour by striking not only at military installations but also at key economic targets such as the dams, the oil pipeline and the ports, and also conceivably at civilian enclaves. Soviet leaders were equally concerned that the Syrians themselves might use the advanced weaponry to start a war of attrition with Israel or to challenge Israeli incursions into Lebanon. Irrespective of the source of any new round of conflict, it was generally agreed that without Egyptian participation forcing the Israelis to fight on two fronts, the military outcome for the Syrians would be disastrous, even with the support of Iraq. The Soviet strategic nightmare therefore was of a Syrian military collapse that would necessitate direct Soviet involvement, which might save an ally but which would almost certainly risk a confrontation with the United States. Syria's own cautiousness in avoiding direct confrontation with Israel in Lebanon indicated that this argument was appreciated by Assad. The Syrian leader was reported to have been influential in persuading the PLO to withdraw from Southern Lebanon, following a Soviet news-agency release on 6 June 1979 that Israel was preparing a second invasion. The warning came after a trip to Syria, Lebanon and Iraq by Oleg Gruncivsky, the head of the Soviet Foreign Ministry's Near East Department.[33] The losses incurred by the Syrians in June 1979, when their MiG-21s challenged the vastly superior Israeli F-15s during an Israeli bombing raid over Lebanon, indicated both that the Soviets were attempting to restrain Damascus by withholding MiG-27 deliveries and that such a policy was having only a limited effect.

RECENT DEVELOPMENTS

The only way for the Soviets to improve their position was to break out of the isolation of being seen only as an arms supplier. In this respect, the most interesting development was the Soviet attitude toward Saudi Arabia. The Saudis were applauded in Moscow whenever they took a stand contrary to Western interests, as in the 1973 oil boycott; and the emergence of Saudi influence on Middle Eastern politics (especially after the Riyadh conference in October 1976 which brought about a cease-fire in the Lebanon) was generally welcomed by Soviet officials and analysts.[34] With Saudi condemnation of the Sadat initiative, the Soviet leaders became even more interested in improving relations with the moderate Arab states. Brezhnev was reported to have sent two messages to Saudi Arabia's King Khaled in December 1978, one written, setting out the Soviet position on Camp David, and one oral, expressing Soviet interest in the purchase of Saudi oil. Jordanian and Syrian officials confirmed that the Soviets had put out unofficial feelers regarding the establishment of diplomatic relations with Saudi Arabia. Gromyko's subsequent statement during his visit to Syria in April 1979, that the Soviet Union has 'no prejudices' against any Arab state holding a 'realistic and worthy position' on the Egyptian–Israeli treaty, coincided with a series of important articles in the Soviet press claiming that 'contrary to Soviet wishes' Saudi–Soviet relations had been broken since before the Second World War, thus creating an 'abnormal situation'.[35]

The Soviets were clearly doing everything possible to achieve a unity of all those forces opposed to the Israeli peace treaty, and were especially keen to encourage a union between Syria and Iraq. Such was their interest in this project that the large-scale clamp-down on the legal Iraqi communist party and the execution of 27 of its members in Spring 1979 (for activities within the army) went without mention in the Soviet press. Although a delegation of Ba'athis and Communists went to Moscow in March for mediation, nevertheless, as Naim Haddad, the Secretary General of the Iraqi National Front, sub-sequently confirmed, prior to the 1972 signature of the Soviet–Iraqi Friendship Treaty, the Soviets had agreed that relations between the Iraqi Communist and Ba'ath parties was purely an internal affair and that under no circumstances would the Soviet Union conduct its relations with Iraq through the Communist Party.[36] Equally, calls in the Arab world for Sadat's overthrow found their muted echoes in Moscow where, for example, the first major *Pravda* editorial following the peace treaty pointedly reminded its readers that such a superficial reconciliation was meaningless since no-one could guarantee how long Sadat would remain in power.[37]

In the years from the October War to the invasion of Afghanistan, the Soviets pursued a relatively low-key policy in the Middle East and refrained from involving themselves in domestic politics. The major cause of the Soviet Union's more pragmatic approach stemmed first of all from lack of options. Following the October war, they were really not in a position to make excessive demands on their Arab partners, who with their new wealth could seek any number of alternative suppliers. Neither did they have the military capability to invade and hold any of the Arab states whose socialist and pro-Soviet orientation might be threatened, as in Afghanistan. Thirdly, the Soviets were entirely excluded from the peace process and were in any case more interested in East–West *détente* than in furthering their policy in the Middle East.

However, following the Soviet take-over in Kabul, Soviet policy in the Middle East was thrown onto the defensive. Just as the USSR has benefited from Islamic unity against the American-backed Israeli occupation of Arab Jerusalem, now it was the United States who profited from Islamic condemnation of the invasion of Afghanistan. The Soviet action was condemned by the January 1980 meeting of Islamic Foreign Ministers which included representatives from Iraq, Algeria and Libya. Of the Soviet-backed Arab states, only Syria and South Yemen stayed away. The Soviets rewarded Syria with the supply of advanced weaponry in addition to a guarantee of support delivered by Gromyko in Damascus on 27 January 1980 that 'the Soviet Union will not allow aggression against Syria'.[38] Yet unlike the pattern of Soviet involvement in Africa, Gromyko gave no indication that the Soviets were considering the introduction of Soviet or Cuban combat forces in any of the Middle Eastern states (this does not include South Yemen where an estimated 2000 Russians and Cubans were stationed during the 1979 border skirmishes with North Yemen).[39] Moscow clearly learned from the 1973 war that the best way to prevent her regional alliance commitments from coming into conflict with *détente* was to prevent crises from breaking out. This was achieved by cautioning her Arab clients to give Israel no excuse to invade, while at the same time strictly limiting their own capabilities to pursue ambitious military objectives.

The Soviet Union was forced essentially into a defensive posture by the Egyptian–Israeli treaty, refusing to fulfil its traditional role of arms supplier to a side weakened by Egypt's 'defection', and prevented from participating in the peace-making process. Nevertheless, the Soviet *role* was not by any means eliminated. Events in Afghanistan and Iran, the union between Syria and Egypt, and the rift between the United States and the moderate Arab *regimes* presented ample opportunities for Soviet involvement. But the nature of that involvement had shifted from offensive to defensive, from long-term to short-term, from ideological to pragmatic, from within their control to largely outside their control. To a certain extent, this was not a failure of Soviet policy as such, but rather a situation in which both superpowers found themselves incapable of controlling their clients or achieving any satisfactory correlation between investment and influence. The bi-polar age had passed, and the simplicity of the Cold War had been replaced with a world in which economic power had been diffused, making client states far more capable of extracting maximum advantage from their patron-allies. Under such circumstances the necessity of strengthening *détente* as a means of preventing crisis escalation clearly increased in importance for both superpowers.

SUMMARY

For the Soviet Union, the three factors central to its assessment of objectives in 1955 remained true twenty-five years later – the perception of Western intentions, the assessment of the national liberation movements, and shifts in Soviet capabilities. Whereas, in 1955, the Soviets believed the existence of Western bases in the Middle East to be a major threat to Soviet security, the increase in Soviet military power and the shift from containment to strategic missile confrontation had downgraded, if not eliminated, that particular source of tension. Fundamentally, however, the continued Soviet belief both that the United States was willing to take greater risks to protect its Middle East interests, and that the Soviets themselves were unable to challenge American military superiority strategically or in the Eastern Mediterranean, still shaped and determined the parameters of Soviet action. This was combined with a marked lack of optimism in Moscow's attitude toward the national liberation movements. Recognition of the fundamental instability of these new *regimes*, of the central if capricious influence of leading personalities, of the endemic corruption and consumerism of the ruling groups, of the near impossibility of communist parties establishing themselves – all these factors produced a recognition in Moscow that the course of the national liberation movement certainly could not be determined in advance, nor could it be ruled out that a right-wing shift, as occurred in Egypt, could frequently, if not cyclically, follow periods of socialist upsurge.

The net effect of these considerations has been to make Soviet policy-makers more sober and cautious in their calculations, while at the same time fundamentally convinced that the Soviet Union still has legitimate interests to protect in the region. Certainly geostrategic realities are not likely to decrease Soviet convictions that they are a Great Power in the region. Indeed, looking over the record of some of Moscow's predecessors in that glorious and largely unscripted role of 'Great Power', surely after twenty-five years of practice at swan-songs, love-duets, and pistols at dawn, at being alternatively cast as the *éminence grise* and the *enfant terrible*, it is time that the Soviet Union be cast alongside the United States and the other 'Great Powers'. However, unlike bygone days, these actors now increasingly are receiving only supporting roles. The real leading parts more and more are being reserved for the Middle East states themselves.

NOTES

1. See Helene Carrere d'Encausse and Stuart R. Schram, *Marxism and Asia*, (London: Allen Lane, Penguin Press, 1969); and Jane Degras (ed.), *The Communist International*, 1919–43, vol. 3. (London: Macmillan, 1964).
2. *Izvestiya* (5 November 1956).
3. Khrushchev's interview with James Reston, *New York Times* (10 October 1957).
4. I.P. Belyaez and Ye. M. Primakov, *Egipet: vremya presidenta Nasera.* (Moscow, 1974) pp. 281–3, 313.
5. Robert G. Weinland, 'Land Support for Naval Forces: Egypt and the Soviet Escadra, 1962–1976', *Survival*, vol. 20, no.2, 1978, p. 74.
6. Ibid.
7. Sadat's speech before the UAR Peoples' Assembly, on *Cairo Radio,* 3 June 1971, quoted in *USSR and the Third World*, vol. 1, no.6, 1971, p 317,
8. Sadat's ASU speech in BBC, *Summary of World Broadcasts, Part IV,* ME/4050/A/1–17, 26 July 1972; Sadat's interviews in *al-Hawadith,* 19 March 1975 and *Al-Anwar,* 27 June 1975.
9. Sadat in his memoirs claims 15 000 were expelled (*The Observer;* 19 March 1978). Also Mogamed Heikal, *The Road to Ramadan* (London: Fontana, 1976) pp.171–5, and Jon Glassman, *Arms for the Arabs* (Baltimore, Md: Johns Hopkins University Press, 1975) p.96.
10. Weinland, op.cit, p.74.
11. SIPRI, Arms Trade Registers, (Cambridge, Mass: The MIT Press, 1975), pp.154–5; and SIPRI, *Worksheets for Soviet Arms Exports to the Middle East* (Stockholm: SIPRI, unpublished papers, 1977).
12. Figures derived from Karen Dawisha, *Soviet Foreign Policy Toward Egypt* (London: Macmillan, 1979) Table 9.1., p.169.
13. *USSR and the Third World*, vol. 2, no. 9, 1972, p.514.
14. Sadat interview with Arnaud de Borchgrave, *Newsweek*, 9 April 1973.
15. Text of Brezhnev released to the *New York Times*, 10 April 1974.
16. Brezhnev's speeches to the March 1977 Trades Union Congress (*Pravda*, 22 March 1977) and to a Party *aktiv* in Baku (*Pravda*, 23 September 1978) reaffirmed the Soviet stand,
17. *Arab Report and Record, 1975*, no. 24, 16–31 December, 1975, p.685; *Al-Ahram*, 2 January 1976.
18. From Dawisha, op.cit, Table 6.5, p.105.
19. US, Central Intelligence Agency, *Prospects for Soviet Oil Production*, ER 77-10270, April 1977, p.9.
20. Drew Middleton, quoting NATO military intelligence, in *New York Times*, 5 July 1978.
21. *International Herald Tribune*, 26 June 1978.
22. The author's interview with Syrian embassy officials in Moscow on 6 May 1977; and Dr. A.I. Dawisha's interview with Ahmed Iskendar, the Syrian Minister of Information, in Damascus on 13 January 1978.
23. The Brezhnev letter is contained in *Events* (London) no. 1, 1 October 1976, p.23. Assad's allegation is made in an interview in the same issue.

24. *International Herald Tribune*, 26 June 1978.
25. See the authoritative editorials in *Izvestiya*, 19 September 1978; *Izvestiya*, 7 January 1979; and *Pravda*, 2 April 1979, plus Gromyko's remarks during his visit to Syria in April 1979 (reported in *International Herald Tribune*, 2 April 1979), and reports on the letters sent by Brezhnev to King Hussein, Assad and Arafat (*Financial Times*, 26 March 1979).
26. *Pravda*, 7 October 1978.
27. Interview with Ahmed Iskendar, in Damascus on 19 December 1978.
28. Interview with Nasser Qadoor, Syrian Deputy Foreign Minister, in Damascus on 17 December 1978. Also see *The Observer*, 17 December 1978.
29. *The Times*, 24 November 1978.
30. Interviews with Adnan Nashabi, Director-General of the Soviet and East European Department, Syrian Ministry of Foreign Affairs, Damascus, 21 January 1979; and with Zuhar Ginan, Director-General of External Relations Department, Syrian Ministry of Information, Damascus 18 December 1978. Also Foreign Minister Khaddam's interview in *Al-Mostaqbal* (Paris) 30 December 1978, p.14; and *The Financial Times*, 11 January 1979.
31. *Syrian Yearbook*, 1977 (Damascus: Central Bureau of Statistics, 1978) p.351.
32. According to Dr Rafiq Jawajati, Director-General of the West European Department, Syrian Ministry of Foreign Affairs, in an interview in Damascus on 4 January 1979.
33. *Financial Times*, 8 June 1979.
34. Interviews with E.D. Pyrlin, Deputy Head of the Near East Department of the Soviet Ministry of Foreign Affairs, and Professor G.I. Mirsky of the Soviet Institute of World Economy and International Relations, in Moscow, May 1977.
35. Ye. Primakov in *Mezhdunaridnaya Zhizn'*, January 1979, pp.48–9 *Literaturnaya gazeta*, no.5, 31 January 1979; *Sovetskaya Rossiya* 30 March 1979; *Pravda* 2 April 1979. Gromyko's comments were quoted in *International Herald Tribune* 2 April 1979.
36. Interview with Naim Haddad, member of the National Command of the Baath Party, member of the Revolutionary Command Council of Iraq, Secretary-General of the Iraqi National Front, in *Ad-Dostour*, no. 425, 2–8 April 1979, pp.6–7.
37. *Pravda*, 2 April 1979.
38. *The Economist*, 2 February 1980, p.52.
39. *Financial Times*, 10 March 1979.

6 Colossus or Humbug? The Soviet Union and its Southern Neighbours

Malcolm Yapp

'A great humbug': so one of the most renowned of all British Foreign Secretaries, Lord Palmerston, described Russia in 1837.[1] He expressed a view widely held during the nineteenth century by those Britons who, contemplating the ramshackle structure of the Tsarist Empire and the inefficiencies of its government and its economy, declined to be unduly concerned about Russia's threatening movements in Asia. Palmerston's observation may be contrasted with the opinion of other British statesmen and publicists who saw Russia as 'the Colossus of the North' – a fearsome, barbaric giant which threatened both the interests of Britain in Asia and the peace and liberties of Europe and was to be held in check only by great exertions, extensive alliances and the levying of mighty armaments. To those who inclined to the latter view moderate scepticism about Russia's capabilities appeared as self delusion or worse; one of their more extreme spokesmen, David Urquhart, even accused Palmerston of being a Russian agent.[2]

If one excludes that tiny band of devoted crackpots who still regard the Soviet Union as the white hope of mankind, the same two views of Russia may yet serve to represent the attitudes of modern Western commentators on the Soviet Union. Their interpretations of Soviet policy throughout the world and their proposals for strategies of counteraction or accommodation are dictated in substantial measure by their perceptions of the strength of the USSR. It may be well for his readers, therefore, that anyone presuming to comment on Soviet policy should state at the outset to which opinion he or she inclines.

For my part, I confess, I am more impressed by the weaknesses of the Soviet Union than by its strengths. I observe an ideology which, despite the most strenuous and enthusiastic efforts to bring it up to date, becomes less and less suitable as a means of describing the world around us; I contemplate an economy which, despite its undoubted successes in those areas in which resources of skill and capital have been concentrated, can yet neither feed nor house its workers adequately, nor supply the goods to satisfy their modest ambitions; I discern a people of great qualities and potential discouraged by poorly rewarded effort, by the suppression of liberty, by the persistence and enlargement of inequalities, by the stifling of national aspirations and infuriated by the obvious falsehoods with which they are comforted. Finally, I see a government of tired men presiding over a creaking bureaucracy and a party in which time servers threaten to outnumber idealists. In short, to me the Soviet Union is no purposive giant but an ordinary state, admittedly one possessed of a fearsome military strength, but in other respects one much like the rest of the states around us – a collection of ordinary people trying to make ends meet and build a reasonable life – and making a rather worse job of it all than we do.

Such a view inevitably inclines its holder to see Soviet policy as defensive and to regard Soviet policy makers as men intent upon preserving a vulnerable heritage rather than wishing to undertake extensions of their responsibilities. Of course the apparent needs of defence can assume strange configurations and one can well understand the exclamations of those who, contemplating Soviet policies in Africa, the Indian Ocean, the Mediterranean and the Red Sea, wonder what aggression could be like if this be defence. The same puzzle agitated nineteenth-century critics of British activities undertaken in the name of the defence of India and still inspires the deepest scepticism in the minds of Soviet writers on that subject. Nevertheless, the extension of a defensive perimeter may often be a sign of weakness; the more vulnerable the patient is to infection the more care is necessary to keep it at a distance, the more inefficient the heating system the greater the need for additional layers of insulation, and failing companies are often distinguished by a flurry of confident advertising.

SOVIET PROBLEMS AND METHODS

Soviet policy makers, examining the great extent of their land frontiers and studying the hostility and instability of many of the states which border their frontiers must often wonder how they can protect themselves with the resources at their disposal. Traditionally, the greatest danger sprang from Central Europe and there the leaky screen of client states constructed between 1944 and 1948 requires continual maintenance. But in that region *détente* offers some hope of postponing a radical restructuring, even if it makes radical change more likely in the end. Most menacing must appear the long frontier with China, both the direct frontier and that provided by the client stage of Mongolia.

Of all the southern neighbours of the Soviet Union it is China which presents the greatest challenge to the ingenuity, resilience and determination of the Soviet leaders. It is Chinese dissatisfactions which, more than any other factor, have driven the USSR to undertake its new commitments in the whole of the Indian Ocean area, to work patiently for more than ten years in an unavailing effort to construct an Asian collective security system, to cultivate good relations with a variety of curious bedfellows, to sign bilateral treaties of friendship with several states as a substitute for and a step towards the great collective containment scheme outlined by Brezhnev, and to maintain an increasing and expensive naval and *ersatz*-military presence in various parts of the area. And how disappointing the results must appear in Moscow. Against the insubstantial and impermanent gains of influence in Asia, Africa and the Middle East (only to be maintained by diverting valuable resources and incurring perilous liabilities) is the hard fact that the world situation has changed greatly to the disadvantage of the USSR with China more irreconcilable than ever, the United States freed from the trammels of its disastrous entanglement in South-East Asia, and the economic attractions of Western Europe exercising a more and more compelling hold on the attention of all the states in its vicinity.

By comparison with the seemingly intractable problems of the Chinese and European frontiers of the Soviet Union that section which forms the subject of this paper seems at first sight to be more malleable; indeed, to many observers it has appeared that recent events in Afghanistan, Iran and Turkey have led to a major advance of Soviet influence at the expense of that of its adversaries, notably of the West. By means of a discussion of the general aims underlying Soviet policy in this middle section of its frontier and of a necessarily brief examination of developments in each of its three Muslim neighbours it is hoped to suggest that these observers are mistaken and that the events of 1978 have made this frontier more fluid and hence more dangerous to the USSR requiring a greater diversion of resources towards it and away from the more vital eastern and western sectors of the land frontier.

For the Soviet Union there are two major interests involved in its relations with its three Muslim neighbours. The first is the danger of infection. The Soviet Republics of Central Asia and that of Azerbaijan in Transcaucasia are inhabited by a majority of Turkish or Persian-speaking Muslims, who are yearly becoming a numerically more significant part of the Soviet population and, through their acquisition of status and wealth, an element which cannot be merely disregarded in the planning and execution of Soviet policies. It is true that the existence of the Soviet army and of the Communist Party and other agencies guarantees control over these people, and it is also true that there is no obvious general dissatisfaction on the part of the Muslims with their membership of a state which has brought them much material prosperity, cultural development and more freedom than they had known previously; indeed, for the people of Tajikistan, for example, it was the Soviet Union which gave them an independent national life and relieved them from the danger of domination by the more advanced and enterprising Uzbeks to whom they were pre-viously subjected. Only a major internal crisis within the Soviet Union, or an upheaval in the international system, could shake Soviet authority in these areas in the foreseeable future. But even to the most casual observer it is evident that the Muslim subjects of the Soviet Union have not merged their being into that of mythical Soviet man, still less of Soviet woman, and that they remain culturally distinct: working with their Russian and Ukrainian fellow citizens but living apart, governed by a distinct system of values of their own. It is stretching credulity too far to suppose that, given the opportunity, they would not like greater control over their own destinies than they presently possess. Such greater control might take the form of larger autonomy or even political and economic independence.[3]

The assertion that some unsatisfied nationalism exists among any of the peoples of the Soviet Union is one which is regularly and vehemently rebutted by Soviet writers, who argue that nationalism is a problem of capitalist societies alone and that socialism has found a complete answer. The socialist answer lies in the separation of cultural nationalism (which is preserved and fostered in the Soviet Union and, it is claimed, fertilised by contact with other Soviet cultures through the medium of the Russian language and culture) from political nationalism (which is eliminated by socialism which ends the divisions and exploitation on which political nationalism thrives). To Western students of the phenomenon of nationalism this answer seems singularly unconvincing. The transformation of cultural nationalisms into political nationalisms is the work of the process of modernisation, not of capitalism and the Soviet Union is in the same dilemma as other countries: the more it attempts to satisfy wants through modernisation the more it creates new wants which become concentrated in the political field.[4]

In the past it was easier for the Soviet Union to reconcile an illiterate and traditional people to their fate. Coercion attracted little notice or resistance and the condition of their Muslim neighbours seemed to offer the Soviet Muslims little inducement to exchange their improving lot for the lives of those who lived on the other side of the frontier. But the progress of Soviet Muslims, the impossibility of shielding them from news of the outside world, and the general progress of Iran and Turkey in the last twenty years has changed that situation, and the long felt apprehension that movements in Iran and Turkey could find a response in the hearts of the peoples of the Soviet Union can only have deepened in recent years. In the 1957 Soviet handbook on contemporary Iran its government could be dismissed as a reactionary and oppressive feudal dictatorship; in the 1975 edition there was some admission that the White Revolution had accomplished great and beneficial results.[5]

To establish and maintain friendly relations with stable states on her southern frontier seems, therefore, to be as important an objective of Soviet policy now as in the past; only in that way can the danger of infection be diminished. It can never be eliminated. Tsarist Russia could hope to establish a predominant political influence among weak and dependent states; that option is not open to the USSR today except possibly in Afghanistan. Turkey and Iran have reached a state of development and assertion which precludes Soviet dictation and they must be wooed, not bullied. The three Muslim states must each be cultivated. Unstable or hostile governments present two dangers: first, that disturbances may spread across the border, forcing the USSR to devote more resources to its own protection, or even obliging it, at the worst, to undertake an unwanted and dangerous intervention in the affairs of its neighbours; and second, that hostile governments in neighbouring countries may invite as an ally some mighty foe of the Soviet Union, pre-eminently the USA or China.

The second major danger to the Soviet Union is that of strangulation and it derives from the existence of the Straits of the Bosphorus and the Dardanelles which form the only sea passage which links the Black Sea with the Mediterranean. Through those Straits Russia was attacked twice (Soviet writers would say three times), and through them passes one half of Soviet sea-borne trade. The rules governing the use of the Straits have been the subject of continual discussion for two centuries. The two extreme positions are that of the USA, which traditionally argued that the Straits were an international waterway and should be open at all times to all ships of all nations, and that of the USSR, which has argued that the Straits are the exclusive concern of the Black Sea Powers which should control all the conditions of their use, excluding all foreign warships, and that this control should be made a reality by the existence of a Soviet base in the area of the Straits. Between these two is the position of Turkey which insists that sovereignty over the Straits resides with Turkey alone, while accepting the desirability of an international convention to govern their use.[6]

Use of the Straits is at present governed by the convention adopted at the Conference of Montreux in 1936. This agreement recognises Turkish sovereignty and affirms the principle of free navigation, to be regulated by a convention. The convention provides for complete freedom of commercial navigation in peace time. In time of peace, also, small warships are permitted to pass through the Straits, subject to limitations on the tonnage of ships passing the Straits at any time and subject to limitations on the total tonnage of warships which non-Black Sea Powers are allowed in the Black Sea at any time and on the duration of the stay of warships in the Black Sea. In wartime different conditions regulate the use of the Straits. The Montreux Convention was to last twenty years but to continue thereafter until one of the parties to it gave two years' notice of denunciation, in which case a fresh conference must be assembled. The principle of free navigation itself, enunciated in the first article of the convention, has no time limit.

The Montreux Convention represented a compromise which acknowledged the views of each party but which was relatively favourable to the Soviet Union. It ensured that no enemy fleet more powerful than its own Black Sea fleet could threaten its coasts and shipping. It also permitted Soviet vessels to issue forth into the Mediterranean. Nevertheless, the Convention was not wholly satisfactory for it still permitted foreign warships to navigate the Black Sea and imposed limitations on the size of vessels which the USSR could send into the Mediterranean and on the number which it could pass through the Straits at any time. But its greatest disadvantage was that it gave the USSR no direct control over the use of the Straits, thus making the

Soviet Union utterly dependent upon Turkish good will, a commodity which the USSR justly believed was in short supply. 'It was impossible', remarked Stalin at Yalta, 'to accept a situation in which Turkey had a hand on Russia's throat'. To the Soviet Union the Straits were at least as important as Suez to Britain and Panama to the United States and since both those latter states thought the possession of a base was essential to safeguard their interests at that time, why, it was asked, should the USSR be denied the same facility? To many Soviet writers it has seemed that the West has condemned, as wicked aggression by the Soviet Union, the same behaviour which it regarded as a statesmanlike assumption of responsibilities when exhibited by itself. There is in the recent display of Soviet might around the world more than a hint that this is intended to exact the recognition of an equality which was apparently denied in the past.

Stalin's attempt to change the *regime* of the Straits (and to alter the eastern frontier of Turkey in favour of the Soviet Union) ended in disaster for the USSR. After some initial doubts the United States concluded that the Soviet demands signified an aggressive rather than a defensive intent and, while expressing her willingness that the Convention should be altered in favour of the Soviet Union provided that it was by international agreement, backed Turkey in her refusal of any base facilities to the USSR. The episode led directly to Turkey's commitment to the western alliance and thereby to a major upset for the Soviet Union.

The Soviet Union quietly dropped its demands for the revision of the Convention and, in recent years the operation of the Straits *regime* has not been such as to offend the USSR unduly, for US warships have used the passage into the Black Sea less frequently and possible infractions of the rules by Soviet vessels have not been challenged by Turkey. Nevertheless, the matter of the Straits cannot be regarded as closed for control of the passage has become yet more important to the USSR. Apart from their commercial importance and the question of defence, the Straits have, since 1960, become the way out into the wider world for the Soviet Black Sea fleet. Between 1964 and 1971 the number of Soviet warships passing through the Straits increased by a factor of three, the consequence of the Soviet Union's assertion of its *role* as a Mediterranean, Red Sea and Indian Ocean power.

By reference to these defensive preoccupations (including the assertion of national prestige which is a defensive act calculated to deter a would-be attacker or to quieten domestic criticism) it is possible to explain much of the course of Soviet policy towards its southern neighbours since 1921, when the heady fantasies of world revolution were quietly buried in the treaties concluded with Afghanistan, Iran and Turkey. No single theory, of course, can explain all the contortions of Soviet policy for no policy makers are that consistent. Even if Soviet policy makers are not so occupationally inclined towards variety as their opposite numbers in the West they yet include their different species of hawks and doves. But explanations in terms of defence seem to answer more questions than those which rely upon some aggressive intent, whether it is couched in terms of ideology, the control of oil, the mastery of the Middle East, the dominance of western communications or the hegemony of the world. I have briefly surveyed some of these theories elsewhere and others have examined them in greater detail.[7] It is unnecessary to repeat that examination here and, from these general considerations we may turn to a consideration of Soviet relations with Afghanistan, Iran and Turkey.

AFGHANISTAN

The Afghan revolution of April 1978 has been hailed as a triumph for Soviet policy and has been commonly attributed to the work of Soviet agents. The facts do not support this view, although it is not surprising that that unusual revolution should have seemed to require such an explanation. It is not that the overthrow of the Daud *regime* itself was unexpected, but that it was replaced by a left wing civilian government. The Republican *regime* established by the 1973 revolution had failed to fulfil the expectations which had been aroused. Muhammad Daud had won a reputation as an autocratic moderniser during his premiership (1953–63) and it has been supposed that he was impatient of the slow pace of advance under the constitutional *regime* which existed from 1963 until 1973. The constitutional monarchy had not flourished: its economic plans had failed to produce adequate returns – merely empty roads and the great but unfruitful Helmand Valley Project; foreign aid had fallen off and bad harvests had completed the tally of the government's misfortunes. Politically too the monarchy seemed to have reached stalemate for it was apparent that the majority of those who had been newly summoned to the political arena were less sympathetic to reform than were the administrators of Zahir Shah; those who agitated for more reforms were a small minority, principally recruited from Kabuli intellectuals outside government service and from students. The unknown factor was the army. An uncertain line of reasoning by analogy with other armies led to the belief that many army officers might be ready for more rapid change and it was commonly supposed that they placed their hopes in Daud.

The 1973 revolution seemed at first to confirm this belief for it was an army-directed *coup* which thrust Daud into power. The King accepted the result with dignity and settled abroad; the country awaited the emergence from anonymity of a new generation of military reformers who would implement the promised changes. The people of Afghanistan were still waiting in 1978, however, for the Republic turned out to be little more than a conservative dictatorship run by Daud, his family and his intimates. Despite Daud's persistent, revolutionary rhetoric, most reforms remained on paper. The very modest land reform of 1975 was not implemented. In 1976 a new civil code was promulgated and a hopelessly optimistic seven year economic plan announced. The constitution of February 1977 merely legitimised Daud's autocracy; the two party system adumbrated in earlier announcements was abandoned in favour of a single party system and Daud was elected President for a six year term. But the elections for the new, carefully balanced, Parliament were not scheduled to take place for almost three years. Throughout his five year rule Daud was preoccupied with beating off challenges to his authority; plots, arrests and purges were regular features of what passed for political life and involved a large number of desperate and hostile groups. In the last year of his *regime*, amid increased political and economic discontent in the wake of acute food shortages and an attempt to raise money by increased taxation, Daud adopted more severe repressive measures. Security advisers were imported from SAVAK (the Iranian secret police). In November 1977 the government attacked striking workers and attempted to extinguish the newly-founded Muslim Brotherhood. In February 1978 Daud turned against the left and removed the moderate leftist ministers from his government. Political murders became common and the ground was laid for a full scale confrontation between the Government and its opponents.

The episode which sparked off the clash was the murder of Mir Akbar Khaybar, a trade union leader and prominent left wing writer and editor. At his funeral on 19 April 1978 there were mass demonstrations and the government was blamed for his murder. In reply Daud arrested seven of the leaders of the leftist People's Democratic Party, formed in 1976 by the reuniting of the two main leftist factions, Khalq and Parcham, to which was added the right wing Musavat Party of the former Prime Minister, Hashim Maiwandwal, who had been jailed and murdered by Daud's *regime*. Among those arrested were Nur Muhammad Tarakki and Babrak Karmal, the respective leaders of the two leftist factions. Two days later, the government began a purge of civil servants and army officers. The army purge, however, was not carried out immediately and thus an opportunity was provided for discontented and frightened officers to stage a responsive *coup*. The commanders of two armoured brigades and an air force unit near Kabul (two majors and a colonel) met and agreed to strike on 27 April. Forces loyal to Daud resisted and for a time the issue was in doubt but the decision of the 2000 strong commando unit to join the rebels appears to have tipped the balance. In the early morning of 28 April the presidential palace was over-run and Daud, nearly all his family and some leading ministers and military commanders were killed. The fighting was largely confined to the Kabul area: only the garrison at Mazar-i Sharif in the north joined the rebels and all other units waited until the outcome was known before declaring their allegiance to the new government.[8]

Circumstantial reports subsequently appeared which alleged that the *coup* was planned by KGB officers in Afghanistan; that the air force unit commander involved, Colonel Abd al-Qadir, was the chief Soviet agent; and that Soviet control of Afghan security ensured that Daud received no warning of the impending *coup*. There is no direct evidence for these allegations and they appear unlikely. The character of the *coup* itself was wholly consistent with one planned and executed on the spur of the moment by frightened officers; so unprepared were they that they did not think to seize the telephone exchange until nine hours after the beginning of operations, so allowing Daud to maintain contact with loyal units. Abd al-Qadir never looked like a Soviet agent and it was soon apparent that he did not possess the influence claimed for him. The view that the Soviet Union controlled security is inherently unlikely, and is apparently contradicted both by the employment of SAVAK agents and by the episode of the telephone exchange.

Those who hold that the *coup* derived from Soviet influence in the army have not explained why no military government came to power. On the other hand the formation of a government from civilians drawn from the People's Party suggests that the army was unprepared for government; in fact of course most of the army had not joined the *coup*; the officers who had done so were rewarded with places in the government. The reason for its assumption of power could not lie in the strength and organisation of the People's Party. Nur Muhammad's claim that the party had 50 000 members and that it had been preparing the way through propaganda for thirteen years cannot be accepted. The People's Party was only a loose confederation of factions which lacked either organisation or considered policies. Its subsequent career was to make clear how divided it was. It seems most likely that the rebel officers had given little thought to what was to follow their desperate attempt and had turned to the imprisoned leftists for want of any obvious alternative.

There is no reason to suppose that the Soviet Union wished to get rid of Daud. Daud had won a special place in Soviet hearts with his policies in 1953–63 when he had drawn Afghanistan closer to the USSR. His fall from power in 1963 had occasioned momentary Soviet perturbation. And although the Soviet Union had maintained good relations with Afghanistan throughout the constitutional period they were quick to welcome Daud back to power in 1973. In 1975 President Podgorny visited Afghanistan and it was agreed that the Soviet–Afghan treaty of neutrality and non-aggression should be extended for ten years. In 1977 Daud was very warmly received when he visited the USSR. On foreign policy the two countries had similar views and Afghanistan supported the Soviet collective security plan in Asia. There were agreements on trade and economic aid. If there were differences on some subjects, as for example, on Cuba's proposed chairmanship of a non-aligned conference and on Daud's drawing closer to Iran, these were not in themselves reasons to upset the generally satisfactory relations which had existed for so long between Afghanistan and the USSR, and which the Soviet Union displayed with pride as an example to the world of how good relations could exist between countries with different social systems. Certainly the Soviet Union, which had watched with equanimity the suppression of genuine, loyal communist parties by many *regimes* allied to the USSR, was unlikely to be concerned by Daud's rough treatment of what must have appeared as a wild and woolly bunch of radicals.

The swift recognition of the new *regime* by the Soviet Union need occasion no suspicion for the Soviet Union is geographically impelled to strive for the position of most favoured nation in Kabul. No doubt if the Devil emerged as ruler of Afghanistan a Soviet delegation would soon be on his doorstep, offering to keep him supplied with brimstone and to equip his hosts with heat-seeking tridents. Still less should one be surprised that the new Afghan government should seek to increase the already substantial aid which the Soviet Union supplied Afghanistan in the form of advisers (military and civil) and economic assistance. Even before the April revolution there were thought to be 3000 Soviet advisers (compared with latest estimates of no obvious authority of 5000), and two thirds of the foreign aid received by Afghanistan in the past twenty years has come from the Soviet Union. The Tarakki government sorely needed friends for it had precious few in Afghanistan. That the traditional leaders of rural Afghanistan had no time for what they regarded as the godless reforms of the Kabuli intellectuals had been amply demonstrated in the constitutional period; the proposed land reforms threatened the economic wellbeing and social authority of these men; the projected reforms of law and education threatened the already disgruntled *ulema*; and all would be excluded from power by the new political system. Nor did the bureaucratic reformers who had been the main supporters of the constitutional period, and who had held aloof from Daud, see any merit in the new government from which they were largely excluded. Tribal opposition was to be expected. Nor could the army be regarded as wholly reliable; only a small fraction had been involved in the *coup*. And beyond Afghanistan's borders were two *regimes* which had good cause to be suspicious of the new radical rulers of the mountain republic; neither Pahlevi Iran nor the new military and Muslim government of Pakistan wanted so uncertain a quantity on their delicate borders. Tarakki's government had to have Soviet aid to survive for it was too weak to live without help.

Subsequent events have born out this impression of the weakness of the new government. It came to power unprepared with any radical programme, instead it offered a few charming and naive sentiments in favour of progress, the uplifting of the poor and the satisfaction of the minorities. The new government would, said Nur Muhammad, be a society in which 'the peasants will have fine clothes and clean and happy faces'.[9] It all sounded more like Wat Tyler than Lenin. The centre piece of the programme gradually unfolded by the government was land reform. In July 1978, a complicated measure for the extinction of agricultural indebtedness was announced and this was followed later in the year by the abolition of dowries and by a major scheme for the confiscation of land from large land-owners and its redistribution to landless peasants. The scheme was evidently based on a most uncertain appreciation of the situation as it actually existed in many provinces, and the government conspicuously lacked the administrative machinery to carry it out. It was, indeed, avowedly political in its inspiration: an effort to break the power of the traditional *elite* and to create a substantial rural basis of support for the few urban radicals of the Khalq.[10]

While this programme was being formulated, opposition to the new *regime* developed and the People's Party factions began to fall apart. In July 1978, Babrak Karmal and others of the Parcham group were sent into diplomatic exile and, in August, Abd al-Qadir was arrested. Further purges of party, government and army reduced still further the pool of capable men. There were risings in the provinces, especially those which bordered Pakistan, and major disturbances in Herat. Its continued use as a police force placed further strain on the loyalty of the army.

From Moscow the situation in Afghanistan must look like a nightmare. The Soviet leaders were unable to turn away an Afghan government and their ideological straitjacket obliged them to make welcoming noises. The old ally Daud was written off as a leader of an aristocratic clique, which carried out a class policy and failed to solve the land problem, and an alliance of patriotic officers backed by the broad masses was said to have removed him. But the new *regime* was described with great caution, the large problems which confronted it were stressed, and there was certainly no acknowledgement of it as a socialist or communist *regime*.[11] Help was given – new trade agreements were signed and on 7 December 1978 a Treaty of Friendship. A close examination of this treaty, however, does not support the claim that Afghanistan has become a Soviet puppet state. The treaty merely reaffirms the principles of the preceding treaties of 1921 and 1931 and provides for co-operation on the basis of equality, respect for national sovereignty, territorial integrity and non-interference in each other's internal affairs. Provision is made for economic, cultural and military co-operation but article 5 explicitly endorses Afghanistan's non-aligned policy. 'The traditional good relations between our countries have acquired' remarked Brezhnev 'a qualitatively different nature'. Mere good neighbourliness has been replaced by profound friendship, comradeship and revolutionary solidarity.[12] But behind this it seems evident that the Tarakki government wished to preserve its independence and the traditionally friendly relations of Afghanistan with the USSR and that the USSR was content with this situation. But whether the two parties can preserve this relationship is another matter and must depend upon developments in the internal and external situation of Afghanistan.

It has been suggested elsewhere that the USSR brought about the Afghan *coup* in order to make Afghanistan into an instrument through which it could destabilise surrounding countries, possibly by exploiting the Pakhtunistan issue with Pakistan and the Baluchistan issue with both Pakistan and Iran. If such was the Soviet intention it has been frustrated for the Afghan government is not a suitable instrument for anything and the only country which has been destabilised is Afghanistan itself. But it is much more likely that the Soviet Union had no such intentions. It was well suited by the existing situation in Afghanistan and had no wish to make an uncertain leap into a hazardous future. No-one in his right mind dumps a load of rubbish on his own back doorstep and sets fire to it and in effect that is what it has been claimed that the Soviet Union has done. There is a danger from the situation in Afghanistan but it is not that which is anticipated. Left to itself it seems unlikely that the revolutionary government can stand for long. Probably the Soviet Union would prefer to let it fall and to come to some agreement with whatever *regime* succeeds it rather than be sucked into a civil war. The danger exists that those elements in Afghanistan which are opposed to the revolutionary *regime* will appeal for help to Afghanistan's neighbours and that help will be given. In this case the Soviet Union might feel obliged to intervene in Afghanistan in order to prevent a hostile *regime* coming to power or, at the worst, to diminish its effectiveness by supporting a separatist movement in northern Afghanistan. Soviet complaints of Pakistani, Iranian, US and Chinese aid to rebels may be desperate attempts to warn off outsiders and avoid what would be the first commitment of Soviet ground troops outside the borders of the USSR and Eastern Europe since 1946.

IRAN

Strange as the Afghan revolution of 1978 has been it does not compare with the Iranian revolution of 1978–9, which must rank among the most unusual revolutions of modern times. For although the Afghan revolution issued in an unexpected left-wing civilian government it was founded upon a simple military *coup*. But in Iran a powerful centralised monarchy was overthrown, not by the action of its own soldiers but by massive, unarmed, urban demonstrations, carried on in the name of a return to a traditional social order. To try to understand this event it is necessary to examine the changing structure of Iran under the rule of Muhammad Reza Shah.

Muhammad Reza Shah wished to transform his country into a strong, independent, modern, national state. His path was blocked by

the traditional political *elites* – the absentee landowners who dominated the Iranian Parliament, the *ulema*, the big international merchants, and the small merchants and artisans of the bazaar who
provided the muscle of political agitation. To break out of the
restrictions imposed by these groups he launched the White Revolution in the early 1960s. In essence, the White Revolution was a grand
plan for economic modernisation and political change. The centre
piece of its first phases was land reform, intended to break the
economic domination of the countryside by the traditional *elites* and so
weaken their political power and also to call to the political theatre
a new class of the grateful underprivileged – peasants, women, and
workers. With the aid of oil revenues, the army, and some able
political allies, the Shah was able to carry out much of this design. In
the event the results were not quite what he had anticipated; the
traditional political *elites* were forced into submission but not co-
operation and the new political groups appeared insensible of the
benefits conferred upon them.[13]

Modernisation has many pitfalls: to go too slowly invites the
possibility of beng outbid by more radical groups; to go too quickly
increases the likelihood of a conflict between those who adhere to the
values of the modern society and those who, brought physically into
contact with that society, maintain values still adjusted to the traditional society. Muhammad Reza Shah believed that he must move
quickly: the opposition of the traditional political *elites* had to be
broken at once, oil revenues would not last for ever, and there was the
desire to establish the new system firmly within his own lifetime so that
a secure succession might be left to his son. It was a reasonable gamble
and for a long time it seemed successful, but in the early 1970s he
became too confident, moved too quickly, became caught in an
economic draught, was obliged to cut back his plans and thereby
suddenly magnified discontent. For whatever reasons – United States
pressure, or too great confidence, or a genuine preference for concilia-
tion – he endeavoured to reach an accommodation with his critics, who
came originally from the traditional political *elite*, that old landowning
class now securely and prosperously established in business and the
professions but which was as hostile as ever to the Pahlevi monopoly of
political power.[14] The Shah's efforts, however, only multiplied his
critics who now united under the banner of Islamic values, articulated
by the *ulema* and especially by the exiled Ayatullah Khomeini.

Who were all those demonstrators who, despite spasmodic brutal
repression, repeatedly returned to the streets calling for the overthrow

of the Shah and the establishment of an Islamic Republic? The Shah denounced them as Islamic Marxists, agents of the Soviet Union operating under the guise of religion, but this description fits very few of them. They were young, male, and urban; the disturbances were concentrated in Isfahan, Tabriz, Shiraz, Ahwaz and above all in the capital Tehran, the city which had grown much faster than any other in Iran and which overshadowed the rest of the urban scene. Among the demonstrators were many students and it is observable that the university students of Tehran and Shiraz, in particular, are relatively well to do, middle class, and secularly minded – often supporters of the National Front and various left-wing groups. These young men had little to gain from an Islamic republic and their support, like that of the senior politicians of the National Front itself, must be seen as tactical. They needed the mass support that Khomeini could bring in order to wrest concessions from the Shah or even to overthrow him, but they believed that they could become the inheritors of power as the only men able to exercise it. The main bulk of the demonstrators, however, came from the bazaar and from the new immigrant suburbs. Within the bazaar there appears to be a clear division between the older genera- tion which forms the main support of the *ulema* and the younger generation which is much less decided in its allegiances. In the new suburbs the situation is much more complex than is often supposed. It is wrong to think that those who come to towns are those thrown off the land, full of discontents and ripe for any radical exploitation. In fact they are usually those with ability and initiative who have come to the towns to better themselves and to get away from the restrictions of rural life; they often form a hard-working, conservative group which eschews political action. Nevertheless, for many there are disappoint- ments and frustrations and the shortages, the inflation and the reduction in economic activity which hit Iran in 1976–8 exacerbated these. Also, studies of similar groups elsewhere suggest that the attitudes which characterise first generation immigrants are not shared by their children, among whom there is often a reassertion of older values. In short, a range of beliefs and attitudes is represented in the new suburbs but among them is a strong feeling that the benefits of modernisation have been appropriated largely by the well-do-do middle classes of business men, professional men, the higher officials and army officers, those who were generally associated with a secular, western style of life. It is not surprising, therefore, that opposition took the form of a reassertion of Islamic values; putting it crudely, the demonstrators were complaining that the rules of the game did not suit them and that under a different set of rules – the original rules – they would do better. The same phenomenon had for some time been visible in the universities, especially those less distinguished than Tehran and Shiraz; poorer students demanded a variety of changes in university administration and teaching, changes which were couched in the form of a return to Islamic practice.[15]

The Iranian revolution seems to be a consequence of modernisation, not of left-wing plotting, with or without the aid of the Soviet Union. It was not a rejection of modernisation but a demand that it should be carried out by different men under different rules. The secular middle class element, which wanted modernisation under different men but the same rules, was carried along by the Islamic movement, partly conniving but partly helpless before it. And the middle class received the reward for its fidelity when the government of Mehdi Bazargan was formed largely from the National Front elements; its difficulties came when it discovered that the rules were still being set by the Islamists and it was called upon to operate a system which it believed to be unworkable and undesirable. The National Front must choose whether to temporise, in the hope that the steam will go out of the Islamic movement, or to form an alliance with other modernisers. Of these the orthodox Marxist left is too weak to provide much support by itself. That leaves the modernisers associated with the Shah and particularly the army, or what is left of it. It is not an enviable choice for the National Front or for Iran. To temporise seems the best way of avoiding conflict, but in the meantime the rundown of government proceeds apace, separatist and other revolutionary movements appear in various provincial areas and the government has few reliable means of coercion at its disposal. To rely on a popular militia would be to condemn Iran to civil war; to restore the professional army too quickly would be to risk a clash with the Islamists or a military *coup.*

The attitude of the Soviet Union to these events is a matter which has been hotly disputed. It has been suggested above that the Iranian revolutionary movement is explicable in purely Iranian terms. The features which might have been expected if there had been Soviet involvement have not appeared or did not appear until a late stage, when they were explicable on other grounds. Little significance need be attached to the reports, even if they are true, of meetings between agents of Khomeini and Soviet representatives; the revolution made clear that no-one could speak for Khomeini and the revolutionaries evidently received no help from the USSR. The swift Soviet recognition of the new *regime* may be accounted for in the same way as the similar action in Afghanistan; and the absence of serious Soviet comment on the events in Iran is good evidence of Soviet uncertainty.

On more general grounds there appears to be no reason why the Soviet Union should attempt to bring about a revolution in Iran. In an effort to establish control over Iran the USSR supported separatist movements in Azerbaijan and Kurdistan in 1945–6 (Soviet writers deny this and claim the movements were purely indigenous in inspiration).[16] This policy ended in disaster and contributed to Iran's subsequent alignment with the West; it was not the only factor in that alignment for the Shah's domestic concerns also made an alliance with the West appropriate.[17] In 1953 the Soviet Union, realising the sterility of the policy of blank hostility to Iran, began a long courtship of that country, which began to find a response in 1962. Since that time economic links between Iran and the USSR have developed and political relations have become much easier, although they have never been warm. In recent years, while acknowledging the achievements of the Shah's *regime* and welcoming his more independent foreign policy, the Soviet Union has criticised Iran's military build-up and Iran's effort to organise a collective security system in the Persian Gulf and Indian Ocean which conflicted with the Soviet Union's own scheme and, by offering a rival attraction to non-aligned *regimes*, threatened to weaken the influence of the USSR.[18] These disagreements, however, must be considered in the general context of the improvement of Soviet–Iranian relations and, although the Iranian military build-up was plainly directed in large part against the Soviet Union, it still offered no threat to the USSR. In these disagreements there would not seem to be a reason for the USSR to undertake so hazardous a step as to disrupt Iran. Nor is there any good evidence that the Soviet Union, for all its denunciations of the continuation of imperialist influences in the affairs of the Gulf states, would have wished to take such a risk to disrupt western oil supplies, which it could not in any case control. All in all there seems to be nothing in the present situation to warrant a belief that the USSR has abandoned the policy of seeking friendly relations with a stable Iranian government which it has pursued consistently since 1953 and which, in recent years, had begun to yield reasonable dividends.

But if the Soviet Union did not wish for the present situation nor attempt to bring it about, it still has to live with the possible consequences and these do not look very attractive. Two possibilities exist in Iran. First, a stable government may emerge, either under an Islamic group, or under a National Front-style group, or under a military group, or under some combination of these. None look so attractive as the stable *regime* of the Shah, for all the objectionable features which the Pahlevi government had from the Soviet viewpoint. An Islamic *regime* would be quite unpredictable and might appeal to Soviet Muslims. A National Front *regime* might adopt a more neutralist policy in foreign affairs, as this has long been a demand of politicians of that school, but its internal rivalries would make it less dependable and in its external relations generally it would be at least as assertive of Iranian claims as was the Shah; Bazargan was one of the critics of the Shah's abandonment of Iranian claims to Bahrain. A military *regime* would be the Shah's *regime* over again, without his steadying hand on the tiller. The second possibility is that no stable government will emerge in Iran for some time, leading to the development of separatist movements in Azerbaijan, Kurdistan, Khuzistan and Baluchistan, to movements for tribal independence, and to a struggle for power by local groups in the provincial cities and in Tehran. The upshot would be a dangerous growth of disorder on the borders of the Soviet Union and the fear of foreign intervention in Iran.

Between these two possibilities the Soviet Union must hope first for a stable government with which it could come to some arrangement. No doubt a National Front government would suit it best, for the political freedom would allow the growth of orthodox communist movements through which the USSR could hope to influence the Iranian political scene. Past experience has shown, however, that Iranian communists rarely come up to Soviet standards and it is unlikely that any political movement avowedly attached to the USSR could make any headway in the strongly nationalist situation of Iran.[19] An unstable situation would be more dangerous and the Soviet Union would then be tempted to protect its interests by supporting selected movements within Iran in the manner in which it supported the Kurdish and Azerbaijani movements in 1945–6. Such a strategy would be dangerous, however, for it would make reconciliation with any government in Tehran impossible and would threaten to replay the unsatisfactory situation of 1946–62. It would also permit the enemies of the USSR to gain a footing in Iran in support of rival groups or of a 'legitimate' government. And, finally, it would severely damage the image of the Soviet Union in other areas of Asia where it hopes to find support for its policy of collective security aimed chiefly against China. On balance one must conclude that the present uncertainty in Iran suits the USSR no better than it does the West, although the Soviet Union begins its assessment from radically different premises.

TURKEY

Many of the features of the Iranian scene are also present in Turkey. There is the same rush for modernisation, the same pace of urbanisation, the same clash of modern and traditional values intermingled with that of more traditional, regional, religious or ethnic rivalries, and the same evidence of political violence. Like Iran, Turkey has recently met severe economic difficulties, Turkey, however, has some distinctive differences which may help to account for her so far escaping the revolution which engulfed her neighbour. In the first place the Turkish democratic political system, as it has developed since the Second World War, has shown itself able to accommodate changes without breaking under the impact of the great pressures to which it has been subjected. Secondly the Turkish army has assumed a *role* unlike that of the Iranian army. The Iranian army was loyal to the Shah in so far as it was loyal to anything, and without clear direction from him it lacked purpose. The Turkish army, since the creation of the Republic, has seen itself as peculiarly charged with the protection of the state and nation and has been willing to intervene when it saw the principle on which the Republic was founded endangered, or the unity of the Republic threatened. At the same time, it was anxious to restrict its interventions so as not to upset completely the development of political life. And, thirdly, the Turkish economy is much more diversified than that of Iran and therefore not so vulnerable to pressures exerted from a single direction. Despite continual predictions of disaster Turkey has so far staggered on from success to success.[20]

The pattern of Soviet relations with Turkey has closely followed that of Soviet relations with Iran.[21] The period of hostility which followed the Soviet demands of 1945–6 endured until the early 1960s when Turkey decided, partly in the context of the general atmosphere of *détente*, partly through doubts about the firmness of US support both against the Soviet Union and against Greece over the Cyprus issue, and partly through the changing balance of forces in the Middle East, to shake the hand of friendship which the Soviet Union had unavailingly extended since 1953. Turkey did not shake it warmly because hostility to the USSR was too deeply rooted in Turkey and especially in the minds of its political *elite*, but a series of economic agreements, cultural exchanges, and border agreements followed. Differences over the frontiers in eastern Asia Minor and over the exploitation of the Black Sea were settled and relations between the two countries became much closer, although Turkey remained loyal to the western military alliance and continued to look towards membership of the EEC. The improvement of relations between Turkey and the USSR was signalled in 1978 by the signature of a political agreement, in itself an innocuous document which mainly rehearsed the principles of the Helsinki Final Act. It was, however, hailed warmly in the USSR as an important landmark. 'The atmosphere of prejudice and mistrust has given way to one of mutual goodwill and confidence,' one Soviet commentator remarked.[22]

From the Soviet point of view, the improvement in Soviet–Turkish relations is a welcome reward for a generation of patient diplomacy. From the Turkish point of view, it reflects some degree of dissatisfaction with the West. The failure of the United States to sympathise with the Turkish action over Cyprus in 1975, which led to the US arms embargo, and the failure of the EEC to be sufficiently forthcoming with aid and other economic help has seemed to Turks to be a poor reward for their sustained loyalty to the Western alliance both through NATO and through CENTO. As they have watched one uncertain convert after another being welcomed into the western fold with open arms, they must have felt rather like the brother of the prodigal son. It is unsurprising, therefore, that they have sought to diversify their foreign policy options, both through seeking better relations with the Soviet Union and also through approaches to Middle Eastern, Islamic and Balkan groupings. Nevertheless, in the end the western alliance is still the most attractive option for the Turks. Only from the United States is military support likely to be forthcoming on the scale on which they require it, and only from the EEC are they likely to find the economic aid they need. But there is no harm in indicating to these valued partners that they should not take Turkey for granted and that in the present climate of affairs in the area they might be well advised to be more generous with their help.

SUMMARY

Contemplating recent developments in Afghanistan, Iran and Turkey it is undeniable that western influence has decreased and that in Iran an important western economic interest has been placed in jeopardy and a strategic observation site lost. At best the West will have to endure a greater increase in oil prices more quickly than it would otherwise have done, with the ill effects that this must have upon western economies. At worst disruption may spread from Iran to engulf other western interests in the area and thereby inflict much greater damage on the West. CENTO has suffered a final, mortal blow.

To many observers these possible results are sufficient reason to point an accusing finger at the Soviet Union. The USSR, it is argued, is an aggressive power; the West stands in its way; the Soviet Union desires to disrupt western economies in order to weaken the West; and, desiring an end, the USSR wills it. Such an analysis appears to show a failure of imagination as well as of logic, for it sees the region entirely in terms of western interests and fails to recognise that Soviet interests are not the same, and that the people of the region have their own interests and their own determination to shape their destinies. No doubt if there were no other questions at issue the Soviet Union would be glad to see its ideological predictions fulfilled and the capitalist system go down in ruins. But the world is not so simple and the Soviet Union is obliged to establish priorities in its interests. These priorities have been made clear by the policy which it has pursued for twenty five years; to seek friendly relations with stable states. The probable destruction of CENTO is an important advance for the Soviet Union and if a new Iranian government could be persuaded to join with the Afghan government in endorsing the Soviet collective security system in Asia, this would be a further favourable development, to bring in Turkey as well would be a crowning triumph. But against these possible advantages (the last of them very unlikely) and the weakening of western influence in the area, the Soviet Union must set the major disadvantage that stable *regimes* no longer exist in Iran and Afghanistan, and that they cannot be created by Soviet action any more than by Western action. For in the end the internal political development of the Soviet Union's southern neighbours is moulded by forces which have their own internal momentums. No outside power can control them and only the most skilful and restrained hands can help to steer.

Neither the West nor the Soviet Union can take much comfort from recent developments in the northern part of the Middle East. But nor can they do much about them. For both *blocs* the best prescription is to sit it out patiently. Perhaps the Soviet Union is better at this than the West; it is ideologically attuned to disruption as a necessary stage in development and historically conditioned to reverses. In which case, neither humbug nor colossus is an accurate description of the Soviet Union. A better image might be Old Father Time, worrying that relativity is going to put him out of a job.

POSTSCRIPT

The tumultuous events of the past months in what has been called 'the arc of crisis' make it desirable to add a postscript to this paper, which was written in March and lightly revised in July 1979. The Soviet invasion of Afghanistan at the end of December 1979 appears to call into question the thesis that Soviet policy in the region is defensive in inspiration and directed principally towards the achievement of friendly relations with stable *regimes*. Some examination of the circumstances which led to the Soviet intervention and of the implications of that event is required.

The radical land and educational policies of the People's Party Government provoked widespread hostility which was revealed in uprisings, army mutinies and desertions, a flow of refugees into Iran and Pakistan, and the formation of rebel organisations. Alarmed by the extent of the opposition the USSR began to press the Afghan Government to slow down the pace of reform and to pursue a more conciliatory policy. The premature end of land reform in July 1979 may be associated with this pressure. The response of the People's Party was mixed: one faction, led by Tarakki, seemed willing to adopt the Soviet recommendations; another, led by the Prime Minister, Hafizullah Amin, wished to persist with radical policies and beat down all opposition. With Soviet connivance Tarakki attempted to get rid of Amin but his plot backfired and in September 1979 Amin emerged triumphant from an armed clash and shortly afterwards had Tarakki murdered. Amin promptly began to implement his own prescriptions; the campaign against the rebels was stepped up and imprisonments and executions, even of men whom the Soviet Union had wished to bring into the Government, were increased. Presumably Amin calculated that the USSR had no alternative but to continue to support him.

That it took the Soviet Union three months to decide what action to take is an indication of the strenuous debate which must have been carried on at the highest levels in Moscow. One can only guess at its nature. It seemed as if the Soviet Union had two possibilities: to support Amin or to leave him to his fate. The first seemed likely to drag the USSR into a civil war which it could not control and possibly into conflict with neighbouring countries; the second would mean a serious blow to Soviet prestige and the confidence of world communism, and would face the USSR with the prospect of a hostile *regime* on a sensitive frontier. In the end the Soviet Union chose neither possibility but resolved to try the daring expedient of replacing Amin with a more pliant ruler, an operation which could only be accomplished with Soviet troops. At Christmas 1979 the troops went in, Amin was deposed and killed, and the Parchami leader, Babrak Karmal, was extracted from his silent refuge in the Communist bloc, dusted off, and installed as head of the Afghan Government. In the original paper it was suggested that the USSR would send troops into Afghanistan if foreign intervention took place. Foreign intervention was indeed the ostensible reason for the Soviet invasion but it was not the real reason. The Soviet Union intervened militarily to install an Afghan ruler who would pursue a more conciliatory policy, form a broad based government (if possible one which would yet preserve a left-wing appearance), and allow the Soviet Union to wriggle off the hook with which she had foolishly allowed herself to be caught.

Whether Babrak Karmal can achieve such a result must be doubted. His previous reputation as the histrionic leader of the wilder fringes of the left and his present position as a Soviet puppet seem likely to weigh heavily against him in his efforts to win over opponents of the *regime*. If he fails the position of the USSR will be most unenviable: to withdraw without leaving behind a stable *regime* would be still more damaging than the abandonment of Amin would have been – some heads would surely roll in the Kremlin; to stay indefinitely is virtually to decide to convert Afghanistan into a full blown Soviet dependency. The complete subjection and remodelling of Afghanistan would cost a great deal in Soviet money and manpower (how many men would it take to seal off 2000 miles of mountainous frontier?). It would also embroil the USSR with Iran and Pakistan, and the disastrous effect of the invasion on Soviet relations with the rest of the world (including the Soviet bloc and other communist parties) would be magnified. The possible gains hardly seem commensurate with the costs. A base on the Indian Ocean would be a hostage to fortune and could only be achieved by conflict with Iran or Pakistan. The use of Baluchi nationalism as a weapon against Iran and Pakistan would be a very dubious enterprise. Apart from the uncertainty of the weapon its launching seems unnecessary; the USSR has nothing to gain from a quarrel with Pakistan and if it should ever be deemed necessary to disrupt Iran this could be done more easily by fostering separatist movements along the Soviet–Iranian border.

How to retire from Afghanistan with dignity and the least possible danger must still be the principal Soviet problem. One option might be to negotiate an agreement with the Karmal Government by which the

USSR would garrison the north of Afghanistan. If it were then decided to abandon the People's Party the USSR would be able to shield its own frontier from possible anarchy and would have a counter with which to bargain with whatever government came to power in Kabul. But as they rake through such possibilities Soviet strategists must be tempted by the well known Irish formula – it would be better not to start from here. Western observers may cynically reflect that they could scarcely have planned a Soviet operation which would better serve the interests of the West. There was a time, while the USA laboured in Vietnam, that one was tempted to believe that the West had a monopoly of silliness; the Soviet Union's Afghan adventure has at least proved that this is not the case.

17 January 1980

NOTES

1. Palmerston to Melbourne 11 December 1837, Palmerston Papers.
2. D. Urquhart, *Diplomatic Transactions in Central Asia 1834–9*, (London, 1841).
3. On the Muslim Republics of the USSR see G. Wheeler, *The Modern History of Soviet Central Asia* (London, 1964); A. Bennigsen and C. Lemercier-Qulequejay, *Islam in the Soviet Union* (London, 1967); O. Caroe, *Soviet Empire*, (London, 1967); E. Bacon, *Central Asians under Russian Rule* (New York, 1966); T. Rakowska-Harmstone, *Russia and Nationalism in Central Asia* (Baltimore, 1970); E. Goldhagen (ed.), *Ethnic Minorities in the Soviet Union* (New York, 1968); E. Allworth (ed.), *Soviet Nationality Problems* (New York, 1971); C.A. Limden and D.K. Simes (eds), *Nationalities and Nationalism in the USSR* (Washington, 1977); R.A. Lewis, R.H. Rowland and R.G. Clem, *Nationality and Population Change in Russia and the USSR* (New York, 1976); V.A. Aspaturian, *The Union Republics in Soviet Diplomacy* (Geneva/Paris, 1966); and especially the penetrating new study by Hélène Carrère d'Encausse, *L'empire éclaté* (Paris, 1978). There have also been important articles in *Soviet Studies* and *Problems of Communism*.
4. For a recent Soviet statement see E. Bagramaov, 'The Soviet Nationalities Policy and Bourgeois Falsifications', *International Affairs*, June 1977. For an outline of western theories see M.E. Yapp 'Language, Religion and Political Identity: a General Framework' in D. Taylor and M. Yapp (eds), *Political Identity in South Asia* (London, 1979).
5. *Sovremennij Iran*, (Moscow, 1957 and 1975).
6. On the recent history of the Straits Question see H.N. Howard, *Turkey, The Straits and U.S. Policy* (Baltimore, 1974); and Feridun Cemal Erkin, *Les relations Turco–Sovietiques et la question des Détroits* (Ankara, 1968).

7.   See M.E. Yapp 'The Soviet Union and the Middle East', *Asian Affairs*
     Feb.1976, 7–18. Other analyses include John C. Campbell, 'The Soviet
     Union and the Middle East' in Roger E. Kanet (ed.) *The Soviet Union
     and the Developing Nations* (Baltimore 1974), 153–77; Joseph Churba,
     Soviet Penetration into the Middle East (Alabama, 1968); Ismet Girinki,
     Superpowers in the Middle East (Istanbul 1972); Ivo J. Lederer and
     Wayne S. Vucinich (eds), *The Soviet Union and the Middle East*
     (Stanford 1974); A. Yodfat and M. Abir, *In the Direction of the Persian
     Gulf* (London 1977); and Gregor M. Reinhard, 'Strategic Problems of
     the Indian Ocean Area: the Iran–Afghan–Pakistan sector of the Inter-
     national Frontier', PhD. Washington 1968.
8.   This account of the revolution is based on an analysis of reports in
     newspapers and periodicals. Many of these are reprinted in various
     issues of *Afghanistan Council Newsletter*. On the background to the
     coup of 1973 see Hasan Kakar, 'The Fall of the Afghan Monarchy in
     1973', *International Journal of Middle East Studies*, 9(1978) 195–214. On
     political developments in Afghanistan during the constitutional period
     and on the rise of the leftist parties see L. Dupree, *Afghanistan*
     (Princeton 1973) and on the Afghan economy see M.J. Fry, *The Afghan
     Economy* (Leiden 1974). For a brief biography of Tarakki, see K.
     Jaeckel, 'Nur Muhammad Tarakai', *Afghanistan Journal 5*, Part 3, 1978,
     105–8.
9.   *Kabul Times*, 3 August 1978. Tarakki's outline of his programme broad-
     cast 9 May 1978 aiso breathes impeccable benevolence but later pro-
     nouncements by Hafizullah Amin and Sulayman Layeq bore a harder,
     less compromising and more Marxist character.
10. *Kabul Times* 31 January; 7, 8, and 12 February 1978.
11. L. Mironov, 'Democratic Republic of Afghanistan', *International
     Affairs*, August 1978, 137–40.
12. Quoted in L. Mironov and G. Polyakov, 'Afghanistan: The Beginning
     of a new Life' *International Affairs*, March 1979, 52. The same claim,
     of course, has been made by Soviet spokesmen and writers for the
     treaties with India, Angola, Iraq and Ethiopia and for other ventures in
     diplomacy. For earlier Soviet–Afghan relations see the documentary
     collection *Sovetsko–Afganskie Otnosheniya 1919–1969*, Moscow 1971,
     and L.P. Teplinskij, *50 let sovetsko–afgaskikh otnoshij 1919–1969*,
     Moscow 1971.
13. Two recent accounts of the policies of these years are Hossein Amirsa-
     deghi (ed.), *Twentieth Century Iran* (London, 1977) and George
     Lenczowski (ed.), *Iran under the Pahlevis* (Stanford, 1978).
14. For the political background see Marvin Zonis, *The Political Elite of
     Iran*, (Princeton, 1971) and for recent events Yair Hirschfeld and Aryeh
     Shmudevitz, 'Iran' in C. Legum (ed.), *Middle East Contemporary
     Survey I*, (New York, 1978), 369–402.
15. On the process of urbanisation see H. Adibi, 'An Analysis of the Social,
     Economic and Physical Aspects of Urbanisation in Iran', PhD, US
     International University 1972. On the bazaar, see Gustav Thaiss, 'The
     Bazaar in a Case Study of Religion and Social Change' in Ehsan
     Yar-Shater (ed.), *Iran Faces the Seventies*, (New York, 1971), 189–206.

On the religious group and especially the events of 1962–3, Farhad Kazemi 'Social Mobilisation and Domestic Violence in Iran 1946–68' PhD. Michigan 1973 is excellent. It is instructive to compare the role of Islam in 1978 with its role in an earlier period: see Abdul-Hadi Hairi, *Shiism and Constitutionalism in Iran*, (Leiden, 1977).

16. See George Lenczowski, *Russia and the West in Iran 1918–1948* (New York, 1949); W. Eagleton Jr., *The Kurdish Republic of 1946* (London, 1963); R.K. Ramazani, *Iran's Foreign Policy 1941–1973*; P.E. Weaver 'Soviet Strategy in Iran 1941–1957', PhD Washington 1958. The most recent Soviet account is E.A. Orlov, *Vneshnyaya politika Irana: posle vtoroj mirovoj vojny* (Moscow, 1975). *Iran: Ocherki novejshej istoril* (Moscow, 1976), takes the other course of ignoring the episode completely.

17. This is the argument of Hormuz Hekmet 'Iran's Response to Soviet–American Rivalry 1951–1962', (PhD Columbia 1974).

18. See, for example, A. Kunov, 'Developing Good-Neighbourly Relations' in *International Affairs*, May 1977, 21–29.

19. On Iranian communism see Sepehr Zabih, *The Communist Movement in Iran*, (Berkeley, 1966).

20. A good account of recent Turkish history is Feroz Ahmad, *The Turkish Experiment In Democracy 1950–1975*, (London, 1977) and a valuable analysis is C.H. Dodd, *Politics and Government in Turkey*, (Manchester, 1969). On the Turkish economy see Z.Y. Hershlag, *Turkey: The Challenge of Growth*, (Leiden, 1968); on recent political movements see J.M. Landau, *Radical Politics in Modern Turkey*, (Leiden, 1974) and E. Özbudun, *Social Change and Political Participation in Turkey*, (Princeton, 1976).

21. The best study of recent Turkish foreign relations is K.H. Karpat *et al.*, *Turkey's Foreign Policy in Transition 1950–1974*, (Leiden, 1975). See also Ferenc A. Vali, *Bridge across the Bosporus*, (Baltimore, 1971). On the war period see E. Weisband, *Turkey's Foreign Policy 1943–1945*, (Princeton, 1973).

22. V. Shoniya, 'An Important Landmark in Soviet–Turkish Relations', *International Affairs*, September 1978, 75–8. For a more recent assessment see V. Alemik, 'Soviet–Turkish Ties Today', ibid., April 1979, 15–19

7. The Soviet Union in South-East Asia

Michael Leifer

THE BACKGROUND

In the course of its emergence as a global power, the Soviet Union has not expressed a major direct and consistent interest in South-East Asia. Indeed, the region east of the Indian sub-continent and south of China has never enjoyed a prominent place in Soviet strategic and political priorities arising from any perception of its intrinsic importance. Apart from a general disposition to encourage non-capitalist modes of development as a way of facilitating a transition to Socialism, the interests and policies of the Soviet Union have been governed essentially by the condition of its principal adversary relationships whose prime *foci* have been located in other regions. Thus, any special significance attached to any part of South-East Asia has arisen from a need or opportunity to engage in competition with notable political rivals and not, for example, from any pressing concern to ensure the exercise of influence in a zone of critical geopolitical importance. Nonetheless, the *role* of the Soviet Union in South-East Asia is a matter of considerable interest and importance, because of the impact of critical adversary relationships which, since the onset of the 1950s, have been conducted with both the United States and the People's Republic of China.

Soviet policies towards and in South-East Asia have been a direct consequence of these adversary relationships, although their respective significance has varied in the period since the beginning of decolonisation in the region.[1] Undoubtedly, the most important relationship which Soviet governments have maintained within South-East Asia has been with counterparts in Hanoi: a relationship consummated by treaty in November 1978 and consolidated as a consequence of China's military intervention into Vietnam in February

1979. However, in any general assessment of objectives and policies in the region, it is necessary to be aware from the outset of a Soviet willingness to neglect and compromise the interests of the Vietnamese Communists. For example, after the capitulation of Japan in August 1945, the Soviet Government behaved with studied neglect towards the Communist-led Viet Minh. Ho Chi Minh's plea for recognition of the Democratic Republic of Vietnam (DRV) made no visible impact on Stalin, who had not only come to terms with the *regime* of Chiang Kai-shek but also countenanced its post-war occupation of Vietnam, north of the sixteenth parallel. At the time, Stalin was much more concerned to advance the political prospects of the French Communist Party, which as a member of a coalition cabinet endorsed repressive measures against the insurgent Viet Minh until May 1947. Soviet support, of a verbal nature only for the movement led by the former Comintern agent Ho Chi Minh, was not forthcoming until after the French Communist Party had left the coalition. Even then, recognition of the DRV was not extended until January 1950, shortly after it had been proferred by China. A willingness to compromise interests was demonstrated by the Soviet Union at the Geneva Conference on Indochina in 1954 when, in harmony with China, pressure was applied to the DRV to ensure its acceptance of a provisional territorial settlement in Vietnam which was less than a full reflection of Viet Minh psychological, if not military, advantage over the French. An indication of the extent to which the Soviet Union was prepared to tolerate the transformation in the status of the line of provisional demarcation in Vietnam along the seventeenth parallel to that of a political boundary was indicated by a proposal, in January 1957, that both North and South Vietnam as well as North and South Korea should be granted membership of the United Nations.

Prior to the death of Stalin, the Soviet Union had applauded the process, if not the political consequences, of decolonisation in South-East Asia and also exhorted revolutionary movements in Burma, Malaya, Indonesia and the Philippines, even though without direct physical involvement. With the abandonment of Zhdanov's 'two camp' doctrine, Moscow's contemptuous view of post-colonial successor governments was replaced by a greater tolerance. Attention in South-East Asia was directed to the encouragement of 'national democracy' and foreign policies of non-alignment as a way of breaching America's global wall of containment. To this end, states like Burma and Cambodia were courted politically and offered limited economic assistance. A major involvement of a political and economic kind occurred in the case of Indonesia in the latter years of the 1950s and into the early 1960s. Opportunity for access was provided in the main by the bitter dispute over the disposition of the Western half of the island of New Guinea (West Irian) which the Dutch had refused to include in the transfer of sovereignty of December 1949. American reluctance to apply pressure on the Dutch, together with evident sympathy for regional dissidents in the archipelago, enabled the Soviet Union to become the major military benefactor of Indonesia whose enhanced capability lent credence to its prosecution of 'Confrontation' against the former colonial power. The practice of coercive diplomacy by Indonesia and the prospect of Soviet and internal Communist advantage motivated American mediation, which resulted in the peaceful resolution of the dispute to Indonesia's satisfaction.

INDONESIA

The Soviet investment in Indonesia was substantial and the form which it took was not logically directed to the transition to Socialism. In the wake of Indonesia's diplomatic triumph over West Irian and despite the scale of military assistance from the Soviet Union, relations between the two states became less cordial as both the Communist Party of Indonesia and the Indonesian Government aligned themselves progressively with their Chinese counterparts. In this context, Indonesia's 'Confrontation' against Malaysia was welcomed without real enthusiasm in Moscow, although the vote of the Soviet representative on the Security Council did save Sukarno's government from the political embarrassment of a critical resolution in September 1964. A symptom of the state of the relationship was Indonesia's unwillingness to endorse Soviet participation in the Afro-Asian conference which was intended to convene in Algiers in June 1965. It is very likely that the subsequent decimation of the pro-Peking Communist Party of Indonesia after the abortive *coup* in October 1965 was contemplated with mixed feelings in Moscow.

The inducement for the Soviet Union in trying to promote a close political relationship with Sukarno's Indonesia would seem fairly self-evident. The largest and most populous state in the region, with allegedly the largest non-ruling Communist Party in the world, represented an attractive political prize in open competition with the United States and latent competition, initially, with China. However, in the case of Indonesia the Soviet Union confronted the classical problem of how to convert benefaction into influence. The short-lived affair with Indonesia was a salutary experience to the extent that it demonstrated that political affections could not be readily purchased with hardware. It proved also to be a costly encounter as, by the end of 1965, the Indonesian Government owed approximately US $1400 million to the Soviet Union and its East European allies. In the event, the Soviet Government cut its losses in pragmatic manner rather than rupture any residual relationship with the successor Suharto Administration. Although aid projects were suspended and cultural cooperation ceased, it reached an agreement in 1970 on a rescheduling of outstanding debts on the same basis as Western states and also sustained a diplomatic presence despite the intensely anti-Communist nature of the Suharto Administration. No doubt an appreciation of the fragile basis of political order in Indonesia contributed to the decision to maintain such a presence, as did the state of Sino Indonesian relations. Tensions have persisted, nonetheless. For example, the Soviet Government was hostile towards the convening of the Jakarta Conference on Cambodia in May 1970. Its news media have expressed criticism of the conduct of general elections in Indonesia and also of the role of the Association of South-East Asian Nations (ASEAN), at least until the middle of 1978. In addition, the Soviet Government has provided asylum for a faction in exile of the Communist Party of Indonesia, whose anti-Chinese pronouncements appear from time to time in its press.[2]

INDOCHINA

The Soviet objective in Indonesia was related initially to the potential and standing of the Republic in the region, in the context of competition with the United States. Although costly, the involvement was not of a critical nature and the successive political disadvantages arising first from Chinese and then American special association could be readily tolerated. A more important Soviet exercise in competitive intervention occurred in Laos between 1960–2. Whereas the Indonesian affair had been undertaken primarily in the context of a central bilateral adversary relationship, at least at the outset, the involvement in Laos occurred at a juncture when competition with China had begun to complicate the pattern of global relationships.

After the settlement of the Geneva Conference on Indochina of 1954, the formal independence and unity of Laos was tested by an incipient civil war sustained in part by external patrons. In August 1960, a paratroop captain in the Laotian army mounted a *coup* against the right-wing government in Vientiane in an attempt to force a change in the international orientation of the fractured state to that of non-alignment. In response, the government of Thailand inspired a blockade of the River Mekong in order to deny essential supplies to the Neutralists. At this juncture, the Soviet Government organised a large-scale airlift of military supplies *via* Hanoi in order to sustain the position of the Neutralists, who had attracted the support of the pro-Communist Pathet Lao and their Vietnamese Communist patrons. Soviet objectives were mixed in this enterprise. One can presume an intention to promote the advantage of the adherents of 'national liberation' ranged against the clients of the United States and Thailand. However, the manner and form of assistance was not such as to alter dramatically the internal balance of forces; it served to maintain political equilibrium in the fractured state. More to the point, it has been argued that Soviet Premier Khrushchev assumed the risks of intervention 'to retain the allegiance of North Vietnam in the developing quarrel with China'.[3] In the event, the Soviet initiative helped to check right-wing military dominance in Laos and thus safeguarded Vietnamese Communist interests in the eastern uplands of the country through which passed the very important 'Ho Chi Minh trail'. Notably, after the negotiation of the formal neutralisation agreement for Laos in July 1962, the Soviet Union did not sustain its interest in the political future of the state. This sense of neglect extended also to Vietnam until after the deposition of Khrushchev by his Party colleagues in October 1964. The Soviet Government responded with some indifference to the Gulf of Tonkin episode in the previous August.

A major revival of Soviet interest in Indochina occurred early in 1965. It was promoted by the initial bombing of North Vietnam in February concurrently with an official visit to Hanoi by Premier Kosygin, in an attempt to encourage a negotiated settlement to the war as well as to plead a case in the quarrel with China. The Soviet Government found itself caught by conflicting pressures. On the one hand, it wished to prevent the establishment of a close alignment between North Vietnam and China; on the other hand, it was concerned to urge moderation on the politburo in Hanoi in the interest of consolidating a relationship of *détente* with the United States in the wake of the partial nuclear test-ban treaty of August 1963. But, with the untimely coincidence of Kosygin's visit with the onset of 'Operation Flaming Dart', the Soviet Government found itself obliged to sustain the military capability of the Vietnamese Communists. Indeed, it had little alternative. It has been well argued that 'Vietnam now became the testing ground not only for the Americans' theories on how to cope with wars of liberation but also for the Soviet readiness and ability to protect a Communist *regime* from the superior power of the United States'.[4]

In competition with China, the Soviet Union provided the Vietnamese Communists with both defensive and offensive capability in sufficient measure to make possible ultimate military victory in April 1975. During the final ten years of the Second Indochina War, the Soviet Union sought with some success to reconcile the conflicting objectives of promoting the cause of the government in Hanoi and the attainment of *détente*. If its freedom of manoeuvre in seeking to persuade the Vietnamese Communists of the virtues of negotiation was limited by its competitive relationship with China, which from the turn of the decade involved the United States as well as Vietnam, the extent to which it kept its own interests separate was demonstrated in May 1972, when the American mining of the port of Haiphong was not permitted to prevent President Nixon's visit to Moscow. In the event, it may be argued that the Soviet Union secured the best of both worlds. For example, in the final years of the war its leadership played a *role* in persuading the Vietnamese Communists to accept elements of compromise which were incorporated in the short-lived Paris Peace Agreements concluded in January 1973. After Paris, the Soviet Union sought to encourage economic priorities and showed some willingness to cooperate with President Ford's Administration while pursuing an accord on the limitation of strategic arms. But, it was not reluctant to help expose America's sense of global weakness after the Jackson amendment on Soviet Jewry was tied to the issue of most favoured nation trading status with the United States. It has been maintained that, in late December 1974, Armed Forces Chief General Victor Kulikov attended a meeting of the politburo in Hanoi and in the following weeks 'seaborne shipment of Soviet war materials to North Vietnam increased fourfold in volume, as Moscow gave full aid and comfort to Hanoi in its final offensive'.[5]

In the course of pursuing its conception of *détente*, the Soviet Union was engaged increasingly in seeking the political disadvantage of China. As the United States embarked on military disengagement from Indochina from the advent of the Nixon Administration, the interest of the Soviet Union in South-East Asia was governed by its intensely bitter conflict with the People's Republic of China. It was in this context that Leonid Brezhnev undertook a less than precise initiative. On 8 June 1969, at an international conference of Communist parties held in Moscow, he remarked in the course of discussing European security 'We are of the opinion that the course of events is also placing on the agenda the task of creating a system of collective security in Asia'. This laconic statement had been preceded two weeks before by an article in *Izvestiya* which sought to link a Chinese threat in Asia to the notion of a system of collective security which would serve to protect the independence of post-colonial states.

Brezhnev's proposal, which has never received serious consideration by the states of the region, reflected the extent to which the Soviet Union was moved by inter-governmental priorities rather than by ideological ones. Ideology has served primarily as an instrument of debate and abuse in the conflict with China rather than as a means of access to revolutionary movements in the region. Foreign policy objectives have possessed a more practical cast, exemplified in the establishment of diplomatic relations with anti-Communist governments in Malaysia, Singapore and the Philippines. Indeed, a striking example of the Soviet concern to secure the political disadvantage of China was the reluctance to break diplomatic contact with the Lon Nol Government in Cambodia when Prince Sihanouk's government in exile was set up in Peking in May 1970.

The Soviet Union maintained its mission in the Cambodian capital headed by a *charge d'affaires* until he was withdrawn after the conclusion of the conference of non-aligned states in Algiers in September 1973, because of the expectation that the Lon Nol Government was about to lose its seat in the United Nations. The Soviet Union – resentful of Peking's patronage of the *Khmers Rouges* – sought to square the circle by refusing to receive an ambassador from Phnom Penh, while it recognised the former Cambodian ambassador who had rallied to Sihanouk but only as the representative of the Cambodian National United Front and not of the government in exile in Peking. At the same time, a representative of the Lon Nol Government was permitted to occupy rooms in a Moscow hotel and to maintain links with other diplomatic missions but without formal contact with the Soviet Government. In the event, the Russians, through their ambassador in Peking, affirmed recognition and support for the government headed by Prince Sihanouk towards the end of March 1975, only shortly before the fall of Phnom Penh. The Lon Nol mission in Moscow was required to close down but the Soviet

Government did not withdraw its residual staff of three from its embassy in the Cambodian capital before the *Khmer Rouge* victory. This belated recognition was a source of great bitterness on the part of the short-lived Administration of Democratic Kampuchea which refused to resume diplomatic relations with Moscow after April 1975.

In the wake of the Second Indochina War, the Soviet Union has profited from the transformation in relations between Vietnam and China and to an extent from the dominant influence which Vietnam exercises in Laos and where approximately 2000 Soviet advisers and technicians are deployed. Initially, although in closer association with the Soviet Union than China, the government in Hanoi appeared to be more than aligned with that in Moscow insofar as it echoed its diplomatic positions on a range of issues but without endorsing Brezhnev's proposal for a collective security system in Asia. Evident differences existed between China and Vietnam arising from apprehensions over Vietnamese ambitions in Indochina and in the South China Sea and sharpened by an underlying concern that Hanoi would serve as the client of Moscow. But a measure of accommodation was sustained between the neighbouring Communist states until early 1978, when the open armed confrontation between Vietnam and Cambodia drew China to the support of the latter with serious consequences for Sino-Vietnamese relations.

The Soviet Union became a political beneficiary of the dramatic deterioration in Sino-Vietnamese relations and also of the serious economic difficulties which faced Vietnam and which were aggravated by the termination of Chinese economic assistance, the limited ability of the government in Hanoi to attract aid from the Western world, and a failure to reach a political accommodation with the United States. In the circumstances, the Soviet Government would appear to have made an offer which the politburo in Hanoi could not refuse.[6] In consequence, in June 1978, Vietnam became a full member of the Council for Mutual Economic Assistance (CMEA or Comecon) affirming its commitment to the statutes of the organisation.

From this juncture, Soviet and Vietnamese policies in South-East Asia assumed an evident harmony. For example, the two countries embarked concurrently on a change of public heart towards the Association of South-East Asian Nations (ASEAN) which, as a corporate political entity, had been represented as an agent of American imperialism. They expressed also a willingness to look more favourably on ASEAN's proposal for the establishment of a Zone of Peace, Freedom and Neutrality in the region. The Soviet initiative was undertaken in July 1978 through a publication produced by its embassy in Bangkok. This public revision of attitudes towards ASEAN marked a major alteration of policy, at least in declaratory form. Since June 1969, the Soviet government had sought to promote the Brezhnev scheme for a system of collective security in Asia. This much had been evident in October 1973 when the Malaysian Prime Minister, Tun Abdul Razak, had visited Moscow. It was indicated also, within days of the fall of Saigon in May 1975, when a visiting *Pravda* bureau chief called on the Thai Foreign Minister, Chatichai Chunhawan, and made the suggestion that his government consider the Soviet proposal for a collective security system. Soviet academic writings have also expressed interest in the proposal.[7]

The significance of the proposal for a collective security system in Asia was not in its actual terminology, which goes back to the rhetoric of Maxim Litvinov, but in its unstated objective. As Arnold Horelick has pointed out, the collective security proposal was 'a giant trial balloon testing the political climate for a Soviet initiative whose ultimate shape, scope and substance would depend almost entirely on events and reactions'.[8] The ultimate objective, whether through the realisation of some grand design or through an *ad hoc* set of treaties, was regarded universally as directed towards the political disadvantage of China. In this respect, the reversal attitude to ASEAN and its policy platform was intended to serve the same end. The object of the exercise was diplomatic competition for the political affections of the members of ASEAN, which had enjoyed the benign political regard of China from 1975.[9] However, the course of events in the latter months of 1978 dictated the necessity for choice on the part of the Soviet Government with attendant opportunity costs for its relations with the states of ASEAN.

On 3 November 1978, the Soviet Union and Vietnam entered into a treaty of friendship and cooperation. The circumstances surrounding the negotiation of that treaty bear comparison with those at the time of the Soviet–Indian treaty of August 1971, which served to deter any Chinese response to India's *role* in the dismemberment of Pakistan. It is not known which party took the immediate initiative in this enterprise and whether or not the Soviet Union had been pressing for such a treaty for some time, as in the case of India; or was impelled by a desire for a riposte to the Sino-Japanese Peace Treaty of August 1978. But it would seem more than just coincidence that the Soviet–Vietnamese treaty was signed one month before the announcement of a so-called Kampuchean National United Front for National Salvation, in opposition to the government in Phnom Penh with open Vietnamese support and evident inspiration as well as Soviet endorsement. This sequence of events prompted the pungent retort from Singapore's Prime Minister, Lee Kuan-Yew, that 'It always seems that once the Soviet Union concludes such a treaty with any country, the joint signatory nation sooner or later launches agression against other countries'. As if to confirm the validity of Lee's allegation, the Vietnamese, utilising the cover of the National United Front, launched an offensive into Cambodia on Christmas Day 1978 and by 7 January 1979 their forces had entered its capital. The Soviet media applauded this act of 'liberation' and its government accorded speedy recognition to a People's Revolutionary Council as 'the sole legal government of Kampuchea'.

The signature of the treaty between the Soviet Union and Vietnam indicated the willingness and ability of the government in Moscow to make a decisive political choice. And if the complementary diplomacy of the Soviet Union and Vietnam among the ASEAN states was negated by the evident consequences of that treaty for the independence of Cambodia, its outcome has probably served the principal purpose of the Soviet Union in South-East Asia.[10] First of all, the treaty sanctified the ideological position of the Soviet Union through an act of identification on the part of a renowned Communist state. Article Four commits the parties to 'consistently strive to consolidate further in an all out manner their fraternal relations, and the unity and solidarity among the socialist countries on the basis of Marxism–Leninism and socialist internationalism'.[11] The joint expression of ideological commitment goes some way to make up for the lack of access by the Soviet Union to the revolutionary movements of South-East Asia. Indeed, the insurgent Communist Parties of South-East Asia have adhered in ideological terms to Chinese orthodoxy even though the measure of support preferred by Peking has been primarily ceremonial. The clandestine Communist radio stations, the Voice of the Malayan Revolution and the Voice of the People of Burma, have expressed support for the vanquished Pol Pot Government and have denounced the Vietnamese invasion of Cambodia although the Voice of the People of Thailand was conspicuously silent on the matter until 13 May 1979 when it quoted a former Thai foreign minister as saying that Vietnam should pull out of Cambodia.[12] It may be argued that, by securing an expression of fraternal socialist solidarity from the Vietnamese Communists, the Soviet Union has become better placed to assert its ideological rectitude towards a

China which, in terms of internal practice and external affiliations, is open to the charge of deviation from Socialist principle.

A more striking feature of the Soviet–Vietnamese treaty is Article Six which gives the relationship the quality of an alliance. It states *inter alia* 'If either party is attacked or threatened with attack, the high contracting parties to the Treaty shall immediately consult each other for the purpose of eliminating that threat, and shall take appropriate and effective measures to safeguard peace and the security of the two countries'.[13] At the time, the evident connection between the treaty and the unhindered armed intervention of Vietnam into Cambodia served to demonstrate the virtues of the Soviet Union as an ally. Potential signatories elsewhere were shown the utility of a by now standard treaty, should there be a hostile neighbour to be contained or despatched. However, in undertaking a security obligation to Vietnam in advance of its invasion of Cambodia, the Soviet Government assumed the calculated risk that its credibility as an ally might be called into question, although the risk was possibly not contemplated as a likely prospect.

In its response to China's military intervention into Vietnam on 17 February 1979, the Soviet Government behaved with a characteristic caution. Although its obligations under the Treaty of Friendship were reaffirmed and reiterated, Soviet reaction was confined to a vigorous denunciation of China's 'shameless aggression', limited naval deployment and aerial reconnaissance in the Gulf of Tonkin, and an airlift of arms to an ally stretched militarily in containing the intervention across its Northern border and engaged also in a protracted pacification in Cambodia. Soviet prudence would seem to have been governed in part by the preference of the Vietnamese to demonstrate their ability to cope independently of any direct military support. Indeed, in the circumstances of an armed confrontation which did not reach a decisive point to the advantage of either one of the two adversaries, the Vietnamese almost certainly did not expect or require more from the Soviet Union. Its formal credibility as an ally was upheld by the distinguished figure of General Vo Nguyen Giap who publicly expressed his country's profound gratitude 'to the Communist Party, the Government, the People and the Armed Forces of the Soviet Union for their immense support and assistance to the Vietnamese people's revolutionary cause in the past and at present'.[14]

The conduct of the Soviet Union during China's Vietnam War would seem to have been governed also by the realisation that it is easier to initiate 'a limited punitive strike' than it is to bring it to a satisfactory military conclusion, as well as by a reluctance to embark on any course of action which might have prejudiced the concurrent SALT negotiations with the United States. In addition, its evident forbearance gave it some credence in its vilification of China as an international deviant, especially among some of the non-Communist states of South-East Asia disturbed by the sight of Peking acting as a regional gamekeeper.

Although the credibility of the Soviet Union as a reliable ally was not put to a full test, the Chinese military intervention was especially significant for the Soviet Union because it represented a demonstration of resolution in the face of Moscow's support for Hanoi in Cambodia. In addition, it marked the first occasion on which the territory of a formal ally of the Soviet Union had been subject to direct military invasion: except, of course, by the Soviet Union itself. In consequence, in the absence of direct military support for Vietnam, it became incumbent on the Soviet Union to help consolidate the position of Vietnam throughout former French Indochina and in sustaining the public legitimacy of its client government in Phnom Penh.

It should be understood, of course, that the recent burgeoning of Soviet–Vietnamese relations has been encouraged by the force of circumstances which have engaged the complementary interests of Moscow and Hanoi. Seen from the vantage of historical perspective, that relationship has not always been easy or necessarily natural when not forged by the imperatives of the balance of power. In this respect, the treaty entered into by the Soviet Union and Vietnam expressed the complementary and not the identical interests of the signatory states. And just as Soviet–Indian interests diverged somewhat after India's successful intervention into East Pakistan, then there is an equivalent prospect in the future of a divergence between the interests of Vietnam and the Soviet Union, given the strong tradition of commitment to independence of the politburo in Hanoi. Of course, as long as Sino-Vietnamese relations are beset by bitter antagonism, and Vietnamese resources are strained because of internal economic failure and the costs of a protracted pacification in Cambodia, then the government of Vietnam can be expected to assume the role of junior partner to the Soviet Union in the prosecution of a second containment of China. Indeed, the more bitter the antagonism with China and the more protracted the pacification in Cambodia, the greater will be the dependence of Vietnam on the Soviet Union and the greater its influence over the self-proclaimed outpost of Socialism in South-East

Asia.

The advantages of the special relationship between the Soviet Union and Vietnam have not been secured without costs. Indeed, it remains to be seen just what proportion of the heavy economic and military burden which Vietnam has incurred by its occupation of Cambodia and its 'provocation' of China will be assumed by the Soviet Government. In addition, there is the problem of overcoming the set-back to the limited progress in intergovernmental relations with the ASEAN states, whose foreign ministers deplored the armed inter-vention into Cambodia and reiterated their demand for the withdrawal of all foreign troops before and after the Chinese military action against Vietnam. The Soviet Government has sought to make the best of a bad case in ASEAN capitals and to try to exploit the disinclination of its five members to appear aligned openly with China in the public argument over the events in Cambodia, as well as their sense of apprehension engendered by China's so-called punitive action. How-ever, it is only as a patron of Hanoi, able and willing to restrict the political appetite of its client, that the Soviet Government can expect to overcome its notoriety in facilitating Vietnamese dominance in Indochina. Indeed, it was with such a prospect in mind that, in March 1979, General Kriangsak Chamanan paid the first visit ever by a Thai Prime Minister to Moscow.

Soviet policy in its most recent phase in South-East Asia has been governed by the consistent priority of seeking the political disadvan-tage of a principal adversary. To this end, the Soviet Union has demonstrated a willingness to take up opportunities in the pursuit of such disadvantage when they have presented themselves and to make necessary choices accordingly. Its involvement, however, has been characterised by a measure of caution and by the avoidance of undue risks. The treaty relationship with Vietnam marks its most successful diplomatic engagement in the affairs of the region. Indeed, the Soviet Union has never before enjoyed such an exclusive association with any state in South-East Asia. The quality of the relationships, between the Soviet Union and Vietnam on the one hand and China on the other, will be the key to its enduring quality. In this respect, one cannot rule out the prospect of a positive Soviet response to a Chinese attempt at limited accommodation motivated by a desire to reduce Moscow's support for Hanoi in Indochina. Just as relations with the United States are ultimately more important for the Soviet Union than those with Vietnam, so its relations with China possess a corresponding order of priority.

SOVIET MARITIME INTERESTS

In the main, South-East Asia should be regarded as a region of competitive opportunity for the Soviet Union and not as an important security zone. One partial qualification which must be entered against this generalisation arises from Soviet naval activity through the region over the past decade. This activity has attracted a revival of attention because of speculation that the government of Vietnam might permit the establishment of a naval base for the Soviet Pacific fleet at Cam Ranh Bay. The Soviet Ambassador in Bangkok, Yuriy Kuznetsov, has gone on record more than once that 'The Soviet Union has no intention to have bases at Cam Ranh Bay'. And Vietnam's Prime Minister, Pham Van Dong, has been emphatic that the Soviet Union has not been, and would not be, given military bases in Vietnam, while conceding that the Soviet Union has been accorded normal facilities offered to friendly countries.[15]

In March 1968, a Soviet naval squadron made an appearance in the Indian Ocean, securing access through South-East Asian waters including notably the Straits of Malacca and Singapore. That initial visit occurred shortly after the announcement of an accelerated British military withdrawal from East of Suez and a major set-back for the United States in Vietnam. It set off discussion about Soviet objectives and the debate on this issue has continued ever since, although now in less intense form. There does not appear to be any consensus among observers as to any one primary objective on the part of the Soviet Union in a recurrent deployment which, from its East Asian port of Vladivostock, is along a lengthy and vulnerable route used also by its merchant fleet. That deployment is perhaps best considered as a regional expression of the sense of global standing enjoyed by the Soviet Union. It is, of course, possible to suggest a list of objectives, from flag showing intended to indicate the prospect of offshore support for onshore clients around the littoral of the Indian Ocean to anti-submarine warfare familiarisation procedures. In recent years, the scale of the Soviet naval presence has been limited, and may be regarded as underpinning a claim to a right of deployment in advance of any circumstances in which Soviet interests may be at stake. In this respect, it merits mentioning the potential importance of the maritime supply route from European to Asiatic Russia, which would serve as an essential alternative in the event of an interdiction of the Trans-Siberian railway.

The waters of South-East Asia, including the South China Sea and the Straits of Malacca and Singapore, provide the most direct route for surface naval vessels from the Pacific to the Northern Indian Ocean. The Soviet Union as a major maritime power has made quite explicit its determination to sustain unimpeded transit rights for its merchant and naval vessels through all straits used for international navigation, including those in South-East Asia. An interesting aspect of Soviet policy towards maritime passage is that while actual naval vessel deployment has taken place through the Straits of Malacca and Singapore on a competitive basis with vessels of the American Pacific Fleet, the Soviet and United States Governments have adopted a common stand on the status of straits used for international navigation. At the present time, Soviet interest in the Straits of Malacca and Singapore is not primarily towards securing access to any part of South-East Asia but in using this maritime facility to deploy vessels beyond the formal bounds of the region. Interest in the straits and waters of the Indonesian archipelago, however, is probably intended as an indication to the United States that it cannot assume that the passage of submerged missile-carrying nuclear submarines into the Indian Ocean will not be subjected to some attempt at surveillance.

Soviet interest in naval passage through South-East Asian waters has grown concurrently with an expansion of its general naval capability. For example, the Soviet Government was conspicuous in not joining with other maritime states in registering an objection to Indonesia's far reaching Archipelago Declaration of December 1957.[16] It subsequently recognised Indonesia's extension of the breadth of its territorial waters to twelve nautical miles. However, in August 1969, when the Malaysian Government extended its territorial waters to twelve miles – with implications for the legal *regime* in the Malacca Strait which is less than twenty four miles at several points – the Soviet Ambassador to Kuala Lumpur submitted an *aide memoire* setting forth his government's objections to the alleged indiscriminate extension of territorial waters.

The Soviet Union itself applies a twelve mile limit to territorial waters but draws a sharp distinction between the legal *regime* of territorial waters and straits used for international navigation.[17] In this respect, its policy is identical to that of the United States with whom agreement was reached on this matter in 1967. Its position on straits used for international navigation was made clear in the UN Seabed Committee which served as the preparatory body for the Third UN Conference on the Law of the Sea, and in that Conference proper whose working sessions began in 1974. Together with the United

States and other maritime powers, Soviet representatives challenged the adequacy of the legal *regime* of innocent passage and, at the Law of the Sea Conference, supported a proposal for a novel legal *regime* of transit passage which would serve its commercial and naval interests.

Consistent with its general position on straits for international navigation, the Soviet Union opposed the terms of a joint statement by Indonesia and Malaysia in November 1971 which challenged the customary legal status of the Straits of Malacca and Singapore and which insisted on their use for international shipping 'in accordance with the principle (*sic*) of innocent passage', A heated exchange between the Soviet and Indonesian and Malaysian Governments in March 1972 followed an attempt by the Soviet Ambassador in Tokyo to exploit Japanese sensibilities on the issue, as well as its current sense of political alienation from the United States. In the event, the issue of passage through the Straits of Malacca and Singapore was ultimately resolved at a session of the Law of the Sea Conference in 1977 within the context of the general status of all straits used for international navigation, as part of a package deal involving maritime powers support for the archipelago status of Indonesia's waters and the institution of a traffic separation scheme in the straits. The Soviet position towards passage through the Straits of Malacca and Singapore has been consistent and firm. For example, in December 1972, Pavel Kuznetzov, the newly appointed Ambassador in Jakarta, announced: 'All authoritative Soviet organs consider the Straits of Malacca and Singapore, in accordance with international law and navigational practices which have been effective since long ago, as an international shipping route for general and free navigation without any limitations whatsoever'.

The attitude of the Soviet Union towards passage through the Straits of Malacca and Singapore is logical, in terms of its expansion in maritime capability and interests. These straits provide a facility which a state with the global standing of the Soviet Union is not prepared to have denied to it through any unilateral alteration of the customary legal status. The use of that facility by the Soviet Union has varied in terms of the scale of naval deployment. It has been governed on peak occasions by crises around the littoral of the Indian Ocean. It should be understood, however, that the Straits area is neither an arena of intra-regional conflict (at least, not since 1966; before the onset of Soviet deployment) nor a focus of indirect conflict between the superpowers. The straits provide a means for competitive intervention but are not, so far, an objective of such intervention. Indeed, there has not been any indication on the part of any one of the superpowers of a desire or an attempt to deny passage to the other through the Straits of Malacca and Singapore. Their relationship over the Straits has been that of adverse partners who have adopted a common position with respect to a maritime facility utilised to prosecute mutual competition.

The Soviet Union has important commercial shipping interests in South-East Asia but no local clients or secure repair and servicing facilities in the Straits area. Singapore is used but only by commercial vessels. Naval interest in Singapore was indicated in July 1971 when the ASW destroyer *Blestyashchiy* accompanied by a tender paid an unannounced visit to Singapore. From that juncture, the government of Singapore adopted a policy of demanding a request for prior diplomatic clearance before permitting the entry of Soviet naval vessels into its circumscribed territorial waters. The willingness of the government of Singapore to make available its dockyards to Soviet naval vessels on commercial terms was reported first in 1970.[18] But such an offer, whenever it was made formally, has never been taken up by the Soviet navy. Only Soviet fishing vessels and merchantmen have entered Singapore's dockyards for bunkerage and repairs, because the government of Singapore has refused consistently to permit Soviet marine agencies access to and exclusive facilities within its port to conduct repairs on Soviet naval vessels. Indeed, early in 1976, the Soviet Government made its third unsuccessful request for separate bunkering facilities for its vessels passing through the Straits of Malacca and Singapore. The Soviet general maritime interest in Singapore has continued to grow, nonetheless, because of its *role* as regional repair centre for Soviet commercial and fishing vessels and also because of the volume of rubber re-exported through Singapore.

SUMMARY

South-East Asia has been a region of marginal direct interest to the Soviet Union. Involvement has arisen in the course of the prosecution of competition with principal adversaries; this has been a prime factor in its concern to uphold the customary legal status of the Straits of Malacca and Singapore. Its mainland engagement in this decade has had China as its focus. Force of circumstances have enabled a formal cementing of relations with Vietnam, with the objective of incorporating the whole of former French Indochina which abuts Southern China within the sphere of influence of Moscow's alliance partner. The

Soviet Union would appear to regard the prize of attracting and sustaining the political affections of a Vietnam dominant in Indochina as well worth any disadvantages which might accrue in the rest of South-East Asia from being regarded as the patron of a state which has visibly violated the independence of a regional neighbour. Its prime objective in South-East Asia, and especially in its mainland sector, has been one of denial of advantage to the People's Republic of China and its special relationship with Vietnam has served that purpose. The problem which this relationship has posed for the Soviet Union as a global power is somewhat similar to that which once faced the United States, which also has never possessed a direct interest in mainland South-East Asia. But because of the perceived imperative of containing a principal adversary, prestige and resources have become committed to a faraway country. Nonetheless experience of the nature of Soviet involvement in South-East Asia would appear to confirm a practice of policy evident elsewhere in the Third World, namely that the Soviet Union is opportunist rather than adventurist. Such opportunism, however, is no cause for complacency in the West for it is now underpinned by strategic parity.

NOTES

1. Agreements to establish diplomatic relations with the states of the region were concluded as follows: Thailand, December 1946; Burma, January 1948; Democratic (now Socialist) Republic of Vietnam, January 1950; Indonesia, December 1953; Cambodia (Kampuchea), May 1956 (not sustained between April 1975 and January 1979); Laos, October 1959; Malaysia, March 1967; Singapore, June 1968; the Philippines, June 1976.
2. For example, *Pravda*, 13 December 1978.
3. Arthur J. Dommen, *Conflict in Laos: The Politics of Neutralisation.* (New York: Praeger, (Revised Edition) 1971) p.179.
4. Adam B. Ulam, *Expansion and Coexistence: Soviet Foreign Policy, 1917–73,* (New York: Praeger, 1974) p.701.
5. Frank Snepp, *Decent Interval* (New York: Random House, 1977) p.138.
6. See the background discussion by Derek Davies in *Far Eastern Economic Review*, 2 February 1979.
7. For example, V. Vorontsov and D. Kapustin, 'Collective Security in Asia', *Far Eastern Affairs*, Moscow (1) 1976.
8. Arnold Horelick, 'The Soviet Union's Asian Collective Security Proposal', *Pacific Affairs*, Fall 1974, p.273.
9. See Khaw Guat Hoon, *An Analysis of China's Attitudes Towards ASEAN, 1967–76* (Singapore: Institute of Southeast Asian Studies, 1977).

10. At a banquet for Vietnamese leaders after the signature of the treaty, Brezhnev was quite explicit: 'At the present complex time when the policies of the Chinese leadership have created considerable difficulties for the socialist construction in the land of Vietnam, the strength of our friendship and the strength of the solidarity of the states of the socialist community are of special significance'. BBC *Summary of World Broadcasts* (SWB), SU/5961/A3/5.

11. BBC *SWB*, SU/5961/A3/3.

12. BBC *SWB*, FE/6118/A3/1-2.

13. BBC *SWB*, SU/5961/A3/3. Note the corresponding similarity between this article and article nine of the Soviet–Indian Treaty of 9th August 1971, reprinted in Robert Jackson, *South Asian Crisis* (London: Chatto and Windus, 1975). p.188.

14. BBC *SWB*, FE/6051/A2/1.

15. See Kuznetsov in Bangkok Post, 2 December 1978 and 5 June 1979: Pham Van Dong Statement (24 May 1979) in BBC *SWB*, FE/6127/A3/5. The Soviet Government confirmed that its warships were using the facilities of Cam Ranh Bay under the terms of its treaty of friendship with Vietnam on 4 May 1979. See *International Herald Tribune*, 15 May 1979.

16. For a consideration of Indonesia's maritime initiatives, see Michael Leifer, *Malacca, Singapore and Indonesia* (vol.II, International Straits of the World). (Netherlands: Sijthoff & Noordhoff, 1978).

17. See P.D. Borabolya *et al, Manual of International Law*, Part I. (Moscow: Military Publishing House of Ministry of Defence, 1966). (Translated by Department of Navy, Washington, D.C., June 1968). p.155.

18. *The Straits Times*, 17 July 1970.

8 The Soviet Union and Africa: How Great a Change?

James Mayall

It is wisest to begin with a confession of ignorance. The experts have not contributed much to our understanding of the Soviet Union's relations with Africa. No one foresaw Soviet intervention in Angola, at least on the scale that occurred. By way of compensation after the Soviet intervention in the Ethiopian/Somali conflict in 1977/8, most Western observers have spent their time watching nervously to see where next in Africa Soviet power would be projected. One reason for this lack of analytical confidence may be that the forensic problems which are associated with the analysis of Soviet intentions anywhere are compounded in sub-Saharan Africa by the lack of any obvious historical, geo-political or economic foundation on which Soviet policy can be seen to rest *regardless* of ideological considerations. Of course, such considerations must affect any assessment of Soviet intentions but since the Soviet Union, no less than any other power, must accommodate principle to contingency, it is relatively easier (or at least less obviously risky) to analyse Soviet policies in terms of the external pattern of restraints and rivalries than to rely primarily on an interpretation of the Soviet commitment to world communism and national liberation, or the complex workings of the Soviet bureaucracy. Soviet policy along the Northern Tier, that is roughly from the Middle East through to Afghanistan, and even in South-East Asia, in this sense has a geo-political, strategic and historical depth which is lacking in Africa. In the strategic competition of the major powers, Africa remains something of a footnote.

THE RANGE OF THE DEBATE

Against this background, the analysis of Soviet African policy has
never been successfully divorced from the history of the Soviet ideological commitment to world revolution. The two main views which
have battled for supremacy differ in the relative weight accorded to the
broad strategy which Soviet governments are held to be pursuing and
to the tactical adjustments which they make in their relations with
particular countries and at particular times. On the first view, which
appears to have regained the ascendancy since 1975, the objective of
Soviet policy is unambiguous and maximalist; it is to overthrow the
world capitalist system and pave the way for its replacement by an
international community of socialist states under the leadership of the
Soviet Union. The need for tactical flexibility in pursuing this objective
was recognised as early as July 1920 when Lenin persuaded the second
Congress of the Comintern to oppose Western capitalism through its
colonial rear, that is by a policy of support for revolutionary movements of liberation carried on by both the bourgeoisie and the
peasantry.

   If Africa did not feel the full impact of subsequent reversals of this
policy and the encouragement of active Communist-led revolution,
this was largely because the European imperial powers did everything
possible to isolate their African colonies from Soviet influence and to
transfer power to nationalist *elites* who shared their own suspicion of
communism. They were helped in this endeavour by the fact that in
most African territories the social relations of production had given
rise neither to an indigenous nationalist bourgeoisie nor to a landless
peasantry as both these social groups were conceived within orthodox
Marxist theory. Presumably for this reason the French Communist
party, which did have ties with French-speaking African nationalist
movements, opposed independence in the early post-war period. Consequently at independence, the Soviet Union could do little but compete for marginal advantages with the Western powers, whose
influence in their former African colonies remained overwhelming.
The competition was conducted through the provision of aid, diplomatic support at the United Nations on anti-colonial issues and by
'seed bed' policies of technical assistance and educational training in
the Soviet Union. But after fifteen years of independence, it can be
argued, these policies are beginning to bear fruit, not least because the
long struggle against the Portuguese in Mozambique, Angola and
Guinea-Bissau has brought to power genuinely radicalised *regimes*,

and because the revolution in Ethiopia occurred in the one African country where the *ancien regime* could be described, without a total distortion of the facts, as feudal.

In the last four years the political map has been substantially altered; for while there are still some dubious and self-styled 'radical' *regimes* such as Benin and Congo (Brazzaville), the Soviet Union now has long-term treaties of friendship and co-operation with Mozambique, Angola and Ethiopia in addition to its long-standing treaty with Guinea. All these countries are under the control of *regimes* which describe themselves as Marxist–Leninist, while with the MPLA in Angola there is also an inter-party agreement with the Communist Party of the Soviet Union (CPSU), on the face of it an additional public acknowledgement that the Russians recognise the legitimacy of this claim. For those who conceive of the Soviet Union as a power with a world mission (and it does not follow from this view that they will also hold that the Soviets have a preconceived strategic plan) the main danger from recent developments to both Africa and the West is the assumed permanence of the new dispensation. And it follows – or so the full sweep of the argument runs – that the case for backing even corrupt and tyrannical *regimes* such as that presided over by Mobutu in Zaire is that this policy does not betray future generations.

The second view, which dominated Western perceptions at least from the establishment of the Organisation for African Unity (OAU) in May 1963 to the Portuguese *coup* in April 1974, is less apocalyptic. It stemmed, on the one hand, from the belief that with the promulgation of the doctrine of peaceful co-existence at the twentieth Party Congress, the Soviet Union had finally abandoned any real, as distinct from symbolic, attachment to the historic goal of overthrowing capitalism and that it was now formally committed to playing the 'game of nations' as traditionally understood in the West; and, on the other, from the belief that this concession to 'realism' had been forced on the Soviet leadership as much by the necessity of co-existing with nationalism in the Third World as by the logic of nuclear stalemate. To be sure, between 1955–62 the new policy led to an intensification of ideological competition in the Third World as much as to a trial of strength and nerve in the central balance, but in Africa Khrushchev's policy of seeking non-communist allies, that is of concentrating Soviet aid and diplomatic effort on a few countries notably Guinea, Ghana and Mali, fairly quickly came unstuck. These relationships with *regimes* which it was said had chosen 'the non-capitalist road' lacked the geo-political underpinning which, for example, has secured India's relations with the Soviet Union since 1955, despite India's much deeper commitment to the doctrine of non-alignment and the presence within the Indian political culture of a much more coherent Marxist element, challenging first the Congress and latterly the Janata estab-lishments.

By contrast, in Africa, the Soviet position proved no stronger than the faction which they had chosen to support, and none of the 'Casablanca radicals' proved a stable ally. Guinea, whose government under Sékou-Touré has survived and which maintains its treaty with the Soviet Union, nonetheless expelled the first Soviet ambassador for interfering in Guinea's domestic affairs, and in neither Ghana nor Mali did the Soviet special relationship survive the military overthrow of the two leaders, Kwame Nkrumah and Mobito Keita. Under the impact of these reverses, a more conventional and pragmatic Soviet policy emerged in the mid 1960s. During the Nigerian civil war (1967–70), when the Soviet Union and Britain together acted as the major external backers of the Federal government, ideological rivalry was not a genuine issue.[1] Nigeria was, in any case, a most unlikely candi-date for the 'non-capitalist' road so that Moscow had no alternative but to confine itself to modest diplomatic and commercial gains while the United States looked on unmoved.[2]

Those who hold to this second minimalist view do not contest that with the Angolan crisis a new element was introduced into Soviet African policy, namely its willingness to use force in support of an ally. But three kinds of arguments can be advanced to question the signi-ficance of this change. First, in the case of the Portuguese colonies it has been suggested that the major influence on Soviet decision making was the need to combat Chinese influence with the liberation move-ments. The MPLA victory in Angola dramatically turned the tables on China and there have been repeated reports of Soviet gains at the Chinese expense in Mozambique also. Having secured these limited objectives, so the argument runs, the Soviet Union is likely to return to its traditionally cautious policy in an area where its real interests are minimal rather than to pursue further gains where Western interests are prominently entrenched.

The second minimalist argument seeks to draw a geo-political distinction between Soviet policy in the Horn and in Southern Africa. Soviet policy in Ethiopia and Somalia, on this argument, is properly viewed in the context of the Middle East, Red Sea and Northern Tier confrontation with the West and with China, areas in which the Soviet Union does have historical security, geo-political, and even economic interests and where, since their expulsion from Egypt in July 1972, they have sought to make compensating gains. But the fact that the Soviet Union went quietly, albeit under protest, from both Egypt and Somalia, with both of whom Moscow had treaty relations, strongly suggests that the Soviet connection is not proofed against Afro-Arab nationalism, and that there is no reason to believe, therefore, that the same will not hold also in Southern Africa where there is not the same geo-political urgency.

Finally, the same conclusion may be drawn from a consideration of the external economic relations of the African states. For not only has the Soviet Union not directly challenged the status quo in any independent African country where major Western interests are heavily entrenched, but Soviet support for the former Portuguese colonies has failed to make a significant impact on their involvement in the Western international economy. In such circumstances, whether any future domestic political change would be prevented under the Brezhnev doctrine must remain extremely doubtful

THE IMPACT OF THE AFRICAN DIPLOMATIC SYSTEM ON SOVIET POLICY

We shall return to a more detailed consideration of these arguments in the final section of this paper but, from this broad outline of the current debate, there is an obvious and arguably all-important omission, namely the African view (or rather competing African views) of Soviet policy. And since, except on the most uncompromising structuralist analysis, it is the policies of African states, both singly and collectively, which set the limits of Soviet and Western initiatives, it is to these that we turn first.

The major tension between African states and the Western powers arises in connection with the all-African commitment to Southern African liberation. This is the one issue which is still capable of transcending the conflicts of interest and ideology amongst African *regimes*. It is also an issue on which they have always been able to rely on Soviet support and never on that of the West. As Ali Mazrui has put it 'temporary flirtations with the Communist world have been basically flirtations on the re-bound, a response to the fundamental cleavage between the colonised African and the colonising Westerner'.[3] Of course such flirtations have not been without their risks, but so long as the West was not prepared to bring effective pressure to bear upon

Portugal to de-colonise, on the Smith *regime* in Rhodesia to abandon its rebellion, and not only refused to take action against South Africa under Chapter 7 of the United Nations Charter but used the veto in her defence, even the most anti-communist *regimes* such as those in the Ivory Coast or Senegal have been forced to acknowledge that on this issue at least there is a convergence of Soviet and African interests.

The significance of this 'anti-colonial alliance' for Soviet policy is precisely that, until recently, such *regimes* were *forced* to acknowledge the convergence when, in most other respects, they viewed the Soviet Union with the deepest suspicion. Between 1960–3 the internecine feuding between African *regimes* was aggravated (although certainly not caused) by the introduction of extraneous ideological conflicts. When their neighbours accused Ghana under Kwame Nkrumah and Guinea under Sékou-Touré of subversion, they also indicated the Soviet Union which was believed to have provided the financial backing for their policies and the military training and hardware for the exiled politicians and their supporters who carried them out.

In this context the agreement to establish the OAU constituted a victory for the 'conservative' *regimes*, an ideological cease-fire under which they traded Pan-African sentiment for a public ban on subversion and political assassination.[4] Its establishment therefore introduced an indirect constraint on Soviet policy; for while OAU members were formally bound (for what it was worth) to pursue policies of non-alignment, this could no longer be interpreted as legitimising policies aimed at overthrowing 'neo-colonial' neighbours: all manner of *regimes* conservative and radical, military and civilian, were now to be judged equally Pan-African. It followed that any attempt to establish a bridgehead for wider Soviet influence by concentrating on a few states which had opted for 'non-capitalist road' would run into difficulties even if their governments proved stable.

Most probably, by 1963, the Soviet leaders were ready to discard this policy in any case. Certainly, like their major adversaries, they were quick to welcome the establishment of the OAU and to endorse its major objectives: the sovereignty and territorial integrity of African states, the peaceful settlement of African conflicts and the elimination of colonialism and racism. It is also probably true that those groups within Africa, the Lumumbists in the Congo for example, who had previously looked to the Soviet Union for support, had exaggerated both its ability and willingness to provide assistance on the scale they had expected.[5] But in so far as the creation of the OAU represented a victory for the traditional western principles of state-craft, it reduced the opportunities to the Soviet Union (or any other power) to pursue 'ideological' foreign policies. After 1963 the activities of the front organisations, the AAPSO for example, became much less important in African diplomacy. This was partly because their meetings were increasingly dominated by Sino/Soviet rivalry, which many African leaders regarded as an unnecessary complication in the difficult task of maintaining solidarity against the remaining outposts of white supremacy, and partly because after independence the state every-where became more important than the party, and governments pre-ferred to concentrate foreign relations in their own hands and to deal with the Soviet Union, on a bi-lateral state-to-state basis.

For the most part the Soviet Government accepted these constraints on its policies with good grace. From the mid-1960s, as Roger Kanet has argued, the Soviet leaders ceased to pay close attention to any theoretical analysis of the African situation and were instead guided by the strategic and economic interests of the Soviet state. [6] As a conse-quence of this new pragmatism, the Soviet Union was now prepared in principle to establish correct diplomatic relations with all states: by 1971 they had relations with 32 out of the then 41 African states, and as their interests have diversified their diplomatic representation has been extended; in 1978 for example Ambassadors were appointed to Botswana and Djibouti, possibly the two most pro-Western govern-ments in their respective regions. But while their policy may have become increasingly opportunistic, they have been consistently careful not to put themselves 'off-side' in terms of the 1963 settlement. In the conflict in the Western Sahara between Algeria and Morocco, the evidence suggests that while the Americans made it clear to King Hassan that they wanted an OAU solution and would not back a Moroccan appeal to the Security Council, the Russians restrained Algeria, at least to the extent of slowing up the supply of arms. Similarly, although the Soviet Union already had considerable influence with the Somalis as a result of the 1963 arms deal, there is no reliable evidence that Moscow ever encouraged Mogadishu in its irredentist ambitions.

But, if the Soviet authorities were constrained from pursuing an interventionist policy, conservative African *regimes* could not but welcome Soviet support in the liberation struggle, since the OAU Charter contained a balancing commitment to eliminate colonial and white supremacist rule throughout Africa. The Soviet Union had always supported this objective at the United Nations (for example, the General Assembly's resolution 1514 calling for an immediate end to colonialism had been inspired by a Soviet initiative at the 1960 session) and continued to do so. Moreover, unlike the Western powers, they made it clear also that they supported the new element in this commitment, namely its extension to cover all forms of confront-ation including armed struggle.

It is doubtful whether the comprehensive nature of the OAU liberation strategy (that is the combination of both diplomatic and military pressure) ever commanded the full support of the more con-servative *regimes*, who feared that its methods could be turned against themselves;[7] but there was little that they could do about it. The proposal by President Houphouet-Boigny of the Ivory Coast in 1971 that the OAU should adopt different, and more conciliatory, policies toward the white South, threatened the precarious solidarity on which the organisation depended, and was abandoned for that reason. The countries which were in favour of the change – the Ivory Coast and its allies in the Entente Council, Lesotho, Swaziland, Malawi, Madagascar and more equivocally Ghana – were all strongly anti-communist, but even so several of them flinched from opposing the majority opinion when the matter was debated by the Council of Ministers.[8] In a material sense, of course, the issue was academic before 1974; the liberation movements had made little visible impact on the structure of white power and there was no immediate threat of any Soviet backed challenge to the leadership in any of the countries north of the Zambezi. In such circumstances there was little to be gained from re-opening the ideological conflict. Nonetheless, the 'dialogue' episode clearly foreshadowed the radicalisation of OAU liberation strategy after 1974, and the relative ease with which the MPLA Government in Angola was able to legitimise its dependence on Soviet and Cuban support.

In one respect, Soviet and African policies on liberation diverged, although in the face of their shared anti-colonialism, it never became a major issue of contention. This was the Soviet refusal to channel its military assistance to the liberation movements through the African Liberation Committee (ALC), which had been set up in 1963 with the dual function of mobilising financial and material support for them and resolving the bitter conflict between rival factions in most of the territories still under colonial rule. But the monopoly over resources, on which this policy depended, never materialised: the movements resented being demoted to mere observers within the OAU structure and refused to give up the external relationships which they had already developed; the financial support provided by the independent

African states, although mandatory under the Charter, was sporadic, came from a few states only and in any case represented only a fraction of what was required. With most African *regimes* in default with their payments, the ALC could hardly complain about Soviet practice. And in fact the ALC soon abandoned its original tactic of granting official recognition to particular movements as an incentive for reconciliation.

Had the ALC resolved its internal difficulties and succeeded in asserting its authority, both the Soviet Union and China might possibly have been persuaded to take it more seriously. But since the two Communist powers (and between them they accounted for more than 40 per cent of the equipment supplied to the liberation movement) were engaged in a competition to establish their revolutionary credentials it seems a very doubtful possibility. By 1969, this competition was so intense that when the Soviet Union sponsored a conference of Liberation Movements in Khartoum, both China and its client organisations were excluded.[9]

CHANGE AND CONTINUITY IN SOVIET–AFRICAN POLICY

Although the scale of Soviet intervention in Angola and the Horn cannot be explained simply in terms of either the historic Soviet commitment to African liberation or Sino/Soviet competition, these aspects have deliberately been emphasised to underline the element of continuity in Soviet policy and, in African eyes, the legitimacy which it enjoys. On the fundamental question of confrontation in Southern Africa, just as on the fundamental question of territorial integrity in the Horn, the Soviet Union has never departed from the official OAU line. One consequence of having legitimised its African policies in this way is that the West has no secure diplomatic ground on which to build a counter strategy. For example, when President Carter visited Nigeria in March 1978, he was subjected to strong pressure from his hosts over US policy towards Southern Africa, but failed to secure the Nigerian condemnation of Soviet and Cuban intervention in Africa which he sought.[10] After the second Shaba crisis, the problem of external intervention dominated the agenda of the OAU Summit in July 1978. On this occasion General Obansango, the Nigerian Head of State, appealed to the USSR not to overstay their welcome but was careful to balance this request with appeal for Western restraint. And although the Assembly passed a compromise resolution on neo-colonialism, and foreign military intervention, which condemned 'the policy of force and intervention in Africa regardless of its source', it also reaffirmed 'the right of every African people to choose the political system it deemed best', which left matters much as they were before. Indeed, it would be difficult to quarrel with *Pravda's* assessment that the attempt by 'conservative' African *regimes* and their 'imperialist' patrons to use the OAU 'to cast shadow on the relations between African countries and the nations of Soviet Socialist community', had failed.[11]

Yet, if in one respect the abandonment of the search for ideological allies has helped to gain a broader base of support for Soviet policies, in another way the new Soviet pragmatism has paradoxically helped to undermine the ideological ceasefire on which the OAU settlement was based. After 1963, Soviet policy towards the Third World appeared to be guided by three sets of considerations: first, the actual or potential strategic importance of a country to the Soviet Union; second, its economic importance as a market for Soviet manufactures (including arms) and a source of raw materials: and third, the possibility of gaining influence at a rival's expense when there was no significant economic or security danger to the Soviet state. But once the state interests of the USSR were accepted as the major criterion for policy, any domestic ideological constraints were correspondingly weakened. And what no doubt appeared as pragmatic opportunism to the Soviet leaders was viewed in Africa in terms of fraternal support or ideological threat. In attempting to weigh the extent of the changes brought about by this unleashed pragmatism, let us return to the three arguments referred to at the beginning of this paper.

(1) *Strategic and military considerations in Soviet–African policy*

The pursuit of a forward policy in Africa has generally been viewed as a consequence of the Soviet determination to compete with the United States, not merely as a nuclear power, but also in terms of its global intervention capabilities. The expansion of Soviet naval activities in the Indian Ocean since the mid 1960s, the development of compensatory ties with *regimes* in the Middle East, North and North-East Africa following the Soviet expulsion from Egypt in July 1972, and the acquisition of 'mobile armed forces appropriately trained and equipped' for 'the task of averting local wars' and supporting 'peoples fighting for their freedom and independence against the forces of internal reaction and imperialist intervention' are all expression of this new emphasis on Soviet Third World Policy.[12]

The implications of these developments for Africa cannot easily be disentangled although, except in the Horn, it is arguable that the naval expansion has so far had the least general impact. One of the advantages of the alliance with Somalia, which developed rapidly after the 1974 treaty, was the maritime facilities which the Soviet Union gained: a base for fleet units at Berbera, an airbase near Mogadishu and a communications base at Kismayu for the control of Soviet submarines in the Indian Ocean. But their loss following Somalia's abrogation of the treaty in November 1977, while no doubt inconvenient, does not seem to have seriously weakened the Soviet position. The airlift into Ethiopia was handled from Aden, and in the long run the facilities at Berbera are likely to be replaced by others at Massawa and Assab. In any case, they were presumably judged expendable when the Soviet authorities decided on an all-out policy of support for the Ethiopian Derg which was bound to put their relationship with Somalia at risk.

The argument, much favoured by both the South African and Chinese governments, that the Soviet intervention in Angola (and to a lesser extent the increasing Soviet support for Mozambique) is to be explained as part of a determined geo-political drive to gain control of the West's strategic sea-ways, is also unconvincing. No doubt the Soviet authorities would welcome such control could it be achieved, but apart from the technical problems for any policy of interference with Western shipping around the Cape, the Soviet Navy is itself vulnerable to counter attacks elsewhere. Moreover, despite the deterioration of superpower relations, it is still difficult to envisage the kind of crisis in which the Soviet Union could directly challenge vital Western oil supplies without risking a much more general confrontation. Obviously the Soviet presence in the Indian Ocean and Southern Africa is facilitated by good relations with the littoral states. But even assuming a major East–West crisis it is not clear that Soviet naval facilities in Mozambique and Angola (and at present, in a formal sense, these do not exist) would be a material factor.

Finally, on the strategic level, the Soviet Union has appeared anxious to engage in negotiations with the United States, aimed at an Indian Ocean Arms Control agreement. In January 1978 they even announced that such an agreement need not require the dismantling of existing superpower bases (their previous position) but merely an undertaking not to acquire new facilities. Since then the talks have been stalled but not because of a change in the Soviet position; rather the United States has become increasingly disenchanted with the concept of Indian Ocean arms control following what they regard as the lack of restraint displayed by the Russians in Ethiopia.

To the extent that there is a single trigger to the projection of Soviet military power into Africa, it is more likely to be found in the Egyptian expulsion of Soviet experts in July 1972 than in the search for distant anchorages. In the wake of that reverse in an area where the Soviets had been deeply involved since 1955, they moved quickly to repair the damage. Although they were presumably concerned primarily with their strategic position in the Middle East, their reliance on military aid agreements as the main vehicle for securing Soviet influence, increasingly spread to Africa as well. After France, which in the early 1970s provided over half of the annual arms transfers to African *regimes*, the Soviet Union is currently the second major supplier with about 12 per cent of the total African market, not counting direct shipments to the liberation movements. [13]

There are no doubt various motives in Soviet arms exports. It has been suggested that the pattern of sales has more to do with the domestic politics of resource allocations for arms production in the Soviet Union than with the pattern of external crises. [14] Be that as it may, once Egypt was 'lost', the Soviet authorities concentrated on strengthening their military relationship with Algeria and with Libya which, under a Military Assistance Agreement in 1974, emerged as the main recipient of Soviet military aid after Iraq. Since Colonel Qadaffi pursues an active foreign policy in Africa as well as the Middle East (for example in Chad and Uganda) the Soviet policy of Middle Eastern diversification began to spread indirectly further afield.

For the most part the Russians have been fairly successful in finding alternative outlets for their arms. Until 1975 over half of all Soviet military aid (US $205 million) to countries south of the Sahara went to the Sudan and Somalia. The loss of Somalia in 1977 was compensated for by the new military relationship with Ethiopia, while the Sudan's earlier break with the Soviet Union had been partially retrieved by the improbable policy of military backing for Amin's *regime* in Uganda which was abandoned only when his fall seemed inevitable. More significant, however, was the new demand for conventional military hardware as distinct from the small arms on which they had relied during the guerrilla struggle, from the independent governments of Angola and Mozambique.

To the extent that more is involved than the opportunistic acquisition of outlets for Soviet exports of military equipment, the dis-advantage, from the Soviet point of view, of a policy based primarily on the provision of military aid and training has been its volatility. Hence the increasing emphasis in Soviet military thinking on the development of mobile intervention forces. If the Soviet authorities were to support 'progressive' *regimes* they would need to be proofed against the kind of fate that had overcome the governments which opted for 'the non-capitalist road' in the early 1960s. In this context, it is probably correct to perceive Soviet policy in the Horn as a continuation of their intervention in Angola. The point is not that it provides evidence of a closely co-ordinated geo-political plan, which has replaced the *ad-hoc* opportunism of earlier years: even now and assuming that Cuban capabilities could be stretched to take on an additional commitment in Rhodesia or Namibia, it is not at all clear that the Soviet Union would consider this a risk worth taking. The point is that twice in quick succession the Russians have demonstrated that they *can* intervene effectively at long distance and in operations of considerable technical and logistical complexity. To that extent, the credibility of the Friendship Treaties (and they preserve these for *regimes* with which their relations are particularly close) was clearly strengthened. In a continent where few governments feel secure, this demonstration effect is unlikely to have gone unnoticed.

(2) *The new foreign economic policy*

A more assertive economic policy towards the Third World has been developing since the beginning of the decade. The imprimatur of orthodoxy was accorded to the new line at the CPSU Congress in 1976 when Premier Kosygin confirmed the policy first announced five years previously, under which the Soviet Union has sought to establish with the developing countries 'a stable division of labour counterposed to the system of imperialist exploitation'. The countries which were singled out for special mention in connection with this policy, India, Afghanistan, Iran, Pakistan, the UAR, Syria, Iraq and Algeria, were not selected because they had opted for 'the non-capitalist road' but because of their strategic and political interests to the Soviet Union and more particularly because through the expansion of trade the 'Soviet Union will receive the opportunity to satisfy the requirements of its own economy more fully'. As Richard Loewenthal has argued, the public announcement of this policy represented 'a distinct shift from old style anti-imperialism to a new concept that can best be described as 'counter imperialism': a strategy of fighting Western imperialism by using the familiar 'imperialist' methods of establishing zones of political and economic influence linked to the Soviet Union by firm ties'.[15]

There is an obvious problem in applying this line of argument to the new Soviet policy in Africa. Although it seems likely that a re-assessment of Khrushchev's African adventures contributed to the new thinking (Egypt, Ghana and Mali all rescheduled their debts to the Soviet Union in the mid-1960s), no sub-Saharan African state and only two countries on the African continent, Egypt and Algeria, were included in the original list of mainly state capitalist countries favoured by the Russians. Of these, Egypt broke out of the 'reserved area of Soviet power' in July 1972, although it continues to trade substantially with the centrally planned economies. Indeed of all the African coun-tries only Egypt conducts more than 30 per cent of its trade with the Soviet Union (Imports 37.4 per cent: Exports 30.6 per cent) after which only Mali gets into double figures (14.1 per cent and 11.8 per cent respectively). Of the remaining states with a sizeable stake in trade with the Soviet Union, the figures range from 5–6 per cent for Morocco and Algeria down to Nigeria and Ghana between 2–4 per cent.

Of course, percentage figures do not tell the whole story, and there is certainly an increasing number of mutually advantageous trading agreements with African countries: for example, in recent years the Soviet Union has been the largest market for Egyptian and Ugandan cotton and it has been an important market for Ghana's cocoa and to a lesser extent for Nigeria's: not least because by taking supplies off the Western market during periods of surplus such sales can exercise an upward pressure on the free market price. Fishing agreements of various kinds have been concluded with several African countries, including Angola and Mozambique. There are also a growing number of joint enterprises such as the construction in Guinea of a bauxite mining enterprise to be paid for by annual exports of 2 million tons for 30 years and a similar arrangement negotiated during 1976 with Algeria (bauxite is one of the few raw materials in which the Soviet Union is not self-sufficient), or the various joint marketing companies such as those in Nigeria, Ethiopia and Morocco which market Soviet trucks and cars. But, overall, the figures illustrate the intractability of established trading patterns except under conditions of quite literally revolutionary change.

It may reasonably be objected that since the Soviet treaties of friendship and co-operation with Angola and Mozambique were negotiated in 1976 and 1977 respectively, and are to run for 20 years, it is plainly too early to predict with any confidence their long term economic yield. But the World Bank's figures of their current trade with the centrally planned economies (less than 1 per cent of merchandise exports for Mozambique and a fall from 2–1 per cent for Angola between 1970–6) hardly suggests a very dramatic restructuring of either countries' trade.[16]

For both Mozambique and Angola, their traditional role within the Southern African economic system also militates against any rapid or wholesale realignment; Mozambique's dependence on South Africa has even increased since independence despite political tensions, with the Republic replacing Portugal as the country's main trading partner. The Frelimo Government has continued to encourage South African use of its rail and port facilities in Maputo and has supplied electricity from the Cabora Bassa Dam to the South African grid. In Angola's case, not only is the revenue from the Benguela railway a powerful incentive for normalisation of its economic relations with Zaire and Zambia, but the bulk of Angolan foreign exchange earnings are accounted for by Gulf Oil's exploitation of the Cabinda oil field. Ethiopia, whose trade has undergone a modest reorientation towards the centrally planned economies, 1.3 per cent,[17] seems at first sight a more likely candidate for economic satellite status, but then Ethiopia, like Mozambique, is one of the world's poorest countries and lacks the resource base to which the Soviet Union might look in the future for the satisfaction of its own needs.

It is, of course, possible to argue that a position of influence even in peripheral countries may help to alleviate some of the Soviet Union's own problems in its economic relations with the Western powers, while protecting its position against future shortages of raw materials. There are, (or so it is claimed), precedents: in 1973, it was rumoured that the Russians had advised OPEC countries to use 'the oil weapon' for two reasons unconnected with the Middle East crisis. One was the Soviet need for foreign exchange, the other the underpricing of Soviet oil supplied to Eastern Europe. The quadrupling of oil prices allowed the Russians to reap windfall profits from its sales in the open market and to revise upwards the price of their oil exports to their Socialist trading partners. As a potential supplier of many other raw materials at the margin, the Soviet Union stands to gain at the West's expense from any general improvement in the developing countries' terms of trade; and as the major supplier of other *bloc* countries at present, the Soviet Union is bound to welcome special relations with raw material producing countries such as Mozambique and Angola, against the day when its own domestic demands will leave little over for the rest of the Socialist Commonwealth. As yet, however, there is little evidence to support such forensic arguments and it is difficult to avoid the conclusion that, for the most part, Africa remains an area of only marginal economic interest to the Soviet government.

(3) *The balance of power and the international competition for influence*

No account of Soviet–African policies would be complete which did not pay some attention to the element of pure competition in Soviet relations with both the United States and China. If there is one persistent theme in Soviet relations with African countries since the fall of Khrushchev, it is that the Russian leaders have always proceeded cautiously, but have seldom missed an opportunity of pressing their advantage when they could do so without risk. Thus, in the Nigerian Civil War, they overcame their scruples about the reactionary nature of the Federal Government once it became clear, not only that they would be supporting the OAU majority, but that the Americans would not become involved.[18] More than a decade of influence in Somalia followed the Western refusal to arm the Somali *regime* on the scale demanded; close relations with Algeria stemmed from Soviet support for the FLN during the struggle against France, while the more volatile relationships with Libya and the Sudan were in the first instance a response to developments within these countries. Unless, following Dr. Kissinger, one credits the Soviet Union with having deliberately encouraged the second Shaba crisis,[19] even now there is no case where the Soviet Union has directly challenged a position of entrenched Western interest. And there is only one case – Angola in 1975 – where they have directly challenged an OAU policy.

   Given this tradition of cautious opportunism, it seems likely that the recent assertion of Soviet power in Africa is as much a reflection of Western, particularly American, weakness and indecision as of Soviet design. The support for the liberation movements was perfectly in keeping with this tradition. Since the Western powers were not competing for the patronage, the Soviet authorities were able to ingratiate themselves with the movements at very low cost (military aid to Angola between 1964–75 has been estimated at only US $54 million compared with over US $200 million in 1975–6) and at virtually no risk at all. The Russians would have supported the successor governments to the Portuguese in Mozambique, Angola and Guinea-Bissau in any case, but, as the trade statistics reveal, this did not have to involve any significant outlays either.

It seems reasonable to presume, therefore, that Angola was made a test case because the circumstances were favourable. Three reasons suggest themselves; first, the balance of restraint on superpower intervention generally had shifted dramatically since 1973; second, in terms of both African opinion and their Cuban alliance, the Russians were in an intrinsically stronger position than the Western powers; and third, once it had become clear that the basis of a coalition government in Angola did not exist, Moscow had a clear prestige interest in preventing victory passing to the movements which enjoyed Chinese support. Indeed it has been argued that there was some initial opposition to the Angolan intervention from elements in the Soviet Defence and Foreign Ministries on the grounds that it threatened *detente* and might prove too expensive; but that the Russians finally took a decision in the Autumn of 1974 to increase assistance to the MPLA and prepare contingency plans (which could be activated or not depending on Western reactions) in response to increased Chinese support for the FNLA.[20]

Whether this is an accurate assessment of Soviet motives, we cannot know. But it is certainly true that, ever since the border clashes between the Soviet Union and China in 1969, the Chinese have never lost an opportunity to advance the thesis that the Soviet Union now represents the most serious imperialist threat to world peace and the independence of Third World states. In this context, their influence with African governments was bound to be viewed with distaste in Moscow. And in 1974, Chinese standing in Africa was still high. After President Nixon's overtures to Peking, the African states had played a significant, if formal, part in voting China into the United Nations, while the Chinese leaders were encouraging African governments in their relations with the EEC, on the grounds that these represented a case of co-operation against hegemonism.

Quite apart from the disturbing prospect of Western collusion with the Chinese, there are two further reasons why the Soviet authorities may have wanted to curb Chinese influence. The first is simply that, while the Soviet Union had backed the more established liberation movements, until 1974 China's African diplomacy was more visible and more dramatic. This was partly because of the success of the Tanzam Railway (its construction, not operation) which was represented as simultaneously a contribution to the liberation struggle and a practical demonstration of the Chinese theory of collective self-reliance; and partly because Chinese theories of guerrilla warfare and peasant revolution were said to be favoured by the Frelimo and PAIGC leaderships in Mozambique and Guinea-Bissau, where the two relatively more successful campaigns against the Portuguese had been waged.

The second consideration is more general. As Marxist–Leninist states, both the Soviet Union and China habitually defend their policies in the language of Marxism and in the name of Marxist orthodoxy. This language has a deep appeal to Third World students and intellectuals who, as Ernest Gellner has put it, 'speak Marxism as automatically and self-evidently as they speak prose . . . They do so because it is the most easily available, optimally orchestrated theory which accounts for the visible, luminous illegitimacy of the old order. Moreover, it simultaneously explains both the necessity and the immorality of the impact of more advanced countries'.[21] No matter that once in power African intellectuals frequently shed their Marxist categories even more readily than the Soviet or Chinese leaders themselves (or alternatively employ them in a shamelessly populist manner), this vast external constituency no doubt helps to legitimise the Soviet leadership, at least in its own eyes, and is unlikely for that reason to be surrendered quietly to a schismatic rival.

NOTES

1. Except in Britain where the threat of Soviet influence was used by the Government to justify its policy of support for the Federal Government and to contain the Biafra lobby.
2. See John J. Stremlau, *The International Politics of the Nigerian Civil War, 1967–70,* (Princeton, 1977) Ch. 3.
3. Ali Mazrui, *Africa's International Relations* (London, 1978) p. 175.
4. Article III (IV) of the OAU Charter.
5. See Christopher Stevens, *The Soviet Union and Black Africa* (London, 1976) pp. 16–17.
6. Roger Kanet, *The Soviet Union and the Developing Nations* (Baltimore, 1974) pp. 27–51.
7. The Ghanaian National Liberation Council which deposed Nkrumah in 1966 claimed that he had been training 'freedom fighters' at the Winneba Ideological Institute from neighbouring West African countries as well as from the Portuguese colonies, Rhodesia and South Africa.
8. See Michael Wolfers, *Politics in the Organisation of African Unity,* (London, 1976) pp. 37–41.

9. Those present represented most of the leading movements, FRELIMO, MPLA, PAIGC, ZAPU, SWAPO, and the South African ANC. Although the Chinese had links with FRELIMO, and PAIGC, their clients were mostly the smaller 'breakaway' parties, FNLA, ZANU, SWANU and PAC.

10. *Africa Research Bulletin,* 1–30 April, 1978. p. 4833.

11. Ibid., 1–30 June, 1978. p. 4895.

12. V. M. Kulish (ed.), *Voyennaya sila i mezhdunarodnyye otnosheniya* (Moscow, 1972) p. 136, quoted in David L. Morrison, 'African policies of the USSR and China 1976', in Colin Legum (ed.), *Africa–Contemporary Record 1976–7.*

13. I.W. Zartman, 'Les Transfers d'Armements en Afrique', *Etudes Internationales,* (September, 1977). pp. 478–86.

14. Raymond Hutchings, 'Soviet Arms Exports to the Third World; a pattern and its implication', *World Today,* October, 1978. pp. 378–89.

15. R. Loewenthal, 'Model or Ally?' *The Communist Powers and the Developing Countries* (New York, 1977) pp. 359–376.

16. See Table B. *World Development Report, 1978* (Washington D.C.: World Bank, 1978) pp. 90–1.

17. Ibid. See also above, chapters 3 and 4, particularly pp. 85–8 and 137–54.

18. O.I. Natute, 'Soviet Policy towards African Regimes', *Survey,* Winter 1976. pp. 93–111.

19. See 'Dr Kissinger on World Affairs, An Interview', *Encounter,* February 1978.

20. Peter Vanneman and Martin James, 'The Soviet Intervention in Angola: Intentions and Implications', *Strategic Review,* Summer 1976.

21. Ernest Gellner, 'Plaidoyer pour une Liberalisation Manquee', *Government and Opposition,* Winter 1979, p. 61.

9 The Soviet Experience in the Horn of Africa

Christopher Clapham

THE REGIONAL SETTING

The massive military involvement of the Soviet Union and its allies in the local conflicts of North-East Africa raises immediate problems of analytical scale. On the one hand, one may view it from the level of the superpowers, as one particular ramification of a Soviet foreign policy which must be assessed in a global perspective. On the other, one may see it as an essentially regional conflict into which the Soviet Union happens to have wandered. Either of these angles, in casting light on some aspects of the subject, will inevitably cast shade on others, and some juxtaposition of the two is obviously required. Of the two, moreover, it is more useful to take the local viewpoint first, since the way that Soviet involvement has been received in the Horn of Africa, and its consequent successes and failures, has been critically affected by the internal politics of the region. It is only by embroiling themselves in local controversies that the Russians have been able to acquire any appreciable influence, and their position remains in important respects that of a prisoner of the local environment.

The Horn of Africa currently encompasses three independent states of very different size, resources and internal composition. The largest by far is Ethiopia, independent (with only a few very short breaks) since the earliest times, and with an ethnically, culturally and religiously heterogeneous population of some 29 million.[1] The Somali Republic, formed from the union at independence in 1960 of the former Italian Somalia and British Somaliland, has only about 3 million people, though by contrast with Ethiopia (and nearly every other independent African state) these almost all belong to a single ethnic group, the Somali, who, despite internal factional divisions, share a fierce sense of national and cultural identity. Finally, there is the minuscule Djibouti Republic, until 1977 a French colony (under the name first of the French Somali Coast, later the French Territory of the Afars and Issas), whose 110 000 population is divided roughly equally between Issa Somalis and the Afar of Danakil of the Red Sea coastal plain. The ramifications of international politics in the area extend frequently to the Sudan and Kenya, both of which include frontier peoples engaged in one way or another with conflicts in the Horn, and more distantly to the states of the Middle East on the one hand, and the rest of black Africa on the other.

The most important single feature of political life in the Horn is the intensity of the longstanding and ultimately irreconcilable conflicts between many of its peoples. It is worth emphasising, too, that these conflicts are fundamentally ones between peoples, and not simply between states, even though states will naturally articulate the values and goals of the dominant groups within them. Still less are they mere quarrels between *regimes*, and least of all disputes between secular ideologies, a point which the Russians have discovered to their cost. The most basic line of division is that between highlanders and lowlanders: between the Amhara and Tigrean peoples of the Ethiopian plateau and those of its lowland periphery. The plateau peoples are for the most part Orthodox Christians, with a traditional economy founded on arable agriculture which has given rise over the centuries to a society very markedly based on the twin principles of hierarchy and territory. In the past, both of these principles have been embodied in the Ethiopian Empire, a political institution which survived over a remarkably long period and was an empire, not simply in having an Emperor at the head of it, but also in the rights of territorial domination which it claimed over surrounding areas. The lowland periphery, dropping down to the Sudan plains, Red Sea, Gulf of Aden and Indian Ocean, is inhabited by peoples organised on very different principles: originally nomadic, almost all Islamic, and with few of the hierarchial political institutions so characteristic of the plateau.

This drastically simplified excursion into regional anthropology may seem a long way from the strategic preoccupations of the Soviet Union. In fact, the two are very closely linked. Though the last Emperor of Ethiopia was deposed in 1974, the attitudes which underlay the institution are as alive as ever, and most strikingly shown in the intense determination of the new military government to hold on to every inch of territory inherited from the previous *regime*. Despite the domestic upheavals which accompanied the change of government, and the switch in external alliances from the United States to the

Soviet Union, the *rationale* for Ethiopia's foreign and much of its domestic policy remains the maintenance of territory, and there has never been any suggestion that this goal might be subordinated either to the desirability of peaceful coexistence with socialist *regimes* and movements in the periphery, or to the immediate need to lessen external pressures while building a revolutionary *regime* at home. The Brest-Litovsk solution was ruled out both by the particular commitment which the military government, as soldiers, had to the inviolability of the frontiers, and to the disastrous effects which any territorial concessions were thought likely to have both on the insecure *regime*'s standing in the Ethiopian heartland and on the aspirations for autonomy of other peoples remaining within Ethiopia.

The hostility of the peripheral peoples towards Ethiopia's territorial pretensions has resulted in two main threats. The first of these, Somali nationalism, derives from the Somali desire to complete the work of unification started by the union of Somalia and British Somaliland in 1960, by bringing all Somalis within a single state.[2] Since a large number of Somalis – perhaps 1 500 000 – normally live within an area acquired by the Ethiopians in the late nineteenth century and now falling, to Ethiopian eyes, within the inviolable frontiers of Ethiopia, conflict between the two countries is inevitable and irreconcilable. Even if one government were compelled to accept a settlement favourable to the other, this would be likely to last only until it was overthrown or until the relative strengths of the two contestants had changed. Somali nationalism is also directed towards the incorporation of Somalis living in North-West Kenya, a fact which accounts for the continuing close alliance between Kenya and Ethiopia despite the differences in their internal *regimes* and other external connections, and in the Djibouti Republic. Even though Somalis account for only a small percentage of the populations of either Kenya or Ethiopia, they occupy a large proportion of their land areas: a full capitulation to Somali demands would result in Ethiopia losing some 20 per cent, and Kenya 35 per cent, of their respective territories. Somali governments have consistently demanded 'self-determination' for extra-territorial Somalis, assuming with some justice that were these given the chance to express their opinions they would opt for union with the Republic, but have been inhibited in the amount they have been prepared to do in practical terms to support this goal by the Republic's own weakness, the need to observe the conventions governing acceptable state behaviour in the international system, and the composition of the government itself, the desire for unification naturally being strongest among those clans whose own kinsmen straddle the frontier. The initiative in seeking to wrest the Somali-inhabited territories from Ethiopia has been taken since the late 1960s by an organisation named the Western Somali Liberation Front (WSLF), which has some autonomy from the Somali government, but which – unlike most of the other numerous liberation fronts in the region – appears to have no other ideology than a straightforward Somali nationalism.

The second main threat to Ethiopia, in Eritrea, is considerably more complex. The larger part of what is now Eritrea formed part of the Ethiopian Empire from the earliest times, and though the coastal regions were lost in the sixteenth century, the highland area with over half the total population remained in Ethiopian hands until taken over as an Italian colony in 1890.[3] Sufficient identification with Ethiopia remained in the highlands to secure a bare majority of support after the Second World War, when the Italian colonies were disposed of by the great powers and subsequently the United Nations, for reunification with Ethiopia within a federal system allowing considerable local autonomy. The Moslem peoples of the coastal plain and of western Eritrea were for the most part opposed to the merger, which took place in 1952. Few federal systems have survived in Africa, and this one was foredoomed by the imperial government's systematic attempts to undermine the autonomous regional administration, culminating in the incorporation of Eritrea as an ordinary province of the Empire in 1962. In the process, it alienated not only the Moslems but important elements in the Christian Eritrean highlands as well. A guerrilla organisation, the Eritrean Liberation Front (ELF), started operations in Western Eritrea in the mid-1960s, with support from radical Arab states including Syria, Iraq, and later Libya. By the time of Haile-Selassie's fall in 1974, it controlled most of lowland Eritrea outside the big towns, and was extending its operations to the highlands, having split meanwhile into three movements with differing ideological and ethnic orientations and sources of external support. After 1974, the various guerrilla movements extended control over the whole of Eritrea except a few garrison towns when the military government in Addis Ababa rejected possibilities of negotiation in favour of an all out, and in the short term disastrous, attack on the secessionists.

Further threats to the peace of the area come from other peoples within Ethiopia, including the Galla or Oromo, who constitute probably the largest ethnic group within the country, but who have lacked any coherent sense of identity or organisation through which to press a claim to political power;[4] it was plausibly reported during the Somali invasion of Ethiopia in 1977 that many of the attacks on Ethiopian government posts in areas far from those of Somali settlement were actually made by Oromo seizing the opportunity to be revenged on an alien government. There are also divisions within both highland and peripheral groups: in the highlands between Amhara and Tigrean peoples, and between rival provinces within the Amhara heartland, in the periphery between Somali clans, and between the Issa-Somalis and the Danakil-Afar who each comprise about half the population of the Djibouti Republic. And if that was not enough for this unhappy region, it has superimposed on it the conflicts resulting both in Somalia and especially in Ethiopia from the overthrow of an established political system by radical and ostensibly Marxist military *regimes*. At second remove, the Horn is also affected by disputes in neighbouring states, especially the long drawn out problem of the southern Sudan and the Arab–Israeli confrontation.

From the point of view of a superpower, seeking friends, satellites, or bases from which to exercise sea power in the southern Red Sea, Gulf of Aden, or North-West Indian Ocean, the Horn thus offers unrivalled opportunities for fishing in troubled waters. All of these competing states, groups and factions need financial and diplomatic support, and most importantly arms and military backing. These the superpowers are able to supply, subject to constraints arising from their own domestic economies and political systems, and from the need to avoid offending other potential allies; any superpower should consequently have little difficulty in finding local allies who will be ready to enrol themselves as its clients in exchange for the protection which the patron superpower can offer. The snag, for the superpower, is that its clients will have sought its protection in order to achieve objectives very different from its own, and though the two sets of objectives may be made to run in harness for years at a time, particularly when the client's regional enemies are in turn protected by a rival superpower, the client will be anxious to avoid subordinating itself so completely to its patron that it loses the ability to pursue its own goals, independently, should the need arise. Client status, too, is likely in time to arouse feelings of resentment against its protector on the part of the regional actor, particularly when the patron is seen to be demanding concessions which slight the client's national independence or reduce its freedom of action. When this resentment comes to a head, and the client perceives the superpower pursuing goals implicitly hostile to its own, then the former patron is likely to find itself being swiftly and acrimoniously ejected.

A further implication of the structure of conflict in the Horn is that it is virtually impossible for any single superpower to establish a complete hegemony over the region by any means short of an overwhelming military superiority, which enables it to eclipse all rival patrons and impose some kind of settlement on the local actors. In other words, increasing influence over one local actor will automatically result in driving its rivals into the arms of another superpower, while if a patron with one client seeks support from that client's enemies, it will inevitably incur suspicion and resentment which are likely to lead to a break.

THE HISTORY OF SOVIET INVOLVEMENT

Russia has had a longer standing interest in Ethiopia than in any other part of the African continent. Before 1917, this interest was stimulated by the attachment to Orthodox Christianity in both countries as well, even then, as by the possibilities of extending Russian influence in the southern Red Sea. Diplomatic relations were established in 1895, and a Russian hospital, later adopted by the Soviet government, was founded in Addis Ababa. Contacts with the Soviet *regime* date from the Second World War, but although Russia and Ethiopia were nominally allies, the Soviet Union attacked the imperial government in Ethiopia, and opposed the union with Ethiopia of the former Italian colonies of Eritrea and Somalia. During the late 1940s and 1950s, Ethiopia built up close relations with the United States, and contacts with the Soviet Union were limited to the minimum compatible with Haile-Selassie's instinctive desire to diversify his foreign contacts to the greatest possible extent, and avoid overdependence on any single foreign power. He visited Moscow in 1959, and exchanged state visits with other East European countries in the 1960s, but, in terms of ideological affinity, trading relationships and military supplies, Ethiopia under the imperial *regime* was clearly aligned with the west. United States military assistance was supplied from 1954, and by 1960 cumulative deliveries of American arms and military services amounted to $38m, almost all of it in the form of aid.[5] The United States continued to be Ethiopia's principal arms supplier throughout the 1960s, and Ethiopia accounted for over 80 per cent of the USA's military assistance spending in Sub-Saharan Africa during the 1960s and early 1970s.[6] The first opportunity for Soviet penetration of the region therefore occurred when Somali independence in 1960 created a new state which closely represented the desires of Somalis in Kenya and Ethiopia for incorporation into the Somali Republic. Since all of the major western powers – the United States in Ethiopia, Britain in Kenya, and France in the Djibouti enclave – had interests in preventing Somali territorial expansion, they could scarcely promise the Somali Republic military aid on a scale which would constitute a threat to her neighbours. When, in 1961–2, a group of western countries led by the United States offered the Somalis aid of some $10m to form an internal security force of 5000–6000 men, they were thus easily outbid by a Soviet offer to train an army of twice the size equipped with modern offensive weapons.

Throughout the 1960s, the pattern of alliances in the Horn was stable. In Ethiopia, Kenya and Djibouti, a dominant local political group, dedicated to maintaining the *status quo* in terms both of existing territorial boundaries and of domestic power structures, was allied to a powerful external patron each of which (the vagaries of Gaullist France notwithstanding) was broadly in alliance with the others. In opposition to these, a Soviet-supported Somali Republic articulated its desire for Somali unification but was entirely powerless to achieve it. From the Soviet viewpoint, the Somali Republic had only one advantage, its strategic location. Counteracting this were two major disadvantages. Firstly, the Republic was small and weak in terms alike of power, wealth and population, and stood only the most meagre chance of achieving the highly ambitious goals which it had set itself; unification could in practice be achieved only with a high level of external involvement and with a disastrous degree of fragmentation in Ethiopia and, preferably, Kenya. Secondly, it was the only African state actively to challenge the convention of respect for existing colonial frontiers on which the entire African state system was founded, and was consequently diplomatically isolated; this point is well illustrated by Ethiopian support for the Federal government during the Nigerian civil war, and by subsequent Nigerian opposition to any attempt to dismember any other African state.

However, other potential Soviet allies at the time were even more weakly placed. For all the claims of Soviet subversion which pro-western Third World governments are prone to make, the Soviet Union has in practice been extremely chary of dealing with anyone other than formally constituted governments. Though the Soviet Union tacitly supported the Eritrean guerrilla movements, especially as these became increasingly and articulately Marxist, this support was channelled through radical Arab states which also favoured the

Eritreans on their own account. Contacts were also maintained with opponents of the *regimes* in Ethiopia and Kenya, as often as not through diplomatic proxies such as Czechoslovakia, but these do not appear to have had any appreciable influence. In the Sudan, where a government broadly favourable to the Soviet Union was installed by a *coup* in May 1969, the Russians lost disastrously through their involvement in the abortive *coup* against the Nimaeiri *regime* two years later.

In Somalia, therefore, the Russians worked to cement their ties with their one reasonably close ally in the region. Their position was markedly enhanced after 1969, when a *coup* overthrew the government of Mohamed Haji Ibrahim Egal, an anglophil prime minister who had played down, as much as any Somali leader dared, the campaign for incorporation of the lost territories. There were certainly domestic reasons for the *coup*, but Russian military advisers were credited with an active role in it, and in any event the result was to bring to power the section of Somali society which had the closest connections with the Soviet Union. On the Somali side, the new *regime* of General Siyad Barre announced its adherence to 'scientific socialism' and portraits of Marx and Lenin were hung up in all government offices.[7] For the first two years after the *coup*, Somali arms imports remained stable, but from 1972 they increased dramatically. Throughout the period 1972–6, the Somali Republic received substantially greater arms supplies than Ethiopia, despite Ethiopia's much larger population and need to contain a serious guerrilla war in Eritrea; and in 1974 arms accounted for a staggering estimated 47 per cent of the Republic's total imports (see Table 9.1). On the Ethiopian side, the United States refused to supply further arms in response, and arms imports dropped fairly steadily from a high point in 1968 to a low in 1973, offering Somalia for the first time the possibility of combat superiority in tanks and aircraft over Ethiopia. Though the Soviet Union did not explicitly endorse the Somali aim of annexing the Somali-inhabited areas of Kenya and Ethiopia, it supplied the Somalis with weapons for which there was no other possible use, thus providing the means for a Somali invasion of Ethiopia and raising Somali expectations of Soviet diplomatic support. In exchange, the Russians gained base facilities at Berbera, opposite Aden, and at Kismayu, close to the Kenya frontier in the south; and after visits by important Soviet civil and military officials and the signature of a treaty of friendship with the USSR, the Somali Republic by the end of 1976 appeared to be the Soviet Union's most faithful African client. It was suggested, in view of KGB involvement in the security services and Russian operational control over the army, that the Republic might have crossed the line between a client and a satellite.[8]

TABLE 9.1 *Ethiopian and Somali arms imports, 1967–76*

	Ethiopia			Somali Repulic		
	Arms imports (millions of US dollars)	Arms imports (millions of US dollars at constant 1975 prices)	Arms imports (% of total imports by value)	Arms imports (millions of US dollars)	Arms imports (millions of US dollars at constant 1975 prices)	Arms imports (% of total imports by value)
1967	13	21	9	0	0	0
1968	19	29	11	4	6	8
1969	12	17	8	6	9	12
1970	13	18	8	7	10	16
1971	12	16	6	1	1	2
1972	13	16	7	19	24	25
1973	11	13	5	39	47	35
1974	15	16	5	61	66	47
1975	38	38	12	64	64	40
1976	48	46	na	53	51	na

SOURCE US Arms Control and Disarmament Agency, *World Military Expenditures and Arms Transfers 1967–1976* (Washington 1978) pp. 129, 148. This Table is based on information available to the U.S.A.C.D.A., which is likely to be fairly accurate for Ethiopia, which was supplied throughout the period chiefly by the United States and other Western countries, but may be liable to a larger margin of error for Somalia, which was exclusively supplied by the USSR and its allies; problems also arise in converting Soviet arms exports into US $ equivalents.

Meanwhile, the stability of alliances in the Horn had been drastically upset by the fall of the imperial government in Ethiopia in 1974. The reasons for that debacle do not concern us; they had little if anything to do with Ethiopia's foreign relations. Its main effects were two: the accession to power of radical military nationalist officers within the Ethiopian armed forces, and the loosening of the hold of the central government over the ethnically diverse and politically rebellious provinces. The soldiers who overthrew Haile-Selassie's *regime* were motivated chiefly by disgust for the immobilism and ineffectiveness of the government, and the venality of the ageing group of courtier-politicians who ran it. This disgust, as well as the readiness to resort to violence which has never been far beneath the surface of Ethiopian politics, was vividly expressed in the indiscriminate assassination by machine gun in November 1977 of fifty-two leading former civilian and military officials. The new rulers saw their enemies as 'feudalists' and 'reactionaries', terms which encompassed not only the Emperor and his entourage but also rural and urban landlords, the Coptic Church, obstructive (or merely bewildered) bureaucrats and, increasingly, anyone who for whatever reason stood in their way. At the same time, brought up as they were within the institutions of the central government and the traditions of Ethiopian nationalism, they opposed any attempt at separatism or devolution of central government power; one of their first victims was the first chairman of the Provisional Military Government, General Aman Andom, a popular Eritrean who favoured a negotiated settlement with the Eritrean guerrilla groups.[9]

The effect of the military takeover was an instant weakening of political ties with the United States. The Emperor had enjoyed good relations with American administrations dating back to Roosevelt, and was viewed as a major bulwark of the stability towards which America's African policy was directed; shock at his ignominious departure was followed by revulsion at the bloodletting indulged in by his successors. From the Provisional Military Government's viewpoint, the United States was a reactionary power which had for too long propped up Ethiopian feudalism. For two or three years, the two countries were nonetheless held together, despite themselves, by the coalition of interests built up over the previous three decades. The Americans desired both to salvage what they could from their connections with Ethiopia, and to avoid the loss of confidence among other client states which might result from their hasty abandonment of a long-time ally. The Ethiopians for their part were desperate for arms, and with the Russians entrenched more firmly than ever in Somalia and the Chinese in no position to compete, they had only the Western powers to turn to. Paradoxically therefore, United States military supplies to Ethiopia soared during the first three years of the military *regime* to a level never envisaged under the Emperor; from a mean of $11m a year between 1969 and 1974, military deliveries (excluding training) reached a value of $18.5m in 1974/5, $26m in 1975/6, and $79m in 1976/7.[10] This increase was entirely on a cash sale basis, military aid deliveries remaining fairly constant until 1975–6, after which they declined sharply. Even so, these shipments did not match the weaponry which the Soviet Union was pouring into Somalia, and were liable to be affected by American reactions to events in Ethiopia. Supplies were suspended for three months after the executions in November 1974, and in May 1976 the United States made it clear that arms shipments would be affected if Ethiopia proceeded with an intended human wave attack by peasant militia on the Eritrean guerrillas.[11] For the Ethiopian *regime*, therefore, the United States was a dubious ally which provided inadequate arms and that only at an unacceptable cost in interference with Ethiopian domestic policies.

THE REVERSAL OF ALLIANCES

It was at this moment, in early 1977, that Ethiopia started to transfer its international allegiance to the Soviet Union. The herald of the change was Fidel Castro, who in March 1977 visited both Somalia and Ethiopia, and sought to get both sides to agree to a Soviet backed peace settlement at a secret conference held in Aden. The terms of the proposed agreement have not been made public, but must at the very least – in order to be acceptable to the Derg – have included the formal maintenance of Ethiopian sovereignty over the disputed Somali-inhabited area in the South-East. The Somalis, more confident than ever at this time of their ability to achieve their longed-for unification, rejected the proposals. At this point, the prospects for resolving the conflict by peaceful negotiation were more favourable than at any time before or since. The two sides were fairly equal in military capabilities, the numerical and economic superiority of the Ethiopians being offset by internal divisions and rebellions and the poor quality of much of their equipment; they both had military *regimes* which claimed to be Marxist and revolutionary, and which might therefore have been expected to sympathise with one another's predicaments; and the dominant external presence in the area, that of the Soviet Union, was thrown behind a settlement which no other external power sought to oppose. That the *Pax Sovietica* never got off the ground shows clearly the intractability of the conflict and the limitations of great power intervention.

Having failed to produce an agreed settlement, the Russians were forced to take sides, or at least to behave towards one of the con-testants in a way which would be bound to prejudice their relations with the other. In effect, they opted for the Ethiopians, and did so very quickly, by promising to supply the aid and expertise, and especially the armaments, which would be necessary to enable the Derg to regain control over the large areas of the country which were effectively governed by opposition movements. First of all, the Ethiopians cleared the decks by expelling the American military mission in April 1977. In May, Mengistu Haile-Maryam paid the first of what was to become a steady stream of visits to Moscow. In June and July, Soviet military advisers started to arrive in Addis Ababa, in some cases tactlessly transferred there directly from Somalia. [12]

Seeing its long-term prospects slipping away, the Western Somalia Liberation Front launched its pre-emptive attack on the Ogaden in July 1977, correctly calculating that once it came to the point the Somali government would have little choice but to back them; Somali government troops and armour were involved in fighting around Diredawa in August, even though their presence in Ethiopia was not acknowledged until March 1978. Catching the Ethiopians at a low point in both morale and equipment, the Somalis (with the benefit of the Russian arms supplied in previous years) were able to overrun the entire Somali-inhabited area of Ethiopia. Then came the snag. The Somalis, like the Israelis, can never hope to win a final victory. At some point, and in any case long before they reach the main population centres of their opponents, they have to stop and stand on the defensive against an eventual counterattack. In this case the counterattack was hastened, and its success guaranteed, by Soviet and Cuban military assistance to Ethiopia on a scale entirely out of proportion to any previous external involvement in the region. It is impossible to quantify this with any accuracy in financial terms, though the figure of US $1000m has been bandied about for lack of a better one. In terms of hardware, it is reported [13] to have amounted to some 550 T54 and T55 tanks, several thousand other armoured vehicles, about a hundred 40-barrelled rocket launchers, 60 MiG-21 and 40 MiG-23 jet aircraft, and perhaps 200 000 AK-47 rifles and other small arms. The final assault on the Somalis in March 1978 was directed by Soviet advisers and spearheaded by about 10 000 Cuban troops, though the Ethiopians also contributed to their own salvation by their ability to raise a large peasant militia. The inevitable incidental cost of this was the abandonment of the Soviet connections with the Somali Republic, which in November 1977 expelled several thousand Russian experts, renounced the Soviet–Somali friendship treaty, and withdrew all Soviet military facilities. Fighting by Somali guerrillas in the area continued on a scale large enough to tie down several thousand Cuban and Ethiopian troops.

The Soviet Union then assisted the Ethiopian government to reconquer Eritrea, which by January 1978 was entirely, but for four isolated government strongholds, in the hands of local Marxist guerrilla forces. Between July and November 1978, these garrisons were first relieved, and then all of the main population centres in the province were recaptured in a series of ground and air attacks co-ordinated with a sophistication which the Ethiopian forces would have been quite incapable of managing on their own. The guerrillas dispersed into the countryside, where they continued local level fighting but had to abandon any immediate prospect of independence.[14] The foreign support which Ethiopia received in this campaign was almost entirely Soviet, and the Cubans took no active role, a fact which has been pointed to as evidence of Soviet–Cuban disagreement, and consequently of the independence of Cuba's African policy from Soviet dictation. Certainly Cuban policy, which must be discussed later, does spring from different roots from Soviet intervention, and the Cuban support for the Eritrean guerrilla movements up to the mid-1970s would have made it particularly invidious for Cuba to have switched so quickly and directly to fighting against them. All the same, the division between Havana and Moscow over Eritrea was more apparent than real. A Cuban brigade was stationed in the Eritrean capital, Asmara, throughout the later part of the fighting,[15] where it must have released Ethiopian troops and Soviet experts for combat duties, while remaining available as a reserve had it been necessary. Cuban non-involvement thus seems to have been, as much as anything, a cosmetic device designed to protect the revolutionary/ideological purity on which much of the legitimacy of Cuba's African policy depends.

In the aftermath of the main fighting, the Soviet and Cuban presence in Ethiopia remains extremely strong. Over 15 000 Cuban troops still appeared to be in the country in April 1979, mostly around the main town and the line of rail north of the Ogaden, and some 1500–2000 civilian technicians were involved in medical services and managing the economy – including, appropriately enough, the sugar plantations.[16] The Russians were less directly in evidence, as well as less popular than the Cubans, but provided security advisers to the government as well as being the *regime*'s most important creditors. A twenty-year friendship treaty between Ethiopia and the Soviet Union, similar to the one previously renounced by the Somalis, was signed in November 1978. The financial terms on which Soviet weaponry was provided have not been made public, but half of the cost is reported to have taken the form of gifts and loans of equipment, with the other half to be repaid in cash over ten years at 2 per cent interest.[17] Since

Ethiopia was consistently running a large trade deficit even before the fighting (except in 1973 and 1974 when coffee prices were exceptionally high),[18] the enormous arms imports of 1977–8 seem to be quite beyond Ethiopia's capacity to pay for. Ethiopia has not however joined Comecon, though it has observer status which does not amount to very much, and since the end of the major fighting it has sought to renew economic ties with the West, which in any case accounts fo· far the larger part of Ethiopia's external trade. The Somali Republic, for its part, has put out a few tentative feelers towards restoring some contacts with the Soviet Union, though the close relationship of 1969–76 has been ruptured beyond redemption.

SOVIET INTERESTS IN THE HORN

A full explanation of Soviet involvement in the Horn would call for an analysis of Russian decision-making, which is beyond the scope of this chapter. It is however possible to outline a number of Soviet interests in the area which might provide some *rationale* for intervention, and then see to what extent each or any of these can be made to tally with the actual course of events.

One first potential *rationale* which can be excluded from the start is a directly economic one. The countries of the Horn are all desperately poor, and none of them appear to contain any important minerals or other resources in quantities large enough to make it worth anyone's while to try to control them. While Somalia is poor because of a simple lack of exploitable resources, Ethiopia's poverty is due quite as much to the fact that her undoubted agricultural potential has scarcely started to be developed, but there is little prospect of its being developed in the near future, and little point in speculating that the Russians might have pumped large quantities of weapons into the country from motives of developmental altruism. Any economic benefits which a presence in the Horn might bring would spring entirely from the opportunities it might provide for influencing developments elsewhere.

This brings us immediately to the strategic value of the Horn, which has a lot more to be said for it. Ethiopia, Djibouti and Somalia are all immediately adjacent to the southern entrance to the Red Sea, and Somalia in particular is within striking distance of the entrance to the Arabian Gulf. A well-established Soviet naval presence in the area, even though it could not interdict western oil supplies except at immediate risk of provoking war, would nonetheless provide a threat against which western naval planners would have to guard, and might also be a useful source of pressure in local conflicts in East Africa and the Middle East. How important this threat actually is, is more difficult to assess. Farer has argued strongly that there is no plausible threat to Western naval interests in the area, though his case, made in the context of a general argument seeking to dissuade the United States from intervening on the side of Ethiopia against a Soviet-backed Somalia, has now to some extent been overtaken by events.[19] The naval interest was however always most plausible in the context of Russian involvement in Somalia, which was accompanied by visits from top-ranking Soviet naval officers, notably Admiral Gorshkov, and the development of naval facilities at Berbera and Kismayu.[20] Russian readiness, first to risk and then to abandon these facilities, in order to cement the alliance with Ethiopia which is navally not so well placed, indicates that they were not in any case of crucial importance.

A second potential strategic interest looks not to the Gulf and the Indian Ocean, but rather to the Middle East. In this respect Soviet influence in Ethiopia might be seen as balancing, in some degree, the loss of influence in Egypt. The case, however, is not convincing, in that Ethiopia's role in the Middle East is no more than peripheral, and the Arab states which constitute the Soviet Union's natural allies in the region have tended, for reasons of Islamic solidarity, to support the Somalis and the Eritrean guerrillas against Ethiopian *regimes* of whatever political complexion. Ethiopia's links have tended to be with Israel, though these have been muted so as not to offend Arab members of the OAU, and Moshe Dayan embarrassed the Derg by supporting them at the time of the 1978 war. Only Qadaffi in Libya switched his stance when the Russians changed sides, and – without the slightest effect – urged the Eritreans to make peace on the grounds that Ethiopia was now ruled by a revolutionary socialist government.

From the viewpoint of Soviet interests in black Africa, a policy of support for Ethiopia makes rather more sense. In this area, a pro-Somali policy was always a liability, since it provided implicit – though never explicit – support for the possibility of changing state boundaries inherited from the colonial partition. Just as Somalia was dedicated to challenging these boundaries, Ethiopia equally inevitably was dedicated to maintaining them, and was able to build the principle of acceptance of existing boundaries into the Charter of the Organisation of African Unity framed in Addis Ababa in 1963. The Russians themselves fortified this principle, and their own diplomatic position in

Africa, through their consistent support for the Federal Government during the Nigerian Civil War of 1967–70; similarly, intervention on the side of the MPLA during the Angolan Civil War likewise enabled the combatant with the most plausible claim to represent central government to extend control over the entire territory within the former colonial frontiers. Support for the central Ethiopian government falls into the same pattern, and the Russians were careful not to overplay their hand by encouraging any Ethiopian invasion of Somalia, after expelling the Somali forces from Ethiopia in March 1978. In a sense, then, this support demonstrates a Soviet willingness to maintain a territorial *status quo* in which almost all African states have a stake, though such support would obviously only be available to states willing to align themselves diplomatically with the USSR, and preferably also to declare their allegiance to 'scientific socialism'.

This raises, inevitably, the question of the role of ideology in Soviet foreign policy. The answer is fairly clear. A *regime*'s willingness to declare its adherence to Marxist–Leninist principles both encourages and legitimises Russian intervention on its side, but does not determine the stance which the Russians will in fact take. To a large extent the link between declared ideology and Soviet support is self-reinforcing, in that *regimes* which like to think of themselves as Marxist will look to Russia for help, and *regimes* which want Russian help will tend to claim that they are Marxist. Scientific socialism in Somalia, always rather an incongruous setting for an ideology of proletarian revolution, was played up before 1977 and has equally been played down since. In Ethiopia, Marxism–Leninism was probably a necessary condition for Soviet support, but in view of the fact that *all* of the Derg's principal opponents, both internal and external, likewise claim the Marxist mantle, it could scarcely be a sufficient one. In the Ethiopian People's Revolutionary Party (EPRP) in Addis Ababa and the Eritrean People's Liberation Front (EPLF) in Eritrea, the Russians have participated in the ruthless extermination of two of the most genuinely Marxist revolutionary movements anywhere in Africa.

For the Cubans, ideology appears to provide a more plausible guide. Indeed, it is hard to think of another, for it would be stretching the evidence to surmise that they are fighting in Africa merely because the Russians are forcing them to do so as some kind of blood money repayment of their Soviet debt; and they have no conceivable strategic and economic interests in the area. Most of the Cubans involved, fresh from their own revolution, seem genuinely to believe it to be their duty to support revolutions elsewhere, and especially in Africa and Latin

America. That said, Cuban decisions as to *which* revolutions are worthy of support display a happy congruence with the requirements of Soviet foreign policy which is far more than coincidental. On occasion, as in Eritrea, the Cubans have been forced into embarrassing shifts which make clear their inability to sustain their support for revolutionary movements independently of Soviet backing, and their willingness to adopt Russian definitions of revolutionary credit-worthiness as their own. Cuban attempts to provide a *rationale* for their actions are, put simply, drivel. The one available Cuban account of the Ethiopian revolution[21] does not try to provide any coherent Marxist (or any other) explanations for what occurred, but is reduced to peddling tales of how, for example, Haile-Selassie used to bathe in the blood of slaughtered virgins in order to revive his declining powers. Eritrea and the Somali-inhabited territories are referred to in passing as elements of the national problem, exploited by 'imperialism, Arab reaction and internal counterrevolutionary class forces' fighting against 'the revolutionary socialist process'.

The inadequacy of other explanations for Soviet intervention forces one back to the residual explanation, opportunism: that the Russians will be happy to extend their influence in any situation where it appears that they can do so without appreciable risk, and will treat as incidental benefits any strategic or economic opportunities which come their way – in the case of Ethiopia, for instance, the exercise value of being able to mount a rapid large-scale military supply and intervention operation at some distance from their own frontiers. Central to this explanation is the assumption that the Soviet Union is concerned above all else with demonstrating power: showing that should it choose to come to the aid of a *regime* which seeks its protection, it has both the will and the capacity to defend that *regime* against all enemies, internal and external. One is struck here by the contrast between, on the one hand, the Soviet Union's readiness to jeopardise its ideological reputation as an agent of global Marxist revolution, and on the other hand, its determination to maintain its reputation or credibility as a patron able to protect its clients. Only this can account for the scale of intervention in Ethiopia, or for that matter Angola. It doesn't matter to the Russians who they protect, it seems, so long as they can ensure that *whoever* they protect will win. And in a continent where most rulers are insecure, this provides a very powerful attraction.

AN ASSESSMENT OF THE SOVIET POSITION IN THE HORN

By mid-1979, the Soviet Union had built up a strong but precarious position in the Horn. It has unquestionably supplanted the United States as the dominant external power in the area, and, with an apparently equally influential presence in South Yemen, in the southern Red Sea and Gulf of Aden as a whole. In the process, it had successfully accomplished the difficult transfer of alliances from a less valued client (the Somali Republic) to a more valued one (Ethiopia), and shown itself able to move into the region forces at a level with which no other power could compete. Any comparison with the position five, ten or twenty years earlier shows a steady and substantial increase in the Soviet presence. The western presence, conversely, has been reduced from one of apparently unchallengeable dominance in 1959 to the single foothold represented by the continued French presence in Djibouti.

The extent of the change was made apparent by the virtual absence of a western response to the Soviet–Cuban military build-up in Ethiopia. Both in the United Kingdom and the United States, there was some resurgence of sympathy for the Somalis, based partly on the simple feeling that if the Russians supported one side, the western powers must have had an automatic interest in supporting the other. As a basis for policy, however, this had nothing to recommend it: the Somalis were so manifestly weaker than the Ethiopians that it would merely have amounted to backing a loser because the Russians were backing a winner. Since support for Somalia implies, as always, a threat to the inherited ex-colonial boundaries, it would also have jeopardised relations with many African states, especially with Kenya, which has more important relations with the United Kingdom than do any of the states in the Horn. An initial American promise to supply Somalia with defensive weapons was substantially reconsidered, and a long series of visits to western capitals by President Siyad produced offers only of humanitarian aid.[22] Western states were thus reduced to the essentially do-nothing of avoiding entanglements in the region and hoping that Ethiopia would eventually wish to re-establish working relations.

This hope, however, is not unrealistic, in that the Soviet Union has lavishly expended both its moral and its material resources without yet obtaining any very tangible rewards. The balance of advantage within the alliance has been heavily on the side of the Ethiopian *regime*. The Derg, recovering from a position of desperate weakness, has been enabled by Soviet help to re-establish government control over the capital and the greatest part of the countryside, defeat (though not entirely eliminate) two major secessionist movements which between them occupied about a third of the national territory, and overcome important internal threats to its tenure of power. In the process, it rejected both Soviet and Cuban pressures for a negotiated rather than an imposed military solution in Eritrea and for sharing power with Marxist movements which it did not wholly control, in each case obliging its allies to help enforce policies which they can scarcely have approved.[23] It has followed the Russian lead in some (to Ethiopia) un-important foreign policy decisions, such as recognising the Vietnamese-supported *regime* in Cambodia, but there is as yet no evidence that it has even offered the USSR naval facilities equivalent to those lost in Somalia.

The essential requirement for continued Soviet hegemony is to build up with Ethiopia the social, economic and political infrastructure for a permanent alliance of interest rather than a temporary alliance of con-venience. This process has scarcely started. Ethiopian observer status within Comecon amounts to little, and there are formidable obstacles in the way of full membership; even the massive military debt to the Soviet Union, from one viewpoint its strongest lever in extending economic control over Ethiopia, is from another perspective a likely source of dependence and thus resentment, while the debt itself can only be paid, if at all, through continued coffee sales on the world market. Socially, it is true, the close connections between the former ruling group and metropolitan centres in the United States, Britain and France have been destroyed, and there has arisen within the new urban and peasants associations a widely distributed group of middle level leaders who (in the urban associations at least) might well look instead to the Soviet Union. There are, however, two barriers in the way of turning this leadership into a coherent political force committed to the Soviet connection in the way in which the old leadership was committed to alliance with the West. The first is that the Russians appear to be generally unpopular, a point which reflects not merely personal dislike, but on the Ethiopian side a pronounced and long-standing suspicion of foreign influence and interference, and on the Russian side insensitivity and inexperience in dealing with peoples and cultures different from their own. The second is not merely the absence but the suppression by the Ethiopian military leadership of any political organisation through which a permanent institutionalised alliance could be maintained. The Soviet Union, as is well known, is much happier dealing with local communist parties than with military dictators, and it has every reason to be. A powerfully organised local party, besides being open to penetration at every level rather than simply at the top, is likely (though not certain) to share both moral attitudes and organisational assumptions with the leading communist party in the world. It is significant here that the Derg in Ethiopia has extirpated any political organisation – especially the Marxist ones – which has threatened to represent any group within the population capable of constraining the powers of the military leadership. The 'red terror' of 1977–8, during which many thousands of young people were killed by the government, was directed against the Ethiopian People's Revolutionary Party, an underground urban party which tends to be labelled Maoist because it is Marxist yet opposed to the *regime*. Another party, Meison, with links especially in the trade unions, grew under government protection but was suppressed the moment it showed signs of gaining an identity and influence of its own; attempts by the Cubans in particular to build links with Meison behind the backs of the Derg were quickly cracked down on. Having enlisted itself so wholeheartedly on the side of the *regime*, the Soviet Union has found itself having to take the most brutal repressive measures – both in Addis Ababa and in Eritrea – against those who might be regarded as its natural allies.

There are evident similarities between Ethiopia's experience and that of radical military *regimes* in the three other major states of North-East Africa, Egypt, the Sudan, and the Somali Republic. In each case, the *coup* which brought the new government to power has been followed by a close alliance with the Soviet Union, which has been gratifying to the military rulers in marking their independence from the West and alliance with global revolution, as well as providing very practical advantages in military aid and protection against internal and external enemies. After this initial period, a cooling off has taken place. Sometimes, as in Egypt, this has followed a decline in the salience of military requirements, in which the Russians have a great deal to offer, and an increase in economic and diplomatic ones, in which the Soviet connection is more of a liability. Partly, it has followed from the Russian tendency to overplay their hand once they have achieved a position of local influence: a legacy, perhaps, of their experience in dealing with satellites, who in the last resort could be coerced, rather than with allies who could if need be go their own way. In any event, too powerful an ally inevitably arouses resentments, and a break may then take place with dramatic suddenness if the Soviet alliance is perceived to be no longer serving the purposes for which it was entered into (as in Egypt and Somalia), or if the Russians seek to capitalise on their position by meddling in domestic politics (as in the Sudan). Thus all of the four principal African states on the Red Sea and Gulf of Aden littoral have entered into close relations with the USSR, and Ethiopia is the only one from which the Russians have not as yet been acrimoniously expelled. One cannot, obviously, be sure that Ethiopia will follow her neighbours. For one thing, the Russians may have learnt something from their mistakes, particularly the need to follow up the initial military component of the alliance with continuous contacts in other fields. For another, the Ethiopian military has presided over a more thoroughgoing social revolution than its fellow *regimes*, and this, if it can be institutionalised, may provide a firmer basis than elsewhere for continuity in foreign policy. But against that, any external patron has to reckon with an Ethiopian national pride and suspicion of foreigners which are so strongly engrained as to be almost pathological, and which are especially marked in the officer corps from which the *regime* draws much of its strength. On the basis of evidence available in mid-1979, therefore, the USSR has so far failed, despite the readiness of all the more important actors in the Horn to espouse a Marxist ideology, to establish a base for Soviet power which in any way transcends local interests and rivalries.

NOTES

1. Population figures are from *United Nations Demographic Yearbook 1976,* pp. 118–9; for more detailed information on conflicts in the Horn, see T.J. Farer, *War Clouds on the Horn of Africa* (New York: Carnegie Endowment, 1976); and *Conflicts in Africa,* Adelphi Paper no. 93, London, 1972.
2. The background to the Somali dispute is discussed in detail in J. Drysdale, *The Somali Dispute* (London: Pall Mall, 1964) and C. Hoskyns, *Case Studies in African Diplomacy: the Ethiopia–Somali–Kenya dispute 1960–67,* (Dar-es-Salaam: OUP, 1969).
3. For background material, see G.K.N. Trevaskis, *Eritrea: a colony in transition* (London: OUP, 1960).
4. See P.T.W. Baxter, 'Ethiopia's unacknowledged problem: The Oromo', *African Affairs,* LXXVII (1978) 283–96.
5. United States Government, Department of Defense, Security Assistance Agency, *Fiscal Year Series December 1978,* FYS39, p. 150.
6. United States Government, Department of Defense, Security Assistance Agency, *Foreign Military Sales and Military Assistance Facts December 1978,* p. 20.

7. Farer, op. cit., pp. 97–8.
8. See B. Crozier, *The Soviet Presence in Somalia,* Conflict Studies no. 54 (London: Institute for the Study of Conflict, February 1975).
9. For the events of 1974, see C. Legum, *Ethiopia: the fall of Haile Selassie's empire* (London: Collings, 1976).
10. *Foreign Military Sales and Military Assistance Facts,* pp. 5, 15, 20, 24; years are US Fiscal Years.
11. Keesing's Contemporary Archives, 1976, p. 27912B.
12. *The Sunday Times,* London, 22 May 1977.
13. Patrick Gilkes (B.B.C. Africa Service), at a talk at the Royal Institute of International Affairs, London, 3 April 1979.
14. Keesing's 1978, p. 29357A.
15. Patrick Gilkes, loc. cit.
16. Ibid.
17. Ibid.
18. United States Arms Control and Disarmament Agency, *World Military Expenditures and Arms Transfers 1967–1976* (Washington 1978) p. 129.
19. Farer, op. cit., pp. 105–23.
20. Keesing's 1975, p. 27134D.
21. Raul Valdes Vivo, Member of the Secretariat of the Central Committee of the Communist Party of Cuba, *Ethiopia, the unknown revolution,* in *Granma,* Havana, 22 and 29 January 1978.
22. Keesing's 1978, p. 28993.
23. Keesing's 1978, p. 29357A.

Index

DATE DUE

GAYLORD			PRINTED IN U.S.A.